TEACHING THE NEW LIBRARY TO TODAY'S USERS

Reaching International,
Minority, Senior Citizens,
Gay/Lesbian,
First-Generation, At-Risk,
Graduate and
Returning Students,
and Distance Learners

Edited by **Trudi E. Jacobson**
and **Helene C. Williams**

**The New Library Series
Number 4**

Neal-Schuman Publishers, Inc.
New York   London

The New Library Series

No. 1 – *Finding Common Ground: Creating the Library of the Future without Diminishing the Library of the Past.* Edited by Cheryl LaGuardia and Barbara A. Mitchell.

No. 2 – *Recreating the Academic Library: Breaking Virtual Ground.* Edited by Cheryl LaGuardia.

No. 3 – *Becoming A Library Teacher.* By Cheryl LaGuardia and Christine K. Oka.

No. 4 – *Teaching the New Library to Today's Users: Reaching International, Minority, Senior Citizens, Gay/Lesbian, First-Generation, At-Risk, Graduate and Returning Students, and Distance Learners.* Edited by Trudi E. Jacobson and Helene C. Williams.

Published by Neal-Schuman Publishers, Inc.
100 Varick Street
New York, NY 10013

Printed and bound in the United States of America.

Library of Congress Cataloging-in-Publication Data

Teaching the new library to today's users : reaching international, minority, senior citizens, gay/lesbian, first-generation college, at-risk, graduate and returning students, and distance learners / [compiled by] Trudi E. Jacobson, Helene C. Williams.
    p. cm. — (The new library series ; no. 4)
    Includes bibliographical references and index.
    ISBN 1-55570-379-8 (alk. paper)
    1. Library orientation—United States. 2. Information services—United States—User education. 3. Searching, Bibliographical—Study and teaching. 4. Library orientation for college students—United States. I. Jacobson, Trudi. II. Williams, Helene C. III. Series.

Z711.2.T43 2000
025.5'677'0973—DC21   00-035117

Table of Contents

List of Tables

Foreword

What an exciting time to be an instruction and reference librarian! How intellectually challenging to be able to design information services so that all library users can easily find needed resources amid the quantity and variety of print and electronic choices. How satisfying and rewarding to see students succeed and to celebrate their academic accomplishments.

Throughout the pages of this book, you will find outstanding examples of how to make library programs and services come alive for a wide range of students.

Today's academic libraries can be overwhelming to our users—the information choices are staggering. Yet, these same conditions inspire our creativity and imagination. The contributors to this book clearly demonstrate how linguistic, cultural, age, and/or gender differences among student populations actually can result in stronger library instruction development and more inventive library services as we work to

- Enhance and expand instructional activities to reach all students, equally and consistently, across the campus.
- Provide an integrated, coherent, quality educational experience for students with library offerings integrated into curricular offerings to deepen and enrich learning.
- Develop convenient access to information from any place at any time.
- Incorporate critical thinking components into the instructional processes.
- Initiate information-literacy programs so that all students

will graduate proficient and competent in the fundamentals and components of the library research process.
• Continually assess programs and strategies to achieve desired learning outcomes.

The challenges and questions before librarians today are similar to those faced in years past: how to excite and motivate students to use the library efficiently and effectively, how to help users to understand the research process in order to sustain the acquisition of knowledge and become self-directed learners, how to reach out to faculty members to develop cooperative and collaborative partnerships through course-integrated or course-related instructional opportunities, how to systematically infuse information-literacy principles across the curriculum, and how to humanize the library-learning experience (especially for those students new to libraries, inexperienced with using networked resources, or overwhelmed by the rapid pace of technological change).

Many libraries have developed and mounted special instructional programs targeted to certain populations, such as international, re-entry, graduate, at-risk, first-generation college, day-time, evening, off-campus, distant-based, lesbian, gay, bisexual, transgender, or older students. An exciting new development is the collaboration between academic libraries and various campus offices to integrate library instruction programs and services into residential or commuter experiences of first-year or transfer students. Such efforts help students adjust to campus life, and support university retention efforts.

In addition, several libraries have been successful in linking formal credit library courses to the general education program for first-year or transfer students, insuring that these students will be exposed to, and benefit from, formal programs in information literacy. Moreover, some universities have established first-year general education "cluster programs" on common themes (such as science, technology, and society) in which information literacy courses are included. Within the "cluster" experience, library assignments are thematically aligned to assignments in the students' other courses so that an integrated and cohesive first-year general education experience for new

students will result. Under such conditions, the educational outcome possibilities are immense—not only for new friendships,
but for new insights and (most importantly) for new lives of
continual learning.

We know that today's librarians spend more time per user
in both "on ground" and "online" instructional environments.
Such instruction occurs in one-on-one encounters at the reference desk; in an Information Commons through the explanation of how to use a local or consortial OPAC or how to select
wisely from a myriad of full-text and subscription-based databases; in a classroom setting through the "one-shot" teaching
of a course-integrated session, or in a sustained learning environment, such as a multi-week credit-bearing library course; on
the telephone; at a workstation through the medium of electronic mail, computer conferencing, or threaded discussions; on
a large screen through interactive video using synchronous or
asynchronous communication; or through the World Wide Web
using a variety of instructional methods, such as interactive tutorials, prepackaged modules, or uniquely created "courses-in-
a-box" or cyber lessons.

Whatever the medium of instruction, the basic pedagogical
purpose remains the same: to make a difference in the life of a
student. As we assist today's library users in becoming successful in their academic pursuits, let us continue to:

- Take risks to anticipate and address user needs.
- Create student-centered environments which are conducive to discovery and learning.
- Provide opportunities for active, cooperative, and expe-
  riential learning to occur.
- Customize learning opportunities to reach and engage all
  users, equitably and efficiently.
- Develop flexible, intuitive, expeditious, and reliable gate-
  ways to knowledge.
- Introduce powerful and easy-to-use teaching and learning tools, taking advantage of the latest technologies to
  help all users to explore, find, organize, synthesize, and
  evaluate information so that new knowledge can be created.

- Recognize and respect cultural, gender, and linguistic values, attitudes, behaviors, and experiences of all users.
- Understand and appreciate the diverse educational backgrounds and learning styles of today's library users.
- Partner and affiliate with other campus and off-campus entities to successfully accomplish our goals.
- Assist all users to transform data into knowledge so that learning continues beyond the time spent earning a degree.
- Celebrate and reward student, and our own, accomplishments on a consistent and regular basis.

This book, so aptly titled, inspires us to achieve all of these goals—and more. It does so within the contemporary cultural environment of academic libraries; it encourages us to reconceptualize, reshape, redesign, and refine our service directions and programmatic offerings to teach the new library to today's students. I applaud the editors and authors for their keen understanding of the issues, and for their generosity in sharing their insights with us.

Ilene F. Rockman
California State University, Hayward

Acknowledgments

Good instruction programs are always the result of a team effort, and this book has not deviated from that model. We have very much enjoyed working with the authors who contributed chapters to this book. Without their knowledge and experience, our idea would still be a dream. The editors would also like to thank Betsy Wilson (University of Washington), Ilene Rockman (California State University, Hayward), and Cheryl LaGuardia (Harvard University), without whom this book would not exist today. Your help and encouragement when we needed it most was invaluable in lifting our spirits. We would like to thank our institutions for providing challenging atmospheres and the support to help us meet those challenges. And most of all, our deep appreciation to John Vallely and Andy Firpo, for their patience in living with us while this project was underway and for their guidance and advice.

Series Editor's Preface

CULTURE-DEFINING ICONS

We define culture in a variety of ways. You will find modern American society expressed in the high art of poetry, painting, sculpture, literature, music, and dance. You can also discover it in the more prosaic entertainments of popular theatricals, the media, and sporting events. To truly understand a culture and its values, try exploring the more widely subscribed realistic customs. One effective icon representing society's image is the tee shirt proclaiming a message. Tee shirts expound profound truisms. Walk down any street and sample every possible philosophy, opinion, belief, and attitude visibly expressed and available in a range of sizes and colors. And how many times do you agree, sagely nodding your head, and say "How true! How true!" Recently I found a tee shirt articulating an innate wisdom with a boldly communicated slogan: "Those who can—do; those who can do MORE—teach!"

I could go one better than the philosophic pronouncement on the quoted garment. Here you discover the connecting thread from that shirt to the series preface of this volume. My ultimately revised adage is "Those who can—do; those who can do more—teach; and those who can do the MOST—write about it!" The authors of *Teaching the New Library to Today's Users* accomplished this exactly: they have done the library work, taught others how to use the library, and now they have written about the experience.

DIVERSE USERS, MULTIPLE CULTURES

The reality in libraries today is that there is no easily defined "user." Instead we find hosts of users from every imaginable background, age, ability, viewpoint, and preparation. The user groups addressed here—international students; students of color; lesbian, gay, bisexual, and transgender students; first-generation college students; at-risk students; returning, graduate, and older students; and distance learners—represent only a slice of our entire "user pie." In the past, we might not have sufficiently focused our library instruction on these groups. Perhaps we thought they were not heavily represented in our patron populations. The students might not have been well identified as a particular group—a concept containing its own contradictions because many of our students may "fit" into two or more of the groups. Possibly librarians and instructors felt they were not sufficiently equipped to address this growing variety of individual needs. The more aware we become of the definable demographic shifts taking place in educational populations, how they change the user composition and our professional requirements, the better we can serve those populations. "Know Your Audience" is the first rule of effective instruction. To prepare an effective class, know who you teach and what they bring to the class. This book will help you define, and understand, the needs of diverse groups of students.

TRIPLE-THREAT DOERS

This book expresses my revised adage. All of the authors here "do" because they work as professional librarians and they also "do more" by teaching about libraries. With the publication of this volume, they "do the most"—research their work and write about it. Consider these authors as "triple threats" in the arena of library instruction. Here you will find the inside information, that realistic "custom of the library instructional culture" difficult to find anywhere else in the library literature. For the first time it is presented in one collective place.

   This volume is a rich collection of the experiences of a teaching group as interesting and diverse as the populations we now serve. I assure you that they "practice what they preach," and practice it effectively. They provide a most valuable service by taking the time to share their work, considered opinions, and philosophies. If you teach in libraries today, or plan to teach tomorrow, *Teaching the New Library to Today's Users* will certainly help you perform your job better.

Cheryl LaGuardia, Editor
The New Library Series
Cambridge, Massachusetts
February 2000

Preface

In the last few years, library instruction has changed tremendously. We have seen our libraries, resources, and systems altered. As our student populations became more diverse, the range of teaching methods expanded. There is a constant sense of struggle as we attempt to keep pace with the changes. Involvement in user education has become fun and frightening, demanding and exciting.

Fortunately, we may call upon a number of resources. We confer with colleagues—locally, across the nation, and around the world. They possess a fount of information, ideas, and assistance. We talk in person at work and conferences, and electronically via e-mail and on BI-L, our incomparable LISTSERV. Print and electronic journals, in the fields of both librarianship and education, assist us greatly. *Teaching the New Library* (also published by Neal-Schuman, and edited by Cheryl LaGuardia and five of her colleagues at Harvard) and other recently published books have also proved exceedingly helpful.

The editors of *Teaching the New Library to Today's Users* roomed together at the "Finding Common Ground" conference in Cambridge, Massachusetts, in March 1996. The conference tackled an intriguing proposition: How do we create the library of the future without diminishing the library of the past? One night we stayed up very late, inspired by the ideas and energy evinced by conference participants. Our discussion started with personal and job-related news, then veered off into professional aspirations. While discussing the challenges of meeting the needs of our changing patron populations, the idea for this book about teaching diverse users came to life.

We had all read literature about new libraries, new systems, electronic resources, and innovative teaching methods. Considering the other changes in our environment, the literature on our new students and patrons seemed scattered and dated. To reach and teach these varied and growing student groups, we needed information written by librarians with experience instructing these populations.

Teaching the New Library to Today's Users set out to accomplish ambitious goals. We gathered a number of librarians working on the cutting edge. We assembled voices that told a story beyond the recounting of personal experiences and descriptions of particular programs. These librarians addressed educational issues and the assessment of instruction.

We designed the volume to assist practicing librarians in academic and public library settings in their day-to-day teaching and to help library school students prepare for the demands of an evolving profession. Library educators will find this volume useful as they look for both real experiences and the theoretical knowledge underpinning the development of successful instruction. Most public service positions in libraries today include teaching patrons, yet many librarians feel they lack adequate training for this instruction. New and experienced librarians alike will find this book a resource for brushing up on their knowledge of effective teaching methods with particular groups.

Good teaching practices translate from one situation to another. Readers will notice that many of the ideas presented can assist in serving and teaching all students; not only the subject group of a particular chapter. Don't be surprised if you read about returning students, for example, and think: "Aha! This technique will work wonderfully with international students." You will also learn more about the theory supporting particular teaching practices. Common theoretical aspects, as practical ideas to be used in the classroom, are woven from one chapter to another into the book as a whole.

Of course, it was impossible to include every potential patron population in this single volume; and each of the groups covered deserves an entire book. The chapters on each group— international students, students of color, gay/lesbian/bisexual and transgender students, first-generation college students, at-risk students, returning students, graduate students, senior citizens, and distance learners—are organized topically. A short essay highlights the main themes of each part, linking them to other pertinent sections. A short chapter, looking to the future, ends *Teaching the New Library to Today's Users*.

We developed this book with one goal: to recognize the diversity of today's college population and to recommend and publicize successful strategies for teaching diverse populations.

Introduction

The demographics of the United States' population are changing, and these changes are reflected on college and university campuses throughout the country. Not only are our students changing, but so too are the methods by which they learn, and indeed, where they learn—will the future even include coming to a campus? And when these students do research, they face a bewildering array of resources from which to choose. Librarians involved with user-education efforts face myriad challenges in their efforts to reach student populations effectively; many instruction librarians find they need to update their well-honed outreach and teaching strategies to meet new situations. New student populations, increased sensitivity to existing populations, and changing technology all play a role in the transformations taking place in education today.

CHANGING DEMOGRAPHICS

The students enrolled in higher education are changing. From 1980 to 1996, college enrollment of students of color increased dramatically: African-American students increased by about a third, the number of Hispanic students more than doubled, Asian students increased by 178 percent, and Native Americans increased by almost 60 percent. International student enrollment grew by 60 percent. In 1983, there were 583,000 college students age 35 and over, while preliminary 1995 data showed 986,000 students in this category (Bureau of the Census, 1998: Tables 302-304). Graduate enrollment increased similarly: from 1985 to 1996, total graduate enrollment increased nearly 27 percent, from 1,376,000 to 1,743,000 (Bureau of the Census, 1998: Table 306). It is more difficult to pin down the number of students participating in distance education programs for several reasons: The first is the changing definition of distance education—what courses does it include, and do all institutions recognize them as such? The second reason is that students enrolled in distance-education courses one quarter may be back on campus as full- or part-time the next quarter, making for even more variable numbers. Although it is difficult to determine the number of distance learners, indications are that their ranks are increasing.

Teaching librarians have always understood that using a "one size fits all" approach to outreach and teaching is inadequate, and will ultimately be unsuccessful. This is even more true in the face of the changes just described. Some students may eagerly seek opportunities to learn research skills, while others will be completely unaware of the chances to learn and the benefits of doing so. Still others are reticent to avail themselves of the array of instruction options offered because of either a past negative experience or fear of failure. To address these varying expectations, the method of instruction, the examples used, and the attitude of the librarian are crucial to a successful experience in the library classroom or distance-learning setting.

CHANGES IN TEACHING AND LEARNING METHODS

Technology has provided access to many new opportunities in education. Even in the fairly recent past, distance education meant correspondence courses. Computer applications, used for teaching both on-campus and off, continue to be woven into students' education. Library instructors have been adapting to and maximizing the benefits of technological changes for many years, sharing what they have discovered with others.

While technology is a driving force in the changed learning culture, it is not the only force. Teaching librarians have been cognizant of the need to address students' learning styles and to expand their own repertoire of teaching styles. Using technology, addressing teaching and learning styles, and recognizing new student populations are all elements of effective library instruction programs.

SCOPE OF USER EDUCATION PROGRAMS

Information literacy, a key concept on many campuses, broadens the scope and content of many user-education programs. While course-related instruction still plays an important role in instructional efforts, there are many additional aspects to a successful user-education program. Library instruction may be incorporated into first-year experience programs or may take the form of credit-bearing courses. Printed how-to guides, bibliographies, and pathfinders are supplemented by (or even replaced by) Web-based guides and tutorials. On-campus classes that are otherwise open to the entire academic community will not reach distance learners. New options must be available to them. Librarians use a variety of formats in their user-education programs, both traditional and technologically based, to reach more students and more groups of students.

Not only is user instruction being provided to more students than ever before, it is also being provided by more instructors than in the past. Librarians who coordinate instruction programs are now joined by subject specialists, library school students, and peer tutors in teaching research skills to a variety of user groups. The liaison role of librarians to departments is more important than ever in reaching some of the less-traditional groups such as transfer or distance-education students. Other units on campus, such as academic computing centers and student services, increasingly collaborate with librarians to support these instructional efforts.

The first rule of library instruction is to know who your students are, so it's essential to be keenly aware of the demographics of your user population. This is where the collaborations and working relationships you build with other units on campus is key. Your contacts in administrative offices (admissions, the Dean of Students' office, etc.) can update you on the changing demographics at your institution.

STUDENTS AS INDIVIDUALS

While librarians may teach classes composed of students who fall within a particular category, such as at-risk students, it is important to keep in mind that labels encompass disparate stu-

dents, all of whom differ in learning style preferences, familiarity with technology, and experience with libraries and research. In addition, many classes are filled with students from
several groups.

The chapters that follow address user education for students
within broadly defined categories: international students; students of color; lesbian, gay, bisexual, and transgender students;
first-generation college students; at-risk students; returning,
graduate, and older students; and distance learners. The authors
all have experience with teaching the student groups they describe, and there is much to learn from their research and their
experiences. However, perhaps what is most striking is how the
techniques and advice transfer to other teaching situations. For
example, some of the suggestions made for distance learners
would help librarians who desire to reach those students who
simply will not set foot in the library, even though they live on
campus.

In her chapter, "Instruction in a Multicultural Setting: Teaching and Learning with Students of Color," Karen Downing
writes, "Perhaps the most positive outcome of cross-cultural
teaching is that all students benefit from informed instruction
based on multicultural learning practices. Being an outstanding multicultural instructor really means being an outstanding
instructor to every learner."

This statement is equally true on a broader level. The editors hope that you will agree, and that the following chapters
will help you in your quest to become an outstanding instructor.

REFERENCE LIST

U.S. Bureau of the Census. 1998. *Statistical Abstract of the United States: 1998*
(118th edition). Washington, D.C. 1996 data is estimated. Available online
at *www.census.gov/prod/www/statistical-abstract-us.html* [cited April 3, 2000].

Part 1

INTERNATIONAL STUDENTS

OVERVIEW

International students may fall into a number of the categories covered by chapters in this book. They may be first-generation students; they might come from a variety of cultures; some may be graduate or returning students; and they may be lesbian, gay, bisexual, or transgendered. Beyond the characteristics and instructional ramifications addressed by these other chapters, though, are unique issues confronted by international students. Many experience language difficulties and may feel disoriented by American culture in general, and by the classroom culture in particular.

Sarkodie-Mensah's article provides an overview of the issues that international students face when they pursue their academic careers in the United States. This background information, which covers the history of these students in the United States, trends in foreign student enrollment, the different classifications of international students, and the adjustment issues that they encounter, will help user education librarians better understand the almost half-million non-U.S. students on American campuses.

DiMartino and Zoe's chapter further examines issues discussed by Sarkodie-Mensah. They investigate some of the cultural differences of international students and, of particular interest to instruction librarians, how these differences create culture-specific learning styles. The linguistic issues that international students face also affect information-seeking behaviors, particularly when these students use the complex information systems now found in American libraries. Familiarity and comfort with technology is a theme that runs through a number of the chapters in this book, but without the added linguistic issues. The effective use of search engines and full-text and other databases requires inputting terms and operators that may not be familiar to international students.

Depending upon the country from which these students hail, other hurdles may include unfamiliarity with the broad range of information formats found in American academic libraries, open stacks, and the classification systems used. Instruction librarians cognizant of these issues, as well as of the linguistic and cultural issues discussed in both of these chapters, will be able to develop programs to meet the needs of these students. Some of the suggestions echo those found in other chapters, such as using relevant examples and exercises (as discussed by Downing and McDowell) and using peer learning (though in a different format than that proposed by Tyckoson and Downing). Other suggestions about teaching methods, however, are unique to this particular, though diverse, population. Some key strategies for teaching international students successfully are:

- Work with appropriate offices on campus to obtain a profile of international students at your institution in order to develop instruction that best meets their needs.
- Become familiar with cultural differences and the effects that these have on learning styles; develop instruction with these issues in mind.
- Specifically structure electronic resources instruction in order to mitigate linguistic issues that affect the quality of searches.
- Emphasize the development of critical thinking and evaluation skills when teaching international students to search electronic resources.
- Develop the habits of speaking slowly and clearly, paraphrasing and rephrasing, using simple sentence structure and vocabulary, and listening carefully.

The International Student on Campus: History, Trends, Visa Classification, and Adjustment Issues

Kwasi Sarkodie-Mensah
Boston College

HISTORICAL BACKGROUND

Even though the end of World War II is usually regarded as the beginning of the influx of international students into the United States, it is important to note that as early as 1784 there was a record of student migration to the United States. In that year, Francisco de Miranda, who later became a prominent Latin American liberation leader, was enrolled at Yale. Thousands of others followed in his footsteps. Dr. Yung Wing, who is credited with being the first Chinese student to receive a degree in the United States, studied at Yale and returned to China in 1859 (Wheeler, King, and Davidson, 1925). Wing designed a program in which thirty students were sent from China to the United States each year beginning in 1871, but the plan was halted in 1881 when Chinese reactionary groups put pressure on the Chinese government to end the arrangement. These groups objected that the students who were sent to America "enjoyed more privileges than was good for them; . . . imitated American students in athletics; . . . played more than they studied; . . . formed themselves into secret societies both religious and political; . . . ignored their teachers and would not listen to the advice of the

3

new commissioner; . . . most of them went to church, attended Sunday schools and had become Christian" (Cieslak,1955: 7).

Forty years later, however, there was a major surge in the number of students from China studying in America. A major factor contributing to this significant increase was Congress's authorization in 1908 of the return to China of a $10-million surplus from the Boxer Indemnity. These funds made it possible for the Chinese government to prepare and send students to the United States and reduced much of the Chinese ill feeling toward America. [Furthermore, American ideas and methods became widely known and accepted in China after World War I, and the United States sent a large number of missionaries to China to establish schools (Meng, 1931).

One of the earliest Japanese youths to come to the United States was Joseph Hardy Neesima, who later founded Doshisha University in Kyoto, Japan. He came to the United States via a sailing ship, studied at Phillips Andover Academy and Amherst College, and returned home in 1874 (Cieslak, 1955).

In 1904, the statistics of the U.S. Bureau of Education indicated that there were 2,673 foreign students in learning institutions in the United States. Among these were 614 British North Americans (Canadians), 30 Mexicans, 236 Cubans, 105 Japanese, and 93 Chinese. Included in the list were more than 150 students from diverse parts of South and Central America, and 46 from the Philippines. In 1911–1912, the number of foreign students had risen to 4,856, and in 1920–1921, there were 8,357 foreign students (Wheeler, King, and Davidson, 1925).

Since 1954–1955, the Institute of International Education has been providing statistics on international students and scholars in the United States and around the world. The number of international students at that time was 34,232. The next section will examine the characteristics of international student flow into the United States.

CHARACTERISTICS OF FOREIGN STUDENT FLOW

In 1997–1998, there were 480,558 international students in the United States from various parts of the world, as follows: Asia, 277,506 (57.6 percent); Europe, 71,616 (14.9 percent); Latin America, 51,368 (10.7 percent); Middle East, 30,962 (6.4 percent); non-U.S. North America, 22,051 (4.6 percent); Africa, 23,162 (4.8

Table 1
Foreign Student Enrollment in the United States: 1954–Present

Year	Number of Students	Numerical Change	Annual Change (%)
1954–1955	34,232		
1964–1965	82,045	47,813	140.0
1974–1975	154,580	72,535	88.4
1984–1985	342,113	187,533	121.0
1989–1990	386,851	44,738	5.6
1990–1991	407,529	20,678	5.3
1991–1992	419,585	12,056	3.0
1992–1993	438,618	19,033	4.5
1993–1994	449,749	11,131	2.5
1994–1995	452,653	2,904	0.6
1995–1996	453,787	1,134	0.3
1996–1997	457,984	4,197	0.9
1997–1998	481,280	23,296	5.1

Source: Davis, 1998: ix.

percent); and Oceania, 3,893 (0.8 percent) (Davis, 1997). The Committee of Foreign Students and Institutional Policy predicted in the 1970s that the United States would attract over a million students in the 1990s (Barber, 1985); it is noteworthy that the United States has yet to attract half the predicted target (see Table 1).

The 1980s and 1990s saw a significant increase in the number of international students from Asia and Western Europe. Since 1987–1988, Asian students have constituted more than 50 percent of the entire U.S. international student population (Davis, 1997). However, many Asian countries experienced economic turmoil and currency devaluation starting in 1997, leading to the fear that the United States will lose a huge number of Asian students unless it identifies barriers and solutions to international education.

AREAS OF STUDY, GENDER COMPOSITION, AND PRIMARY SOURCES OF FUNDS

Ranked in order of popularity, international students tend to concentrate on the following areas of study: business and management (20.9 percent); engineering (14.9 percent); "other" (9.7 percent)—traditionally classified to include areas such as liberal/general studies, communications, law, library and archival science, and home economics; mathematics and computer science (8.5 percent); social sciences (8.1 percent); physical and life sciences (7.7 percent); fine and applied arts (6.5 percent); intensive English language (5.3 percent); health professions (4.1 percent); humanities (3.4 percent); education (2.7 percent); and agriculture (1.8 percent). The remaining 6.2 percent represents undeclared areas of study (Institute of International Education, 1999). These 1997–1998 figures are fairly representative of the 1990s and demonstrate a shift away from the humanities, which was the third most popular area of study in the 1960s, but which has been declining since the 1970s (Davis, 1997).

Traditionally, male international students have consistently outnumbered their female counterparts. For example, in 1954–1955, the male population was 76.8 percent as opposed to 23.2 percent for women. In 1996–1997, the percentages of men and women were 59 percent to 41 percent, respectively. It is interesting to note that Japan, Jamaica, and Trinidad and Tobago send a larger proportion of females than males (Institute of International Education, 1999). The number of undergraduate students has typically surpassed that of the graduate population, even though in the 1960s, 1970s, and mid-1980s, both categories reached a parity point. The majority of international students (in 1997–1998, 67.9 percent) at both the undergraduate and graduate levels are single, full-time students, supporting their education through personal or family finances. Other funding sources include U.S. colleges and universities (18 percent); home governments or universities (5.9 percent); foreign private sponsors (2.5 percent); current employers (2.3 percent); U.S. private sponsors (2.3 percent); U.S. government (0.8 percent); international organizations (0.5 percent); and other sources (0.2 percent) (Davis, 1998).

VISA CLASSIFICATION OF STUDENTS

The three most important documents people from other nations require are a passport, a visa, and the I-94 card. A passport is a repatriation document issued by the person's home country/

government. International students and scholars have to keep their passports valid for at least six months into the future at all times. Embassies or consulates of individual countries located in the United States can renew passports. A visa is a travel document issued by the U.S. embassy or consulate abroad, and it is issued in the form of a stamp in the passport by an officer at the U.S. consular post. It is not a guarantee of admission into the United States; it is a document that the foreign national presents at a port of entry to request admission into the United States. The I-94 is the arrival-departure record issued to all nonresident U.S. citizen travelers, including Canadian and U.S. permanent residents, after immigration officials at the port of entry have examined their documents. Most of the time, the I-94 issued to international students is marked "D/S," or duration of status, implying that the students can stay in the U.S. as long as they maintain their student standing.

Types of Visas

Much of the information in this section on visa classification of international students is summarized from *Boston College's Immigration Regulations for International Students and Scholars* (Nussbaum, 1998). There are various types of visas for which foreign nationals can apply. B-1 is for visitors on business. B-2 is for visitors here for pleasure; evidence of financial support and of tourist plans is required for this type of visa. Many students who come to the U.S. to visit apply for admission on this visa and then through international student offices change, with difficulty, to the F-1 visa.

The most common type of visa is the F-1 student visa, which is given to students admitted to an academic course of study. Students receiving this type of visa must manifest evidence of adequate financial support, adequate command of the English language, or proof that they will be enrolled in intensive English-language training programs. Accompanying spouses and children of F-1 visa students are issued F-2 visas. Before a student or dependents can apply for an F-1 or F-2 visa, they must be issued an I-20–AB or IAP-66 form from the institutions in which they will be enrolled. These forms prove that students can support themselves through their own funds or other funding sources.

Another common type of visa is the J-1 exchange-visitor visa for students and scholars. J-1 exchange-visiting professors and researchers must have a university appointment to teach or conduct research as well as an indication of adequate financial support. Spouses and children of J-1 exchange visitors are classified as J-2 and may apply for permission to the Immigration and Naturalization Service (INS) to accept employment for the support of the dependents, but not for the support of the J-1 visa holder.

By law, F-1 students may not accept off-campus employment at any time during their first year of study; however, the international student office, through the INS, may grant permission to accept off-campus employment after one year or in the case of a financial emergency. Students can accept non-work-study employment on campus for twenty hours per week during school semesters, and full-time during vacation periods without the permission of the INS. International student offices act as the clearinghouses for this type of employment.

Many international students and scholars may have immigrant status, also known as permanent-resident or green-card status. This group includes people who have professional degrees and labor certification for permanent positions. Some of them may have an international reputation, or they may be immediate family members of U.S. citizens or permanent residents, refugees, or people admitted under special diversity programs. Permanent residents can work without any restrictions and can apply for citizenship five years after obtaining the visa. Those married to U.S. citizens can apply for citizenship three years after obtaining permanent residence.

Practical-Training Visas

An important element for visa holders is practical training. F-1 visa holders can have practical training in their area of specialization. Curricular and optional practical training are the two types of this visa.

Curricular practical training

- is for students who have been full time for at least twelve months

- can be for part-time or full-time off-campus employment
- has no limit as long as it is required for the degree or is part of an established curriculum.

Students who complete one year or more of curricular practical training cannot apply for the optional practical training, which is employment in a student's field of study. This type of visa

- is open to students who have completed twelve months of study
- can be used during annual vacation periods and/or while school is in session
- allows students to work up to twenty hours a week and/or after completion of all course requirements excluding thesis, and/or upon completion of studies
- cannot exceed twelve months for F-1 students and eighteen months for J-1 and J-2 visa holders, except in cases where internship and practical work are part of the student's curriculum
- is not open to students who have already received one or more years of practical training.

Graduate students whose programs include immediate participation in internships or on-the-job training do not have to wait twelve months before they start their practical training.

ISSUES AFFECTING INTERNATIONAL STUDENTS

International students go through a lot of difficulties during their sojourn in the United States. In a 1992–1992 article, Selvadurai boldly stated: "The difficulties faced by international students in the United States have not changed radically since the days of Kwame Nkrumah in 1930. Although the population of international students has grown dramatically . . . the higher education community has shown little interest in the special needs of these students, or on the impact of such growth on the colleges and universities" (Selvadurai, 1991–92: 27–28). Following is a discussion of specific problems international students face.

Language

Problems international students face with the English language are featured prominently in the literature. Even though many international students are able to successfully complete in English the application procedures to bring them to the United States, reality sinks in as they begin their studies. The question of language difficulty affects foreign students in many facets of their lives on campus, and the causes are varied. Although some students do come from countries where English is the official language of instruction, or from homes where English was spoken often, most do not, and most find it "difficult to function in an academic context, even though they are able to pass a standardized proficiency examination" (Eddy, 1978: 5).

Thus, although students may be experts in the grammar of English language, and may have been exposed extensively to spoken English, once they arrive in the United States they face the yeoman's task of learning to speak, read, write, and think in English. The much-quoted line of a student is worth repeating here: "I think in Thai, I am fluent in Japanese, I read French, and I cry in English" (Cable, 1974: 40). Even though students tend to improve as the academic year progresses, instructors should recognize their needs. Coleman offers several strategies to alleviate some of these difficulties:

- reviewing and explaining key vocabulary specific to the course
- speaking clearly at a pace that will facilitate understanding
- explaining colloquial expressions used in class
- allowing students to use tape recorders as a means of keeping up with class lectures
- encouraging students to interrupt for clarification
- providing the opportunity for reluctant class participants to talk to the professor outside the class period
- using alternative types of assessment or replacing timed tests
- referring students to appropriate units on campus that assist them with language skills (Coleman, 1997).

The American Classroom Culture

The classroom culture in the United States presents a challenge to students from other countries, especially those from non-Western cultures. Kaikai outlines the major cultural differences between non-Western and Western students along the lines of perceptions of the instructor, attitude toward education, and performance expectations and reactions. For the non-Western student, the instructor is not only "omnipotent, revered, unquestionable, a disciplinarian," but also someone who "mandates conformity" (Kaikai, 1989: 124). The non-Western attitude toward education rigidly adheres to excellence, considers educational accomplishments as the most important manner of attaining status and wealth in society, and involves family members, peers, and society, putting pressure on students to attain status and wealth through education. In the non-Western world, students are blamed if they fail examinations and are informed of examination dates without being told specifically what to study; examination results, promotion outcomes, and completion of programs are made public. When a student fails, the entire family is disgraced. The Western attitudes and beliefs are the reverse of the characteristics outlined here (Kaikai, 1989).

In addition to the differences in expectations that international students experience, there are other classroom-related problems: course selection, advising, class attendance, punctuality, keeping up with the pace of classes (including note taking, asking questions, participating in class discussions as individuals and in groups), asking for assistance with course content, office hours, and quizzes and examinations. All these issues present the international student with a new landscape filled with anxiety, confusion, uncertainty, and bewilderment. This is understandable, because in many foreign countries, university education is so different from that of the United States. A *Denver Post* article summarizes what can be applicable to any U.S. campus: "Students are shocked to learn that they're allowed—even encouraged—to challenge their professors in class. 'You would never do that in Japan' . . . said . . . a senior from Nagoya, Japan's third largest city. 'It's impolite to speak out in public, and we have to respect our teachers'" (Curtin, 1999: B-05).

The International Student Assistant

The classroom culture in the United States takes on a different and distinct perspective when it comes to using foreign nationals in the classroom. Many graduate students from abroad are employed as international teaching assistants (ITAs). Nationwide, the role of ITAs continues to generate controversy. Universities and state legislatures now require a language proficiency screening for international teaching assistants whose native language is not English. This is especially important since standard instruments such as TOEFL (Test of English as a Foreign Language) or TSE (Test of Spoken English) have proven to be unreliable predictors of the classroom success of ITAs. To ensure that ITAs use English proficiently and have mastered the organizational, textual, and strategic knowledge required for effective classroom performance, various alternative tests have been used: Speaking Proficiency English Assessment Kit (SPEAK), the Foreign Service Institute (FSI) Oral Proficiency Interview, and the American Council on the Teaching of Foreign Languages Oral Proficiency Interview (ACTFL OPI) (Halleck and Moder, 1995).

Many universities have even gone a step further by including programs to improve the cultural and pedagogical skills of ITAs. At Louisiana State University, for example, domestic undergraduate students are recruited to evaluate ITAs and to determine their readiness to teach introductory linguistics courses. Among the items included in the evaluation are pronunciation, vocabulary and rhythm of speech, blackboard drawing/writing, and contact with the audience (Yule and Hoffman, 1993). As Halleck and Moder mention, many institutions have implemented tests requiring ITAs to perform teaching tasks. Among the skills evaluated during such tasks are:

- teaching skills, including organization and presentation of materials
- clarity of presentation, relevance of content
- use of blackboard and visual aids
- manner of speaking
- nonverbal communication
- audience awareness

- interaction
- teacher presence
- aural comprehension
- method of handling questions and clarity of response to questions
- pronunciation, fluency, and grammar
- ease of understanding their interactive language skills (Halleck and Moder, 1995).

It is important to note that ITA training varies from campus to campus; where such formal training does not take place, ITAs parading to our libraries may be struggling to master the expertise of classroom teaching on their own. Among the issues they may be battling include the behavior of undergraduate students, the informal and personalized atmosphere in the American classroom, and examination protocol. Coming from cultures where university students are held in the highest esteem and to the highest standard of seriousness, the sometimes laissez-faire attitude of American students can puzzle the ITA.

Culture Shock

Culture shock can take many forms. Wapner and associates list the following under the umbrella of culture shock: "strain in adapting, loss from uprooting, rejection by host, surprise, discomfort, indignation, disgust, impotence linked to unfamiliarity with culture and lack of capacity to cope" (Wapner et al., 1997: 286). In her definition, De Verthelyi includes "language difficulties, financial problems, dealing with a new educational system, pressure to succeed, changes in social status, home sickness, adjusting to social customs and norms, difficulties in making friends with host nationals, and . . . racial discrimination" (1995: 389). Thus, while international students are deeply involved in their academic work, they are simultaneously struggling to adjust to a new environment. International students are used to environments where friendships are established easily, where interaction among humans comes naturally, where the simple fact of being a college student commands the highest form of respect, where foreigners are welcomed with open arms, and where holding and touching people of the same sex are acceptable. They become bewildered as they discover that these human existence traits many take for granted have different interpretations and implications in America (Pedersen, 1991).

Many international student offices have orientations for international students to alert them to the elements of culture shock and to prepare them to deal with it. For example, at Boston College, the international student assistant program, now in its twentieth year, makes it possible for incoming international students to have a "buddy" throughout the year. Assistants are drawn from both domestic and international students, who make a one-year commitment to help their assigned incoming student to become acclimatized to the American culture and life at Boston College (Brancatella, 1999). Denver University uses the I-team, "students who befriend and mentor international students" (Scanlon, 1997: 4A). Team members drawn from U.S. and veteran international students introduce time concepts, class participation, grocery and department store shopping, banking, and other facets of American life to entering international students. Unfortunately, not all international students take advantage of such programs or the resources available to them through the international student and other similar offices on campus. This can lead to stress and other related conditions.

Stress

Here are just a few of the countless ingredients in the recipe for stress: adjusting to a new culture; stringent academic demands; nostalgia, stemming from the loss of close relationships; worry about the well-being of immediate and remote family members; uncertainty about political stability in home countries; the exorbitant costs of health care in the United States, especially compared with the free medical care in many foreign countries; the complicated employment regulations for students and their dependents; and the welfare of an accompanying spouse and dependents. International students seem to have to begin life all over again in a foreign land. However, most international students resist seeking help in times of stress. The reasons vary but most frequent among them are "distrust and lack of understanding of the counseling process, as well as a strong adherence to their cultural value orientation which favors psychological issues to be handled by themselves, by family members or peers" (De Verthelyi, 1995: 402).

Campus programs for incoming international students should continue to educate on the value of counseling, putting an emphasis on professionalism, trust, and confidentiality. Once students are assured that disclosing personal problems will not become CNN news items, they may be more willing to take advantage of campuswide programs designed to deal with even the most personal aspects of their lives.

CONCLUSION

Student migration to the United States has a long and impressive history. Even though the predicted overabundance of international students has never become a reality, it is clear that the United States is a world leader in educating citizens of other countries and that it will continue to attract students at all levels. F-1 and J-1 visa holders and their dependents will continue to populate our institutions of higher learning. During their sojourn, they are not immune from the plethora of conditions experienced in a new cultural and social environment. Language difficulties, the American classroom culture, culture shock, and stress are among the many experiences they must deal with. By understanding the international student flow, visa classification, and issues that affect students' academic and social well-being, we as librarians, and most importantly as educators, can provide better services in unison with many campus agencies to make the experience of our esteemed guests as meaningful and as memorable as possible.

REFERENCES

Barber, Elinor G., ed. 1985. *Foreign Student Flows: Their Significance for American Higher Education.* Newark: Institute of International Education.

Brancatella, Caroline. 1999. "An International Connection." *The Heights* (March 16): C4.

Cable, John N. 1974. "Foreign Students in the United States." *Improving College and University Teaching* 22 (Winter): 40–41.

Cieslak, Edward Charnwood. 1955. *The Foreign Student in American Colleges.* Detroit: Wayne University Press.

Coleman, Susan. 1997. "International Students in the Classroom: A Resource and an Opportunity." *International Education* 26 (Spring): 55–57.

Curtin, Dave. 1999. "A Warm Welcome USC's Key to Foreign Student Recruitment: A Home Away from Home." *Denver Post* (January 31): B-05.

Davis, Todd M., ed. 1997. *Open Doors 1996/97: Report on International Educational Exchange.* New York: Institute of International Education.

———. 1998. *Open Doors 1997/98: Report on International Educational Exchange.* New York: Institute of International Education.

De Verthelyi, Renata Frank. 1995. "International Students' Spouses: Invisible Sojourners in the Culture Shock Literature." *International Journal of Intercultural Relations* 19, no. 3 (Summer): 387–411.

Eddy, Margot Sanders. 1978. "Foreign Students in the United States: Is the Welcome Mat Out?" *AAHE-ERIC/Higher Education* (December): 5–8. Also available as ERIC Document 165524.

Halleck, Gene B., and Caroll Lynn Moder. 1995. "Testing Language and Teaching Skills of International Teaching Assistants: The Limits of Compensatory Strategies." *TESOL Quarterly* 29, no. 4 (Winter): 733–58.

Institute of International Education. 1999. "Primary Source of Funds, 1997/98." *Fast Facts: Open Doors 1997/98.* Available online at *www.opendoorsweb.org/download.htm* [cited 2000, March 30].

Institute of International Education. 1998. "What Foreign Students Study, 1997/98." *Fast Facts: Open Doors 1997/98.* Available online at *www.opendoorsweb.org/download.htm* [cited 2000, March 30].

Kaikai, Septimus M. 1989. "Accommodating Diversity." *College Teaching* 37, no. 4 (Fall): 123–25.

Meng, Chih. 1931. "The American Returned Students in China." *Pacific Affairs* 4, no. 1 (January): 1–16.

Nussbaum, Adrienne, ed. 1998. *Immigration Regulations for International Students and Scholars.* Chestnut Hill, Mass.: Boston College Office of the Dean of Student Development.

Pedersen, Paul B. 1991. "Counseling International Students." *The Counseling Psychologist*, 19, no.1 (January): 10–58.

Scanlon, Bill. 1997. "Easing the Way in a New Land: International Students Learn from DU's I-Team." *Denver Rocky Mountain News* (September 8): 4A.

Scanlon, David G. 1990. "Lessons from the Past in Developing International Education in Community Colleges." In *Developing International Education Programs*, edited by Richard K. Greenfield. San Francisco: Jossey-Bass.

Selvadurai, Ranjani. 1991–1992. "Problems Faced by International Students in American Colleges and Universities." *Community Review* 12, nos. 1–2 (Fall–Spring): 27–32.

Wapner, Seymour, Jack Demick, Takiji Yamamato, and Takashi Takahashi, eds. 1997. "Sojourn in a New Culture: Japanese Students in American Universities and American Students in Japanese Universities." In *Handbook of Japan–United States Environment-Behavior Research: Toward a Transactional Approach.* New York: Plenum.

Wheeler, William Reginald, Henry King, and Alexander B. Davidson. 1925. *The Foreign Student in America.* New York: Association Press.

Yule, George, and Paul Hoffman. 1993. "Enlisting the Help of U.S. Undergraduates in Evaluating International Teaching Assistants." *TESOL Quarterly* 27, no. 2 (Summer): 323–27.

International Students and the Library: New Tools, New Users, and New Instruction

Diane DiMartino and Lucinda R. Zoe
Baruch College, City University of New York

Increasingly, the international student population on American college campuses comes from non-Western countries. Students from South and East Asia comprised 57.8 percent of all foreign students during 1994–1995, a rise of over 27 percent since 1980–1981 (U.S. Department of Education, 1996). In addition to the difficulties most face in adapting to a different language and receiving and understanding communications both verbally and nonverbally, international students must also deal with different cultural norms and expectations. Many are accustomed to educational environments that emphasize lectures, memorization, and recitation over the more fluid American style of discussion and analysis.

Adjustments to this new environment extend to the college library, where information exists in a variety of formats, most stacks are open but arranged by unfamiliar alphabetical classification schemes, and computers are omnipresent. According to Moeckel and Presnell (1995), functional barriers can impede native as well as non-native students in the effective navigation of the library. These obstacles include underdeveloped critical-thinking skills, variations in educational backgrounds, inaccurate expectations of libraries and information technologies, and language problems.

Cultural barriers also exist and can be described as behaviors and ideals specific to individual countries—commonly nonverbal behaviors and communication styles. For instance, international students often arrive with more formal oral and written English-language skills than one tends to hear and use in everyday encounters. Their reading comprehension also is generally not as good as that of native students.

Sophisticated research tools, increased self-service access to a variety of full-text sources, and a growing awareness of learning styles and ethnic backgrounds present reference and instructional librarians with new concerns. The ability to personally observe and guide students lessens with each remote log-in, yet international students may be reluctant to approach library staff for assistance. This situation becomes more complicated for English as a Second Language (ESL) students, for whom vocabulary may be the biggest impediment to effective searching. Creative approaches to assessing user needs, developing innovative instructional models, and partnering with classroom faculty are critical in efforts to better serve and educate students attending universities in the information age.

The growth in full-text databases and information systems has significantly altered the information landscape. Many library networks now offer access to their subscription databases from home, the dorm room, and other off-campus sites. This often means less technical support and fewer opportunities for instruction on the use of these products. It remains to be seen if the World Wide Web will be able to provide new and more effective interactive instructional support. Searchers must now independently learn to select and navigate complex systems and to adapt their choices and approaches to different types of interfaces and databases—from basic bibliographic utilities to statistical machine-readable data files and full-text, multifile information systems, to a World Wide Web of point-and-click hypertext links. Full-text database searching poses even greater challenges to students with varying educational and cultural backgrounds, skills, and English-language proficiency. This chapter will briefly review the literature on international students in American libraries and examine the impact of learning styles, language proficiency, and cultural barriers on the library classroom.

INTERNATIONAL STUDENTS IN AMERICAN LIBRARIES

A number of articles have been written about foreign or international students in American libraries, focusing primarily on language barriers, cultural and communication differences, methods of bibliographic instruction, and suggested teaching models (Anderson and Adams, 1992; Borgman, 1989; Natowitz, 1995). In a 1995 review of the library literature in this area, Natowitz examined eighteen primary articles on the topic and identified the common issues, concerns, and trends regarding international students and American libraries, and noted that there was little in the literature that focused on technological barriers. Ball and Mahony's (1987) paper on foreign students, libraries, and culture identified major differences in foreign and American libraries and presented approaches to putting the international student and the academic library in a cultural context by way of revised instructional techniques and library staff development. They concluded that it is the responsibility of librarians to define the library for international students, to identify and describe services, and to teach them how to use basic research tools.

Differences in how libraries are used and perceived in different countries, and the difficulties encountered by international students in American libraries, have also been addressed in the literature (Macdonald and Sarkodie-Mensah, 1988; Moorhead, 1986; Sarkodie-Mensah, 1992; Wayman, 1984). This literature reviews culture shock and library anxiety and how it impacts international students' abilities to approach an authority figure, ask for help, use computers, and do independent research (Kflu and Loomba, 1990; Lam, 1988; Liu, 1993; Liu, 1995; Moeckel and Presnell, 1995; Onwuegbuzie and Jiao, 1998). Small towns and villages in other countries may have no libraries; those places with a library may have only books that may be out of date or not available for circulation. Censorship, restrictive lending policies, closed stacks, and notions of public service all vary dramatically from culture to culture, but most are decidedly different from what is considered common in academic libraries in the United States (Huston, 1989; Liestman and Wu, 1990). Such cultural factors must be kept in mind; it is not always a question of language fluency or proficiency.

Cultural differences of international students will produce a variety of culture-specific learning styles and information-seeking behavior that may be at odds with traditional American methods of instruction. Lin noted in a paper on library instruction for culturally diverse populations that "different modes of thinking produce different learning patterns that instructors should take into account" (Lin, 1994: 170). DiMartino and Zoe (1996) demonstrated that non-native English speakers had more difficulties than natives using Boolean logic and other vocabulary-based search strategies in a large, full-text database. Although many databases now present transparent interfaces that, in fact, employ Boolean logic and, in advanced search modes, permit one to search in specific fields of a document, many interfaces still require the user to submit a search statement employing the Boolean "and" and "or." Still others encourage the use of natural language searching and relevance ranking.

A review of the literature indicates that librarians, particularly instruction librarians, have been concerned with addressing the special needs of international students in American universities. There is a clear consensus in the literature of this field of what the issues are and what solutions and approaches are needed to address these issues appropriately. Language, cultural and technological barriers, and a heightened awareness of learning styles and cognitive development theories are all identified as primary issues that need increased attention. Of particular interest to librarians is the need to gain a greater awareness and understanding of learning styles and the integration of that knowledge into instruction planning.

CULTURAL DIFFERENCES AND LEARNING STYLES

In order to help students from other backgrounds become comfortable in the library and obtain needed research skills, librarians need to become familiar with cultural differences in learning styles and cognitive processes as well as the cultural and sociopolitical backgrounds of international students. There has been some work in the field of librarianship on learning theories and styles with regard to library instruction, although much of the work that has been done on learning styles and theory has taken place outside of the library literature. Models of intellectual development and basic cognitive development processes were addressed by McNeer (1991) in an article that reviews two major theories of cognitive development and then presents suggestions for their use in library instruction. An article by Mellon (1982) acknowledged that librarians have not been quick to integrate research on learning theories into instructional activities in the library. Both Mellon and Reichel (1988) incorporated cognitive development theories into library instruction design and assessment activities in the 1980s.

There is much to be gained by understanding learning styles and theory and integrating them into library instruction. In order to serve a diverse population of students, librarians and other teaching faculty must learn effective intercultural communication. Basic characteristics of various cultures, as well as the characteristics of individual languages, must be taken into consideration and examined. Kflu and Loomba (1990) pay particular attention to this area in their work and strongly urge librarians to become proficient at cultural appraisal and more sensitive to cultural differences. Others claim, however, that this cannnot be done simply by reading a few articles and having a desire to be more sensitive; specific strategies must be developed and training programs for librarians must be implemented within the context of a strong staff development program (Greenfield, 1988; Jacobson, 1988).

It is important for librarians as instructors to be aware of both their own learning and teaching styles as well as those of their students (Jacobson, 1993). However, this may be difficult to do in an open workshop setting, and one runs the risk of falling into generalities and stereotypes. Staff must be sensitive to students who represent other societies or backgrounds. There is also a move to create positions that specifically address and target the needs of international students, particularly if an institution has a large international student population (Liu, 1993; Welch and Lam, 1991).

One initial approach that is consistently recommended is to work with other departments on campus such as the international student affairs office or the campus ESL program (Greenfield, 1988; Helms, 1995). Instruction librarians can increase their knowledge of cultural differences in learning styles by partnering with ESL teachers who are familiar with diverse linguistic backgrounds. By extrapolating some of the underpinnings found in many contemporary ESL classrooms to the instructional library class, librarians may be better able to understand some of the learning styles international students bring to a library instruction session. In her description of different learning-style theories in the heterogeneous ESL classroom, Reid (1998: ix) states that "learning styles are internally based" and are often unconsciously used characteristics for the "intake and comprehension of new information." Students may exhibit multistyle preferences and may adapt their learning styles with experimentation and practice. Learning styles stand in contrast to learning strategies, which students may consciously use to improve their learning. Learning strategies identified in this context include metacognitive (self-monitoring and self-evaluation); cognitive (note taking and inferencing); and social/affective (clarification questions and cooperative work) (Reid, 1998).

Learning strategies and approaches continue to be addressed and examined in the literature. Onwuegbuzie and Jiao (1998) found that bibliographic workshops do not lower anxiety levels for non-native English-speaking students and recommended that instruction be based on learning styles. Dr. Howard Gardner, Harvard University, challenged the classical assessment of intelligence by presenting a wider and more eclectic range of intelligent behavior in his 1983 book, *Frames of Mind*. His Multiple Intelligences Theory presented seven distinct sets of skills for problem solving, creating new products, and finding or creating new problems—the fertile ground for new knowledge acquisition. Using the skills Gardner identified, Christison (1988) further defined the basic skills and examined the learning activities that help develop specific intelligences. A brief look at these seven skills can provide a point of departure for understanding the learning styles of international students:

1. *verbal/linguistic:* ability to use words effectively, orally and in writing. Skills include remembering information. Activities include lectures, small and large group discussions, and student speeches.
2. *musical:* sensitivity to rhythm, pitch, and melody. Skills in-

volve recognizing simple songs and varying tempo and rhythm.

3. *logical/mathematical:* ability to use numbers effectively and to reason well. Sample skills include understanding the principles of cause and effect and the ability to predict. Activities include logical-sequential presentation of subject matter, story problems, creating codes, logic problems, and puzzles.
4. *spatial/visual:* sensitivity to form, space, color, line, and shape. One is able to represent visual or spatial ideas graphically. Activities include charts, maps, diagrams, videos, and slides.
5. *bodily/kinesthetic:* ability to use the body to express ideas and feelings and to solve problems. Activities include hands-on activities, creative movement, field trips, and role playing.
6. *interpersonal:* ability to understand another person's moods and motivations and intentions. Sample skills involve responding effectively to people and problem solving. Activities involve cooperative groups, peer teaching, group brainstorming, pair work, and conflict mediation.
7. *intrapersonal:* ability to understand oneself and one's own strengths and weaknesses. Skills include understanding how one is similar to or different from others, reminding oneself to do something, knowing about oneself as a language learner, and knowing how to handle one's feelings. Activities include independent student work, individualized projects, options, self-programmed instruction or self-teaching, reflective learning, and goal setting.

Some ESL teachers and researchers have relied upon the Perceptual Learning Style Preference Survey developed by Joy Reid as an instrument to better understand students' preferred learning modes (Reid, 1998). The questionnaire allows ESL students to self-identify their preferred learning styles. Reid's 1987 study of nearly 1,300 ESL students across the United States showed that most of these ESL students liked kinesthetic (learns more effectively through complete body experience) and tactile (learns more effectively through touch or hands-on) learning. They also preferred independent studying and learning as compared to

Table 2
Learning Styles by Cultural Group

Group	No. Students Responding	Preferred Learning Styles
Arabic	193	visual, auditory, kinesthetic, tactile
Spanish	130	kinesthetic, tactile,
Japanese	130	none identified
Malay	113	kinesthetic, tactile
Chinese	90	visual, auditory, kinesthetic, tactile
Korean	118	visual, auditory, kinesthetic, tactile
Thai	47	kinesthetic, tactile
Indonesian	59	auditory, kinesthetic
English	153	auditory, kinesthetic

Source: Reid (1998).

learning in groups, a factor that may work against the one-shot lecture approach to library training. Each language and culture group responded differently in their selection of learning styles. Table 2 gives a breakdown of nine language background groups studied by Reid and their learning style preferences, in order of preference. These particular data should be helpful to instruction librarians planning programs for diverse populations, since possessing even basic knowledge of learning styles by a cultural group can provide insight into how best to reach specific student populations and design appropriate programs.

Reid has also pointed out that the longer ESL students study in the United States, the more their learning style preferences become more auditory and less tactile. Of the language backgrounds indicated above—including English—only the Arabic and Malay did not indicate negative perceptions of group learning. According to Cheng and Banya (1998), most East Asian students are not comfortable with group learning. They reported that individual success over group success is rewarded more in Chinese society, although group cohesiveness is ultimately essential. They also note that age, prior knowledge, gender, motivation, and ethnicity influence learning styles, subject matter, and context.

Collaboration requires that students assert themselves as well as actively listen to other viewpoints and can, especially within a heterogeneous group, promote positive social behaviors and understandings. Kinsella and Sherak (1998) have found that small group learning is recognized within a classroom setting as having substantial educational benefits. Peer working groups, when well designed, can help students learn more efficiently, but many international students show some resistance to working groups. This could be due to expectations, based on their academic backgrounds, that teachers alone, standing in the front of the classroom, have the responsibility to pass on information for students to record, memorize, and recall. Harthill and Busch (1998) report that culture often influences learning type preferences. They submit that students from countries such as Japan or Korea, which are homogeneous or "high-context cultures," have many rules for precise behavior and relationships. In these cultures, the internalization of information through analysis and reflective observation is highly valued. This emphasis on observation rather than action can produce students who are very quiet yet thoughtful and precise, who are vested in "keeping face."

Foley (1984) developed a list of attitudes and cultural traits from Pacific nations that can affect reference service and consequently impact instruction:

- cursory acquaintance with large body of western knowledge and culture
- difficulties with the alphabet
- differences in thinking patterns, resulting in difficulties understanding Western logic
- nonjudgmental acceptance of both sides, resulting in a lack of questioning
- fear of revealing ignorance
- respect for authority, which can hinder asking questions.

Knowledge of these traits as well as language skills and linguistic issues can have a dramatic impact on how a student responds in the classroom and should be taken into consideration by instruction librarians during program planning.

LIBRARY INSTRUCTION AND INTERNATIONAL STUDENTS

The library literature has specifically addressed the delivery of instructional services to international students. Jacobson (1988) reviewed literature on the importance of instructional programs and other specialized library services. Koehler and Swanson (1988) reported in a paper on ESL students and bibliographic instruction that cultural and societal differences make it difficult for international students to recognize that they need help or that they need to ask for help, leaving students ill-prepared to do basic library research. As a result of increasing awareness of such issues, innovations in instruction and new approaches to instruction targeted at international students have begun to appear in the literature (Adams, 1992; Hall, 1991; Hefner and Rhodes, 1988; Helms, 1995; Lin, 1994; Moeckel and Presnell, 1995; Osborne and Poon, 1995). In a survey of 395 international students at the University of Illinois on computer-use and library-use patterns, Allen (1993) reported that many international students arrive in the United States unprepared to take advantage of automated systems. She further noted that not only did they not have appropriate information retrieval skills, but also that libraries need to make changes in their instructional programs in order to serve these students adequately. This particular study was significant in that it, unlike many of the previous studies, was conducted after the use of computers, online catalogs, and end-user database searching had become common tools for basic library research.

LANGUAGE PROFICIENCY

English-language verbal and communication skills and the difficulties encountered by ESL students have been examined in the library setting in a number of studies, which have often addressed the relationship between English-language proficiency/command of the language and effective library use (Allen, 1993; Feldman, 1989; Koehler and Swanson, 1988; Macdonald and Sarkodie-Mensah, 1988). A study by Bilal (1989) examined the acquisition of library research skills by international students in relation to their English-language proficiency. Results of the study indicated that a lack of command of the English language and lack of a basic awareness of library research and resources were major obstacles to comprehension. There has also been some reporting on the use of bilingual presentations—offering instruction in various native languages (Liestman and Wu, 1990; Spanfelner, 1991). This approach, while effective, raises human resources and budget issues, but also questions the appropriateness of offering instruction in a native language when all of a student's other campus work, classes, and activities are in English. Feldman (1989) and Ormondroyd (1989) examined specific learning strategies that might be more effective with international students. Both discuss the benefits of a task-oriented approach to library instruction, and report on programs that are designed around four- to five-step research tasks that include bibliographic instruction.

There has been some research on the potential effects of language background on searching ability and retrieval in automated systems that merits further study. Allen's 1993 study found that the increased reliance on automated systems in American libraries might be one of the most notable differences between U.S. libraries and those in the native countries of international students. This research suggests that much more attention needs to be paid to instruction in the use of automated systems and tools. DiMartino and Zoe (1996) examined the issue in a study on the impact of native language on search success and satisfaction in using electronic information services. Cultural differences and educational backgrounds—how libraries are viewed, how languages are constructed, how people think and view their world—are all factors that may prove to have a serious impact on searching skills and abilities as well as on the instructional methods needed to reach these students. A closer look at linguistic issues and the potential influence of language skills on the ability of students to learn and instructors to teach is in order to fully understand all the factors at play when working with diverse populations in the library classroom.

LINGUISTIC ISSUES

With the growing number of foreign or non-native, English-speaking students in college libraries, librarians are increasingly confronted with the need to communicate more effectively, not only at the reference desk but also in the classroom. A growing awareness of linguistics and communication theory by librarians points to the importance of work already done by scholars and researchers in other disciplines (Radford, 1996).

Linguistic issues play a great role in the delivery of effective instructional services to a culturally diverse population. Linguistic theory is a set of categories, rules, and principles to explain observations about language. Broadly speaking, it covers phonetics, or the sounds of languages; phonology, the function and patterning of sounds; morphology, the study of word structure; and syntax, the study of sentence structure (Parker, 1986). Syntactic knowledge helps us avoid a sentence such as *Jack smiled Dean*. Syntactic knowledge fits a word into the proper grammatical category and indicates whether it is a noun, accepts pluralization, or takes a direct object. Semantics is the study of meaning. Familiarity with semantics helps us avoid such phrases as *the bike whom I rode*. Dewdney and Michell (1996) point out that the "communication accidents" (such as a request for the book *Oranges and Peaches*, not *On the Origin of Species*) that frequently occur between librarians and students often have linguistic explanations or interpretations. For example, a word may be heard as "fie-la" but be written "phyla" (Dewdney and Michell, 1996). Homophones can be truly challenging to the nonnative speaker. Common examples include euthanasia/youth in Asia; China/china; Turkey/turkey. English has many words with more than one meaning, such as fly, hide, and tear. Ambiguity also is found with such sentences as *Chris believes that she is a genius*, which can refer to either Chris or someone else. However, in *Chris believes herself to be a genius*, "herself" refers only to Chris. The linguistic foundations of the native languages students bring with them to the library classroom, coupled with poor English vocabulary skills, may interfere with their ability to construct effective search statements.

According to Professor Gerard Dalgish (1999), director of the ESL program at Baruch College, CUNY, many ESL students make errors that fall into two categories: grammatical errors (use of articles, connectors, and plurals) and semantic/idiomatic/vocabulary errors. As an example of the latter type of error, a non-Latin-language student may write "Children should be obedient and not face their parent," selecting "face" for "confront" from a thesaurus. Many mistakes are over compounds, articles, subject-verb agreement, and confusion over parts of speech, plurals, sentence combining, tenses, and "rooting" of words. Despite different language backgrounds, many students make similar mistakes, with articles the biggest problem for all language groups: the Chinese, Russian, and Korean languages do not have articles; French, Spanish, Italian, and Swedish do; yet students tend to make similar mistakes with articles. Native speakers of these languages also tend to leave out subject-verb agreement and have difficulties determining nouns and whether to use singular or plural forms. Compounds are also difficult to construct or unravel.

Linguistic scholars have closely examined differences in languages. O'Grady, Dobrovolsky, and Aronoff (1989) noted that each language has a different type of grammatical system, and that all are equally complex. Some, such as Spanish, employ patterns of double negatives: *Juan no vio' nada* (John not saw nothing). However, in virtually all languages, negative elements such as "not" either immediately precede or follow the verb; in Spanish, for example, it would be correct to write *a child lost a shoe* or *lost a shoe a child* (O'Grady, 1989). Chinese, however, is a subject-verb-object language, with the topic appearing at the beginning of the sentence, followed by a reference to the topic: *This gentleman have you ever seen him?* (DeFrancis, 1984). Chinese is a context-oriented and terse language that uses sentence or phrase connectors such as *and* or *if* less frequently than English. The answer to the English question, *Do students like him?* would be *Yes, students like him* in English, but simply *like* in Chinese. Like the English word *deer*, DeFrancis goes on to note, Chinese nouns do not change to distinguish between plural and singular; within the language, the context will remove the ambiguity. In Chinese, modifying elements precede the elements they modify, with adjectives coming before nouns and adverbs before verbs. Thus, *This I here yesterday bought book* would be in English *This book that I bought here yesterday*. When compared to other languages, Chinese appears to have a fixed word order. Russian, DeFrancis points out, is the reverse: a highly inflected language, its noun endings indicate subject and object, permitting subject-verb-object to be reversed to object-verb-subject with the exact same meaning. This is in contrast to English, where *Sheila loves Max* does not have the same meaning as *Max loves Sheila*.

Implications of Linguistic Issues on Instruction

Clearly, linguistic issues must be considered, acknowledged, and understood in order to design and develop effective instruction for students with diverse language backgrounds. While search engines and database interfaces have improved over the past several years, especially with the migration to Web-based services, most are still reliant on Boolean logic techniques and still require sophisticated use of vocabulary—truncation, proximity searching, plurals, and field searching. Even the new natural language interfaces employ basic Boolean concepts when breaking down a search statement. This action may take place behind the scene, but users should still be able to understand their search results. The introduction and efficacy of natural language searching needs to be examined more closely in the literature; whether it will help has yet to be determined. The linguistic issues that foreign students bring with them into the library and the classroom must be taken seriously and integrated into professional development and training programs for librarians.

In 1995, two members of the library department at Baruch College explored the ways in which 131 graduate students, trained on the full-text LEXIS/NEXIS system, were searching this information service (DiMartino and Zoe, 1996). (This version was a precursor to the more highly structured Web-based product, LEXIS/NEXIS Academic Universe, currently available on many campuses.) Access to full-text newspapers and periodicals, corporate documents, court cases, and laws have long been the strength of the system.

At Baruch College, 50 percent of all students come from homes where English is not the first language. Given that effective use of LEXIS/NEXIS required specific and complex vocabulary skills (proper use of Boolean operators, synonym searching, proximity relations, segment searching, and truncation), the impact of language background upon search results was an important component of the study. The subjects consisted of 52 native English speakers; 49 speakers of Chinese or Korean; 18 students whose native languages were French, Spanish, Russian, or German; and 13 students with other native languages, mainly from Southeast Asia and the Middle East. The students had varying degrees of experience with the system, and all of them had received basic introductory training.

The study looked at several factors, including satisfaction with search results. Overall, 55 percent of the students indicated dissatisfaction. Of the 49 native East Asian speakers, 67 percent reported dissatisfaction, while only 38 percent of the 52 native English speakers reported any dissatisfaction, as shown in Table 3. Of the 18 European-based language speakers, 13, or 72 percent, reported dissatisfaction. Chi-square tests revealed a significant pattern of association with a Pearson's value of .004.

Students also expressed difficulties in search strategy construction. Chinese and Korean students had more trouble with library and file selections than did native English speakers. All students, however, indicated difficulties in developing search strategies. Moreover, only 21 percent of the East Asian students reported using Boolean connectors, compared to 46 percent of the native English speakers. The East Asian students also reported very little use of truncation (15 percent) or wildcard symbols (6 percent) (see Table 4). This was not surprising, considering the language skills (identifying key words and concepts, specifying proximity relationships, and applying Boolean operators) that were needed to properly construct an effective search. Given the absence of plurals as well as use of the word "and" as a connector in the Chinese language, these results make sense. A closer look at these problem areas reported by non-native speakers of English should provide insight on future instructional approaches and the needs of different users.

COMPUTER/INFORMATION LITERACY

Critical thinking skills, which are increasingly important in this information society, may not be familiar to international students. This ability to select, analyze, evaluate, and appropriately use information is a skill that must be learned and continuously developed. According to Moeckel and Presnell (1995), American higher education tends to be highly participatory, with in-

Table 3
Correlation Between Language and Search Satisfaction

Results	Native Speaker	E. Asian	European	Total
Satisfied	32	16	5	53
(%)	26.89%	13.45%	4.20%	44.54%
(column %)	61.54%	32.65%	27.78%	
Dissatisfied	20	33	13	66
(%)	16.81%	27.73%	10.92%	55.46%
(column %)	38.46%	67.35%	72.22%	
Total	52	49	18	119
(%)	43.70	41.18	15.13	100.00%

Chi-square = 10.933, df = 2, p = 0.004

teraction between instructors and students that helps develop critical-thinking skills. There is a decreased emphasis on rote memorization and the teacher's expertise. A lack of developed critical thinking skills may have a negative impact on a student's ability to use information resources effectively.

Full-Text Databases

The move toward Web-based subscription databases that are accessible outside of the library creates yet more obstacles for the inexperienced international searcher. Many of these new databases, particularly full-text services, are presented as easy, user-friendly services. Yet, by offering full-text retrieval they require sophisticated knowledge of search strategy construction, Boolean operators, and field searching, as well as a great awareness of content. Though too often deceptively simple and replete with help features, these databases are underutilized by students. For example, a recent unpublished study examined the need for training on new user-friendly Web-based databases and found that students are not navigating these services as well as one might expect. Zoe (1999) surveyed 100 users, all students in introductory library science, college-credit courses on information research in business. The students searched Information Access's (IAC) Expanded Academic Index, a full-text periodi-

Table 4
Analysis of Search Techniques Used by Language Background

	Boolean	Proximity Connectors	Modi-fication	Wild Card	Trun-cation	Segment Searching	Date Range
Native Speaker	46%	32%	32%	30%	22%	27%	38%
(37)	(17)	(12)	(12)	(11)	(8)	(8)	(14)
East Asian	21%	49%	57%	06%	15%	34%	34%
(47)	(10)	(23)	(27)	(3)	(7)	(16)	(16)
Total	36%	39%	54%	18%	19%	32%	38%
(104)	(37)	(40)	(56)	(19)	(20)	(33)	(40)

cal database on the Web, as part of a three-month product evaluation project. Four classes, each with twenty-five students, participated in the study. Two classes (fifty students total) received an introduction, brief overview, and short training session on the IAC full-text Web database; the other fifty students received no training or introduction. All 100 participants were given the same research question and asked to use the database and then complete an evaluation form that collected data on their gender, native language, search satisfaction and results, ease of use, and actual search strategy. Statistically significant correlations between training and search results were shown. Eighty-five percent of those who had received training found the database easy to use, but only 57 percent of those not trained found it easy to use. Chi-square test calculations were performed and produced a Pearson's value of .002, a clear indication of significance. Likewise, 42 percent of those trained believed they had retrieved "all of the information" needed, whereas only 26 percent of those who had not received training reported that they believed they had located all of the needed information—producing a Chi-square Pearson value of .046, again statistically significant. These findings suggest that some of the many new "easy" Web-based databases that are being marketed as user-friendly, end-user systems still require training to maximize their potential. Results indicate that although satisfied with their results, the users did not in fact conduct effective searches or net satisfactory results.

Search Engines and Interfaces

Many of today's information services and databases still rely heavily on the use of Boolean connectors, strong vocabulary skills, and, to a lesser extent, knowledge about the source. Even as search engines have become more streamlined and friendly in a Web-based environment—with drop-down menus, point-and-click navigation, and menu-driven interfaces—the sheer number of databases and types of engines continue to grow and become more complex. In any given academic library a student is likely to encounter a variety of engines and interfaces in such services as Dow Jones Interactive, LEXIS/NEXIS Academic Universe, OCLC's FirstSearch databases, UMI's ProQuest Direct, IAC's numerous databases, the Wilson and Silver Platter products, not to mention a plethora of government services and smaller, more specialized services such as Softline's Ethnic NewsWatch. These are usually considered the "easy" user-friendly products—each with their own engine, interface, output options, and special features.

Students are also faced with the more complex products, many of which are used independently, usually without the benefit of instruction or direction. Disclosure's Global Access, for example, provides SEC files, company data, and annual reports—with a very sophisticated front-end engine that allows for extensive manipulation of search results. Yet, many of these services are presented to students as simple and easy to use because they are Web-based, when in fact they utilize sophisticated language-based systems. The LEXIS/NEXIS Academic Universe service, for instance, provides an opening search window that requires a keyword or phrase. It also has a hidden default that searches only the headline or lead paragraph of an article or record. While that default might be apparent to some, search results still can remain misleading. Moreover, searching a full-text system like LEXIS/NEXIS or Dow Jones Interactive requires the use of proximity connectors to focus in on a desired topic. Even native English speakers have trouble navigating many of these systems effectively. One can only imagine how perplexing they must appear to international students whose background has not prepared them for this level of automation in a library. Keeping up with the abundance of databases now available and so common in most American libraries is a challenge even to librarians and trained information professionals.

With the dramatic increase of full-text offerings, search and retrieval continues to be a tricky business. Knowledge of Boolean searching and how to use the basic operators as well as an understanding of proximity searching and relations is critical in order to search these databases effectively. Language skills and subtle linguistic differences can make a big difference in a student's ability to produce relevant results. The use of plurals, articles, and phrase connections in any language will greatly impact a student's success with a full-text database. The ability to understand the concept of field searching is also critical, particularly in the business databases, which offer the ability to search by a much wider range of specific fields such as SIC codes, company name, or product codes.

In order to comprehend "fields" or segments of a document, one has to have some familiarity with the original source documents. This refers not only to the way in which a document is designed and laid out in various fields, but also to the way it relates to similar documents in its discipline. Students need to grasp the difference between a refereed journal article, a popular periodical article, a newspaper article, a press release, a media transcript, and a conference proceeding. They should also be able to distinguish between primary and secondary sources. This is an area of great potential concern where the international student is concerned. Many have never seen the periodicals and newspapers that most American students have grown up with. Their first and only experience with many of these titles may be only in electronic format. *Redbook* may appear to be as credible a source as *American Demographics*. Furthermore, the popularity of the World Wide Web and its multitude of search engines present yet more difficulties in terms of language and search and retrieval. With the variety of basic and advanced Web search engines, subject directories, and meta-search engines from Yahoo! to Excite to AltaVista to HotBot, users must learn and use language-based searching techniques.

INSTRUCTIONAL APPROACHES AND RECOMMENDATIONS

Examining and understanding some of the language problems and difficulties international students may encounter when searching may assist librarians in designing instructional modules and workshops, but helping students obtain critical thinking skills is even more important. Often, social and peer-influenced networks spring up among students of the same language or ethnic background that substitute for the family- or community-oriented networks back home. These peer groups can play a critical role in the way students seek information, and, though comforting to some students, can often result in the dissemination of misinformation, or partial information. Librarians should seek to create ways, either through individual relationships, student clubs or organizations, or the campus international-student office, to "intervene" and provide opportunities for directed peer learning in a supportive environment.

Like all students, international students exhibit a wide range of behaviors. Some may be shy and others demanding. Nodding heads may not mean what we expect. Working in a multicultural environment requires librarians to learn new ways of responding to the changing needs of a diverse student body. For a number of years now, those researching this issue have been providing clear and concrete suggestions and models on instructing international students. Instruction librarians have been urged to develop in-house training programs and to create professional development opportunities to retrain and reorient themselves to the needs of a more diverse population. Librarians must gain a greater understanding of learning styles and cognitive development theories and, indeed, must be taught to become proficient at cultural appraisal and more sensitive to cultural differences. In order to accomplish this, very clear and specific strategies must be developed, and training programs for librarians must be implemented. In institutions with large international student populations, it may be necessary to develop new library positions that specifically serve the needs of international students. Librarians are also strongly urged to partner with ESL teachers who are familiar with the linguistic issues, and to collaborate with the international student affairs office on campus to better prepare themselves with an increased knowledge of cultural differences in learning styles.

A number of articles have appeared suggesting ways in which the library instructor can develop methods to interact effectively with non-native speaking students. Osborne and Poon (1995) and Helms (1995) recommend holding unique workshops for non-native speakers. Helms suggests offering workshops in such a manner that indicates to students that their time will be profitably spent. Publicity and organization remain important components of any library instruction program. Efforts made to reach out to the international student population include contacting the campus international student office, working with clubs and student leaders, and taking advantage of any word-of-mouth, electronic, and traditional campus publicity systems. In addition, the creation of a social atmosphere for the students is important. Getting students to introduce themselves and talk about their expectations will help toward this end. Evaluate each workshop, examine attendees' suggestions, and make revisions for future workshops. Hands-on experience prompts international students to think through the process while overcoming the communication barrier. Macdonald and Sarkodie-Mensah (1988) also recommend that a majority of class time be spent in hands-on activities and, if possible, that librarians partner with faculty or link library classes to ESL courses. Downing and Diaz (1993) also recommend working with instructors both before and after class to strengthen the content and relevance of the workshop, and emphasize that creating an informal atmosphere in the classroom can help to humanize the library and make the students feel more welcome. They stress that improved cross-cultural communication (staying alert to reactions, using the body to communicate, not assuming knowledge of the system, and being friendly) are important steps to take within the classroom setting.

A number of instructional methods and techniques have been suggested when working with students for whom English is not the native language. Below is a compilation of suggestions from the literature cited above based on the experience and insight of instruction librarians working in the field:

- Employ a mix of lecture, discussion, demonstrations, and hands-on activities to appeal to the various learning styles encountered in a typical multicultural classroom.
- Include time for students to ask questions about hand-outs.
- Do as much of a drill as possible during class, as most students will not do the exercises later.
- Create an atmosphere in which students will feel free to come to you, or someone else, with questions or feedback.
- When possible, link a workshop with a class and an instructor.
- Target individual needs by asking students ahead of time their majors or topics of interest.
- Prepare relevant examples or exercises related to those interests.
- Provide tours of the library, explaining how photocopiers and microfiche readers work to make students feel more comfortable.

Common sense also plays a great part in working with international students:

- Speak slowly, clearly, and deliberately, defining technical terms and avoiding slang.
- Use simple sentence structure and vocabulary.
- Explain something several different ways.
- Rephrase rather than repeat to make sure questions have been understood.
- Ask for feedback and verify that students understand; do not assume that they do.
- Listen carefully; be aware of possible cultural influence.
- Be sensitive to the stresses from which students may be suffering.

Kinsella and Sherak (1998), both ESL instructors, provide some guidelines for designing and implementing group workshops—a situation that may be uncomfortable for some students, but are often necessary in library instruction programs:

- Have highly structured tasks, with explicit objectives, procedures, and outcomes.
- Invite multiple responses that build collective knowledge.

- Create tasks with multiple parts that include analysis and creative problem solving, as well as personal relevance and meaningful application.
- Provide a clear and adequate time frame.
- Include different participation formats (independent, partner, small group, unified class).
- Be an involved teacher-facilitator who checks progress and helps students stay on task.

A big issue facing librarians today is the lack of interaction, guidance, or observation we have with students using electronic tools to do research. This is due to the increase in remote access to electronic resources through virtual networks. The situation becomes more complicated for ESL students, for whom vocabulary may be the biggest impediment to effective searching. The impact of the new electronic information environment on instruction cannot be underestimated. Our challenge is to harness the strengths of the technologies so that they work for us in and out of the classroom. The Web can support and supplement instruction through Web-based tutorials and asynchronous interactive computer-based instruction. Students can pace themselves and be in control of their own learning process. Regardless of the format, however, the issues remain the same, particularly when striving to serve an international population. Knowledge of basic searching principles and techniques needed to access electronic information services is still required when using sophisticated vocabulary-based systems. The irony here is that personal interaction may be most beneficial to nonnative students, yet end-user searching produces exactly the opposite—human intervention is often missing. Establishing an effective search query is still critical, maybe even more so now than it was years ago. The challenge in teaching is even greater.

FINAL RECOMMENDATIONS

Although any number of models could be developed, the following recommendations and training guidelines should be considered when developing a program appropriate for your institution:

- *Set up partnerships* between librarians, teaching faculty, and other relevant departments.
- *Develop assignments related to the curriculum*—focus training on specific curricular incentives to put research and information needs into context.
- *Establish multistep training*—develop students' electronic research skills by introducing them to less complex tools first.
- *Teach critical-thinking skills*—focus on the actual content and evaluation of information resources.
- *Direct peer learning in a supportive environment*—develop small group-training workshops that encourage collaboration and learning between native and non-native speakers of English to enhance content and context, and improve listening and oral skills.
- *Prepare for the diversity* of populations and learning styles within the classroom.
- *Promote staff development programs*—sensitize staff to cultural, language, and technological barriers.

REFERENCES

Adams, Maurianne. 1992. "Cultural Inclusion in the American College Classroom." *Teaching for Diversity: New Directions for Teaching and Learning* 49 (Spring): 5–15.

Allen, Mary Beth. 1993. "International Students in Academic Libraries." *College & Research Libraries* 54 (July): 323–33.

Anderson, James A., and Maurianne Adams. 1992. "Acknowledging the Learning Styles of Diverse Student Populations: Implications for Instructional Design." *New Directions for Teaching and Learning* 49 (Spring): 19–33.

Ball, Mary Alice, and Molly Mahony. 1987. "Foreign Students, Libraries, and Culture." *College & Research Libraries* 48 (March): 160–66.

Bilal, Dania M. 1989. "International Students' Acquisition of Library Research Skills: Relationship with Their English Language Proficiency." *Reference Librarian*, no. 24: 129–45.

Borgman, Christine L. 1989. "All Users of Information Retrieval Systems Are Not Created Equal: An Exploration into Individual Differences." *Information Processing & Management* 25, no. 3: 237–51.

Cheng, Mario Hsueh-Yu, and Kingsley Banya. 1998. "Bridging the Gap between Teaching Style and Learning Styles." In *Understanding Learning Styles in the Second Language Classroom*, edited by Joy Reid. Upper Saddle River, N.J.: Prentice-Hall Regents.

Christison, Mary Ann. 1998. "Multiple Intelligence Theory and Second Language Learning." In *Understanding Learning Styles in the Second Language Classroom*, edited by Joy Reid. Upper Saddle River, N.J.: Prentice-Hall Regents.

Dalgish, Gerard. 1999. Interview by Diane DiMartino. February 18, New York, NY.

DeFrancis, John. 1984. *The Chinese Language: Fact and Fantasy*. Honolulu: University of Hawaii Press.

Dewdney, Patricia, and B. Gillian Michell. 1996. "Oranges and Peaches: Understanding Communication Accidents in the Reference Interview." *RQ* 35 (Summer): 520–36.

DiMartino, Diane, and Lucinda R. Zoe. 1996. "End-User Full-Text Searching: Access or Excess?" *Library and Information Science Research* 18 (Summer): 133–49.

Downing, Karen, and Joseph R. Diaz. 1993. "Module 6: Instruction in a Multicultural/Multiracial Environment." In *Learning to Teach: Workshops on Instruction. A Project of the Learning to Teach Task Force of the Bibliographic Instruction Section*. Chicago: American Library Association, Association of College and Research Libraries.

Feldman, Dick. 1989. "The International Student and Course-Integrated Instruction: The ESL Instructor's Perspective." *Research Strategies* 7 (Fall): 159–66.

Foley, May. 1984. "Reference and Information Services in a Multi-Cultural Environment." *Journal of Library & Information Science* 10 (October): 143–62.

Gardner, Howard. 1983. *Frames of Mind: The Theory of Multiple Intelligences*. New York: Basic Books.

Greenfield, Louise W. 1988. "Training Library Staff to Reach and Teach International Students." In *Reaching and Teaching Diverse Library Groups: Papers Presented at the Sixteenth National LOEX Conference*. Ann Arbor: Pierian.

Hall, Patrick Andrew. 1991. "The Role of Affectivity in Instructing People of Color: Some Implications for Bibliographic Instruction." *Library Trends* 39 (Winter): 316–26.

Harthill, Barbara, and Connie Busch. 1998. "Teaching Modals to Multistyle Learners." In *Understanding Learning Styles in the Second Language Classroom*, edited by Joy Reid. Upper Saddle River, N.J.: Prentice-Hall Regents.

Hefner, James A., and Leslie G. Rhodes. 1988. "Excellence in Education: Libraries Facilitating Learning for Minority Students." In *Libraries and the Search for Academic Excellence*, edited by Patricia Senn Breivik and Robert Wedgeworth. Metuchen, N.J.: Scarecrow.

Helms, Cynthia Mae. 1995. "Reaching Out to the International Students through Bibliographic Instruction." *Reference Librarian*, nos. 51–52: 295–307.

Huston, Mary M. 1989. "May I You: Teaching Culturally Diverse End-Users through Everyday Information Seeking Experiences." *Reference Services Review* 17, no. 1: 7–11.

Jacobson, Francis F. 1988. "Bibliographic Instruction and International Students." *Illinois Libraries* 70 (December): 628–33.

Jacobson, Trudi E. 1993. "Module 2: Selecting a Teaching Technique." In *Learning to Teach: Workshops on Instruction. A Project of the Learning to Teach Task Force of the Bibliographic Instruction Section*. Chicago: American Library Association, Association of College and Research Libraries.

Kflu, Tesfai, and Mary A. Loomba. 1990. "Academic Libraries and the Culturally Diverse Student Population." *College & Research Libraries News* 51 (June): 524–27.

Kinsella, Kate, and Kathy Sherak. 1998. "Designing ESL Classroom Collaboration to Accommodate Diverse Work Styles." In *Understanding Learning Styles in the Second Language Classroom*, edited by Joy Reid. Upper Saddle River, N.J.: Prentice-Hall Regents.

Koehler, Boyd, and Katherine Swanson. 1988. "ESL Students and Bibliographic Instruction: Learning Yet Another Language." *Research Strategies* 6 (Fall): 148–60.

Lam, Errol R. 1988. "The Reference Interview: Some Intercultural Considerations." *RQ* 27 (March): 390–95.

Liestman, Daniel, and Connie Wu. 1990. "Library Orientation for International Students in their Native Language." *Research Strategies* 8 (Fall): 191–96.

Lin, Poping. 1994. "Library Instruction for Culturally Diverse Populations: A Comparative Approach at Purdue University." *Research Strategies* 12 (Summer): 168–73.

Liu, Mengxiong. 1995. "Ethnicity and Information Seeking." *Reference Librarian* 49–50: 123–34.

Liu, Ziming. 1993. "Difficulties and Characteristics of Students from Developing Countries in Using American Libraries." *College & Research Libraries* 54 (January): 25–31.

Macdonald, Gina, and Elizabeth Sarkodie-Mensah. 1988. "ESL Students and American Libraries." *College & Research Libraries* 49 (September): 425–31.

McNeer, Elizabeth J. 1991. "Learning Theories and Library Instruction." *Journal of Academic Librarianship* 17, no. 5: 294–97.

Mellon, Constance A. 1982. "Information Problem-Solving: A Developmental Approach to Library Instruction." In *Theories of Bibliographic Education*, edited by Cerise Oberman and Katrina Strauch. New York: R. R. Bowker.

Moeckel, Nancy, and Jenny Presnell. 1995. "Recognizing, Understanding, and Responding: A Program Model of Library Instruction Services for International Students." *Reference Librarian* nos. 51–52: 309–25.

Moorhead, Wendy. 1986. "Ignorance Was Our Excuse: BI for Foreign Students Requires a Shift in Cultural Perspective." *College & Research Libraries News* 9 (October): 585–87.

Natowitz, Alan. 1995. "International Students in U.S. Academic Libraries: Recent Concerns and Trends." *Research Strategies* 13 (Winter): 4–16.

O'Grady, William, Michael Dobrovolsky, and Mark Aronoff. 1989. *Contemporary Linguistics*. New York: St. Martin's.

Onwuegbuzie, Anthony J., and Qun G. Jiao. 1998. "The Relationship between

Library Anxiety and Learning Styles among Graduate Students: Implications for Library Instruction." *Library & Information Science Research* 20 (Spring): 235–49.

Ormondroyd, Joan. 1989. "The International Student and Course-Integrated Instruction: The Librarian's Perspective." *Research Strategies* 7 (Fall): 148–58.

Osborne, Nancy Seale, and Cecilia Poon. 1995. "Serving Diverse Library Populations through the Specialized Instructional Services Concept." *Reference Librarian*, nos. 51–52: 285–94.

Parker, Frank. 1986. *Linguistics for Non-Linguists*. Boston: Allyn and Bacon.

Radford, Marie L. 1996. "Communication Theory Applied to the Reference Encounter: An Analysis of Critical Incidents." *Library Quarterly* 66 (April): 123–37.

Reichel, Mary. 1988. "Library Literacy." *RQ* 28 (Fall): 29–32.

Reid, Joy, ed. 1998. *Understanding Learning Styles in the Second Language Classroom*. Upper Saddle River, N.J.: Prentice-Hall Regents.

Sarkodie-Mensah, Kwasi. 1992. "Dealing with International Students in a Multicultural Era." *Journal of Academic Librarianship* 18 (September): 214–16.

Spanfelner, Deborah. 1991. "Teaching Library Skills to International Students." *Community & Junior College Libraries* 7, no. 2: 69–72.

U.S. Department of Education. 1996. *Digest of Education Statistics*. Available online at *http://nces.ed.gov/pubs/d96/D96T408.html* [cited 1999, March 8].

Wayman, Sally G. 1984. "The International Student in the Academic Library." *Journal of Academic Librarianship* 9 (January): 336–41.

Welch, Janet E., and R. Erroll Lam. 1991. "The Library and the Pluralistic Campus in the Year 2000: Implications for Administrators." *Library Administration and Management* 5 (Fall): 212–16.

Zoe, Lucinda R. 1999. "Search Patterns in Full-Text Web Databases: Implications for Training in a Digital Environment." Unpublished paper. Department of the Library, Baruch College, City University of New York.

Part 2

MULTICULTURAL AND GENDER ISSUES

OVERVIEW

As in Tyckoson's discussion of first-generation college students in the next section, Downing's and McDowell's chapters consider groups that may not be easily identified and that include students who most likely will not come to the library. Students' racial backgrounds and sexual orientations often contribute to feelings of isolation; although some of these students will self-identify during an instruction session, it is important that librarians incorporate teaching techniques and diverse examples to address the needs of these students and to raise overall awareness. There is a further similarity between teaching in a multicultural setting and teaching at-risk students, as discussed later by Jacobson. Many multicultural students will not have had access to technology before arriving at college, which needs to be taken into account when teaching in the electronic environment.

Library instructors may be apprehensive working with these students. They may fear students will be offended by incorrect, or outdated, language used in print as well as electronic resources, or they may recognize their own lack of comfort and preparation in teaching in a multicultural setting or to students of nontraditional sexual orientations. Both authors recommend demonstrating an awareness of the needs of these students, which can be done by incorporating their suggestions for topics or vocabulary terms into an instruction presentation, and by showing students that their relationship with the library exists for more than just a fifty-minute session.

The resources used in instruction sessions are also important. Promoting alternative sources can help these students realize not only that they are not alone, but also that their concerns and interests are being addressed by an increasing number of sources, both in print and online. In the larger picture, librarians must ensure that collections reflect the increasing diversity of the users. Displays, handouts, and outreach activities across campus all promote interaction between the library and these user groups.

Fortunately, much support exists for increasing librarians' confidence, comfort levels, and knowledge of these groups of students. Professional organizations such as ALA as well as local and national groups can provide information and feedback. Programs instituted at other libraries, such as the Peer Information Counselors at the University of Michigan, and the peer mentoring at Cal State Fresno discussed by Tyckoson, can serve as models. Additional teaching methods contained in Downing's and McDowell's chapters include ways to:

- Assess our own strengths and weaknesses in teaching multicultural, lesbian, gay, bisexual, and transgendered students.
- Provide student-centered instruction, with relevant examples.
- Explore bias and different perspectives in vocabulary and types of sources.
- Reflect the diversity of the community at all levels of instructional programming.
- Promote a positive learning environment, both by setting the right tone in the classroom and through building ongoing relationships with these students.

These ideas and more make the following two chapters an excellent place to start for background information as well as for effective teaching and learning techniques for multicultural settings and for lesbian, gay, bisexual, and transgendered students.

Instruction in a Multicultural Setting: Teaching and Learning with Students of Color

Karen E. Downing
University of Michigan

A multicultural classroom is much more than a collection of students who vary according to age, class, ethnicity, gender, national origin, race, religion, sexual orientation, or other such variables that may, like these, be visible or invisible. The critical ingredient is a supportive learning environment fostered by a teacher who appropriately recognizes and values different cultural styles and perspectives and effectively engages students in the learning process.—Schmitz, 1992: 75

Perhaps the most positive outcome of improving one's cross-cultural teaching is that all students benefit from better informed instruction based on multicultural learning practices. Being an outstanding multicultural instructor really means being an outstanding instructor to every learner.

This chapter addresses some frameworks and strategies for increasing the effectiveness of cross-cultural library instruction. It outlines an assortment of multicultural learning theories, research, and best practices related to improving instructional activities aimed at students from under-represented groups.

It is important to note here that, throughout this chapter, the term "minorities" refers to the under-represented and historically discriminated-against groups including African Americans, Asian Americans, Hispanics/Latinos, and Native Americans. The term "minorities" and phrase "people of color" are used interchangeably, as some persons prefer one term or phrase to the other.

DEMOGRAPHIC CONTEXT

Today, library and information professionals are faced with a dilemma. At the very time when colleges and universities are making large gains in recruiting students from under-represented racial groups to campus, our profession is losing ground in terms of its diversity. In 1994–1995, minorities comprised 26.4 percent of the U.S. population, but only 9.86 percent of new library school graduates (ALISE, 1998). Many if not most campuses have strived to match their admissions demographics to state and national demographics. Librarians, then, are faced with the responsibility of doing their best to serve an increasingly diverse student and faculty body and the consequent richness of diversity brought to research interests.

Added to this dilemma are increasingly segregated lives being led within many of our communities. There are significant differences in access to computing resources in K–12 schools in urban and rural areas as compared to many suburban areas. Due to the segregated nature of our communities, these vast differences often coincide with racial minorities being negatively impacted before they reach college.

Given this rather grim context, it is no wonder that many librarians are anxious and uncertain when asked to teach a class of learners who are different from themselves, and are equally anxious to improve their ability to do so. A diverse campus brings diverse research interests, diverse curricula, and the need for effective multicultural library instruction.

IMPROVING OUR MULTICULTURAL TEACHING

Teaching that includes and respects differences is likely to be more effective for learners and more satisfying for teachers.—Schmitz, 1992: 75

Self-assessment is in order when preparing to teach cross-culturally. Self-awareness is vital in order to be more fully aware of what we bring to our intercultural interactions.

History and Societal Ills

There are four basic things to consider when teaching cross-culturally. First is that many of us have grown up and lived in highly segregated and mostly homogeneous communities. We have lived in economic and racially segregated neighborhoods and attended mostly homogenous schools. We must recognize that this may be limiting our natural abilities, and our comfort levels, when working and teaching across differences. As adults, we must think about it, and work at it, much as we do in learning a new language.

Second, because of our societal ills relating to race relations (which span many centuries) and the impact of living largely segregated lives, most of us are not interculturally literate or competent. Sometimes we don't know the differences that exist between cultures or how to bridge the differences when we do realize they exist. Therefore, we don't recognize how our own behaviors, words, and affectations may interfere with our abilities to instruct effectively across differences. While it is possible to become interculturally competent as adults, it is not inherent.

Third, most of us have not had the opportunities to build the skills that are so necessary to operate effectively in a multicultural classroom and society. We have not developed skills like cross-cultural communication and effective diversity management. Many of our campuses have not seen this as a priority because they have been largely monocultural in the past. Our systems of reward and promotion have not recognized this type of skill-building as vital to our individual and institutional success, and to the success of our students.

Finally, many of us would like to improve our skills in areas of cultural competence and communication across differences, but we are afraid to make mistakes or offend others. These fears often paralyze us from taking a positive course of action.

While this is a rather daunting list to consider, there are many concrete things we can do to improve our cross-cultural teaching; some of them do not even require great amounts of time. Some simply require a paradigm shift or a new approach or technique to adapt current material to new audiences.

Recognizing that, as a profession, librarianship lacks the diversity that is vital in order to most fully serve our users, there are several strategies we can employ in our classrooms (and when engaging in outreach on our campuses) to improve our chances of connecting with our diverse users. One important strategy for coping with our profession's diversity deficit is to educate ourselves on how to do the best we can with what we have now. We need to learn how all librarians can overcome the challenges of cross-cultural communication and past and present societal ills to build strong learner/teacher relationships across differences.

Criteria for Excellence

James Anderson and Maurianne Adams (1992) have laid out seven criteria for excellent multicultural teachers:

1. *They assess their own strengths and weaknesses.* In a bibliographic instruction setting, when teaching across racial differences, this means instructors are developing awareness of their limitations and hidden biases as well as building on their strengths, perhaps by team teaching and sharing their successes with colleagues.

2. *They tend to be student centered.* In a racially diverse classroom, this might mean ditching the "canned" program and using examples that the students find interesting, informative, and meaningful; instructors effectively become co-learners.

3. *They possess a repertoire of alternative teaching strategies.* Instructors become learners as they continuously update their teaching strategies via research, observing other strong instructors and co-teaching.

4. *They provide perspectives that reflect a respect for diverse views.* In a multicultural classroom, try using examples from small presses and alternative presses, or using learning cycles such as Bias and Perspective (see section below on learning cycles).

5. *They are well prepared and organized.* In a multicultural classroom, displaying respect for one's students and demonstrating that their success is important to you as a librarian is very important. Poor preparation sends a message of disrespect.

6. *They use techniques that encourage independent and critical thinking.* In a multicultural classroom where many learning styles are present, coaching students through discovery is much more effective than talking at them for fifty minutes.
7. *They develop and utilize interpersonal skills that motivate students and facilitate learning.* The teacher becomes the learner in a multicultural setting; one must continuously update and refresh interpersonal and cross-cultural communication skills, coaching, and motivational skills.

Using these items as a checklist to work through will go a long way to improving any librarian's cross-cultural teaching. Keep this list handy to remind yourself of the continuous nature of improving multicultural instruction.

Interracial Communication

In interracial interactions, power and race are woven together and significantly influence the tone and texture of relationships.
—Bowser, Auletta, and Jones, 1994: 37

As a subset of cross-cultural communication, interracial communication in the United States is intertwined with issues of power and historical oppression. For the instructor in a cross-cultural classroom—especially if the instructor is white and many or some of the students are not—there are many issues of power that are being communicated and assumed without saying even a word. As instructors, librarians must recognize this in order to build relationships across differences.

Bowser, Auletta, and Jones state how communication is "subtle, systematic and multidimensional" (1994: 37) and takes place on two different levels:

1. *content*—the topic being discussed. In bibliographic instruction sessions, this includes all the cognitive material you wish to teach to the student learners, such as the online catalog and the research process.
2. *relational*—the feelings evoked by the communication and the unspoken power each participant possesses. In bibliographic instruction sessions, this relates to the affective

side of learning and teaching. How did the learners feel about the class and the instructor? Did the instructor feel connected to the class?

The authors also explain *racial dividers* and *racial connectors* in communication. *Racial dividers* are any communications (verbal or nonverbal) that the person lacking power may interpret to mean that their experiences related to race do not matter to the person who has power. The implication is that learning about those experiences is not of importance or the responsibility of the communicator in power. If we, as instructors, do not explore (through staff training and development) how to improve our cross-cultural communication, we may be putting up racial dividers without even realizing it. Examples of racial dividers in the bibliographic instruction setting include calling on primarily white students and only affirming those students' answers to whom we most closely relate.

Racial connectors are any communications that imply that each person's proprietary racial experiences matter to each communicator, and that learning more about those experiences is a shared responsibility. In the instructional setting, this includes ensuring that a variety of students are called upon, and affirming your interest in sharing the topics being explored by a variety of students.

In order to successfully communicate the bibliographic content of a class to the students, some understanding of communication norms is also important. At their Website entitled Cross-Cultural Communication, the Northwest Regional Educational Laboratory (1999) outlines the aspects of communication that can cause content to become interrupted and misinterpreted. The site notes, "Being unfamiliar with cultural communication differences can lead to misinterpretation, misunderstanding and even unintentional insult." Knowing that differences exist in these areas of communication can help us to understand our own cultural biases. Some of these aspects include:

- how one opens or closes a conversation
- how participants take turns during the communication
- how interruptions are handled

- how silence is used as a communicative device
- interjecting humor at appropriate times
- using nonverbal behavior
- expressing laughter as a communicative device
- knowing the appropriate amount of speech to be used by participants.

Simply realizing that there are different cultural norms for these elements of communication, and how we may favor our own cultural norms over others, can help build stronger cross-cultural relationships with any instructor's students. At the beginning of a class, sharing with students how you wish interaction to take place (or asking them how they would like to interact, such as formally—raising hands to speak—or informally—just jumping in and interrupting) helps set students on an equal footing.

It is imperative for sensitive multicultural communicators to realize when they may be perceived as being in a position of power, and to understand differences in norms associated with intracultural and intercultural discourse. It behooves an excellent multicultural instructor to devise ways to let students know that many experiences, perspectives, and viewpoints in the classroom are valued and represented. It is equally helpful to share one's own experiences in order to encourage the students to do the same.

COGNITIVE SIDE OF TEACHING AND LEARNING

Making all students feel welcome, fostering their academic success, and embracing many cultural perspectives can be achieved through a variety of ways, including establishing a supportive climate, striving for curricular inclusiveness, and varying instructional strategies.—Collett and Serrano, 1992: 42

The cognitive side of teaching includes the content of what the instructor would like the students to understand by the end of the instructional session(s), and the process of discovery or learning itself. This is the part of bibliographic instruction with which many instructors are most familiar and comfortable.

Learning Styles

Much has been written about the impact of diversity on learning styles. While there have been many quantitative and qualitative studies undertaken throughout the last several decades, many research accounts remain contradictory. It is safe to assume that there exists as much individual variation in preferred learning style within any group or race as between the races. For this reason, it is imperative that excellent multicultural instructors not dogmatically fit learners into an overall "learning-style preference profile" based on minority status. It is equally important to know that different learning styles do exist, and to know how to adapt one's bibliographic instruction sessions so that all learners may benefit.

M. F. Green notes that "no consensus exists as to which differences matter in terms of learning" (1989: 141). Maurianne Adams supports this in her work: "There is no consensus within the research tradition to directly connect cultural ways of knowing based on race or ethnicity to classroom learning" (1992: 11). Adams further states "there is the danger of creating new stereotypes. Broad generalizations about culturally different learning styles can too easily be misunderstood as euphemisms for deficits calling for remediation or acculturation of the student rather than flexibility and responsiveness from the college instructor" (11). Patrick Andrew Hall sums it up nicely: "Too often we either fall into the trap of viewing minority groups in monolithic terms and do not consider the great amount of diversity within that group, or we build instruction around cultural practices that we do not or cannot fully understand" (1991: 321).

With these caveats in mind, it benefits any multicultural instructor to develop a basic understanding of different broad categories of learning styles, because they surely exist within the students of each and every class we instruct. Knowledge of these differences can only enhance an instructor's multicultural teaching to an audience with a diversity of learning needs. Categories of learning styles include:

- *field-dependent versus field-independent*—the need to build relationships before getting down to "the business at hand," as opposed to being very goal-oriented.

- *relational versus analytical styles*—the need to learn the "big picture" before learning the pieces of the picture, as opposed to being detail oriented.
- *competitive versus cooperative styles*—some learners need and enjoy the energy that comes from working toward a goal individually while others need to feel supported during the learning process.
- *concrete versus abstract styles*—some students excel with experiential-based learning, others excel by logical analysis and deductive thinking.
- *active versus reflective styles*—some students learn by doing and exploring, others need time to think and observe.

While these are gross simplifications of each style, there are many resources that expand on each of these learning styles (see Anderson and Adams [1992] in particular). Having an idea of how these different styles impact the way students learn best helps make our classrooms much more welcoming and respectful to all our library learners. When combined with strong knowledge of the affective side of learning, we start to become excellent multicultural instructors.

Learning Cycles that Lend Themselves to Multicultural Content

There are many conceptual frameworks upon which an instructor may base the class content that is explored, in a shared manner, by the instructor and learners together. Tuckett and Stoffle (1984) outline a number of these conceptual frameworks that promote critical thinking and user self-reliance. A few examples of these frameworks that lend themselves to multicultural topics include:

- *Exploring Bias and Perspective.* This framework promotes critical thinking about the inherent perspectives and biases that we all bring to our writing and publishing. It not only explores what is published, but also what is left out of the publishing stream.
  Preparation: Before class, investigate a topic of multicultural interest using a conservative source and a liberal source. Or, using the same topic, explore it in a

mainstream white-owned paper and a minority-owned paper (check Gale's minority directories for sources that would be meaningful for your students). During a discussion with students, make sure they notice the difference in language usage, graphics, and perspective on the issue. An excellent example of this can be found in comparing the front pages of the black-owned *Oakland Tribune* and the white-owned *San Francisco Chronicle* from August 24, 1991. The two papers cover the same two stories side-by-side; one story is about a murder trial and the other story is about the new Oakland fire chief. The white-owned paper shows a picture of the black murder defendant and the black-owned paper shows a picture of the black fire chief instead. It is a subtle way of pointing out how one's perspective influences what news is published, read, and seen by the public.

- *Exploring Controlled Vocabulary.* This framework promotes critical thinking about how information is organized and categorized and the inconsistency between tools and sources.

  Preparation: Before class, trace the subject headings for a topic of multicultural interest, like "interracial dating." Use search tools such as the *Library of Congress Subject Headings, Social Science Index, Psychological Abstracts, Alternative Press Index,* and the *Index to Black Periodicals.* During class, get students to do the same, working in small groups, giving each group several sources. Also, point out the changes in vocabulary over time (miscegenation or mulatto), while being very careful to fit outdated or even offensive language into the historical context, acknowledging that some language is very offensive today. This will help them to understand that subject searches are different from keyword searches, and that if they do not find what they are looking for on first try, they may need to alter their language and ask for help.

- *Exploring "Alternative" versus "Mainstream" Sources.* This framework promotes knowledge and awareness of important sources usually outside of the knowledge of most undergraduate students. Many topics of interest to minority students may not be adequately covered in the so-called mainstream sources found in the library. Students need to know there are tools like the *Chicano Index, Index to Black Periodicals, Multicultural Index*, and the *Alternative Press Index* in order to fill out their research and give alternative perspectives.

Preparation: When using any conceptual framework, including Bias and Perspective and Controlled Vocabulary, make sure you have a selection of fact tools, such as encyclopedias and dictionaries, and search tools, such as indexes, catalogs, and bibliographies, from both mainstream and alternative sources.

Using Multicultural Examples During Class.

Many instructors mistakenly think that if they simply sprinkle some multicultural examples throughout their classes, then they have multiculturalized their classes. Many an instructor has made the mistake of assuming, for instance, that African American students are interested in rap music or Toni Morrison. In attempting to better serve a diverse clientele, they may actually be offending students by assuming that all minority students want to research certain topics. It is much better to use examples that reflect a range of research interests, including sharing some of your own interests. This can be accomplished by contacting the academic instructor ahead of time to get some subject ideas, asking for suggestions during the bibliographic instruction session, or by using a range of topics that are being researched at the reference desk by students' peers. When presenting the topics in class, frame them in a way that tells the students you want to make the examples as meaningful as possible to them.

Teaching and Learning in Electronic Facilities

Because so many of our campuses have been highly computerized for so long now, it is easy to lose sight of the fact that vast disparities still exist and are growing between the computer resources available in many urban and rural school systems as compared to many suburban public schools. This affects the level of technical preparedness that many students of color (as well as disadvantaged white students) bring to college campuses. According to the U.S. Department of Commerce (1993), in 1993 35.8 percent of all white students in K–12 grades had access to computers, compared with only 13 percent of African Americans and 12.1 percent of Hispanics. Though certainly those percentages have changed since that report, "the gap is not only there but it is widening" (Taylor, 1995: 23).

As effective multicultural instructors, we must consider this gap when planning instructional activities for, and follow-up with, our diverse students. Strategies for overcoming computer skills disparities include: pairing up students for cooperative learning exercises involving computer usage, including information on library or campus computer tutorials and help in bibliographic instruction packets, and using overhead projection so students can at least follow along on the instructor's screen if they are unfamiliar with a keyboard or mouse.

THE AFFECTIVE SIDE OF TEACHING AND LEARNING

My basic mistake wasn't in method or preparation but in lack of "affective" pedagogy.—Hall, 1991: 323

So how does an instructor bridge the vast racial, cultural, and socioeconomic gaps that often exist in our multicultural classrooms? It is not unusual for one classroom to contain students who come from very impoverished school systems sitting next to students who have their own PowerBooks and LEXIS/NEXIS passwords; where fifth-generation students sit next to first-generation students; where students who may have rarely left their urban settings sit next to students who rarely left their rural environments. These are some powerful barriers to overcome.

Put these circumstances in a larger campus perspective: think of how many times a day students are treated like interruptions or mere numbers. Then think about how it feels to be told and shown someone cares about your success. This author's experiences with using affective considerations in the classroom have made me realize that teaching without this understanding is usually very ineffective, especially in a multicultural setting. My experiences with coordinating the Peer Information Counseling program (see following section) for six years, along with teaching and learning with thousands of students of color, have shown me that unless I make an effort to connect with my student learners on a more personal, rather than strictly professional, level, I have lost them before they even get a chance to benefit from otherwise academically sound course content.

Knowing something about the affective side of teaching and learning can help to close these gaps by strengthening instructor/learner relationships and making important connections with students who really need our assistance, regardless of race, class, culture, or other differences. Using the tools of affective teaching, instructors have seen these seemingly unbridgeable gaps close remarkably and strong cross-cultural relationships develop and thrive.

Patrick Andrew Hall (1991) uses the term "affectivity" to refer to qualities such as:

- rapport
- concern
- empathy
- dedication to one's students
- high expectations.

Hall refers to these qualities as being imperative for instructors working with culturally diverse students. Most important, effective multicultural teaching is a matter of building *relationships*. He talks about how success in learning and teaching is simply a matter of how well one's concern for success is communicated to students. Hall also discusses the importance, when teaching across differences, of being open to learning as well as teaching. Be willing, and even eager, to learn from your students: What are their paper topics? What difficulties are they encountering? This requires flexibility and agility during classes, rather than rote lectures or activities.

What is affectivity in the classroom? Jane Keefer (1993) talks about three important parts of the affective side of learning:

1. *The psychological process is as important as fact finding.* There is a need, during the learning process, to feel able, competent, and accepted. Students don't want to feel foolish or hopeless.

2. *Coming away with good feelings is as important as coming away with the best answer.* This may seem very counter-intuitive to our profession; however, when you lack confidence, there is a greater need to feel good about an interaction than to be inundated with content. It is important that a learner feels well-treated and positive about the outcome after the experience.

3. *Feelings come first in the learning process, then comes cognition.* We must make certain when setting the tone of our classes that our students know we wish them to feel welcome and respected, or else they will shut down immediately and get very little from the material presented. This is where multicultural barriers often interfere with the learning process. If students do not feel respected by their instructor, or if they feel their instructor is not interested in their success, they will "turn off."

Competence/Confidence/Acceptance

Keefer also talks about the three components of literacy of any type:

1. *Competence.* This is often thought of by librarians as the "real" business of information literacy and is often content based: "I've got to get as much stuff into the fifty-minute lecture as I can!" It is cognitive in nature—"I will tell them X, Y, and Z, and they will walk out of my classroom enriched for my having said it!"

2. *Confidence.* This is the affective or emotional component. It's touchy-feely and it's hard to transfer. It's not thought to be professional. Process is important to confidence building. Building literacy skills is a process that affirms one's own experiences and builds confidence.

3. *Acceptance.* This is a strong predictor of academic success—the better connected and accepted students feel on campus, the greater their success (Steele, 1997). A welcoming environment—an environment that reflects cultures, abilities, genders, and races in artwork, handouts, staff and users, and Web spaces—helps. A welcoming attitude helps, too.

Table 5 outlines issues relating to literacy in a multicultural classroom within this framework.

Other Important Affective Considerations

Librarians are educated in professional schools; we are taught to be "professionals," which includes a set of vocabulary (jargon), a demeanor, a way of approaching our colleagues and nonlibrarians. Because of this environment, some of the following considerations may seem very foreign at first. According to Hall, we have been "socialized to keep a certain professional distance. . . . But it is this very distance that lends itself to low affectivism. Professional distance may be viewed as a sign of rudeness or contempt toward the students on the part of the professor" (Hall, 1991: 322). Consider, and be aware of, the following affective teaching aspects; the sum of these considerations helps build stronger teacher/learner relationships.

Tone of Classroom

The instructor has the power to set the tone of the class right from the outset. The instructor sends verbal as well as nonverbal signals that immediately alert students as to the tone of the class. Nonverbal signals include: body language, manner of dress, professional demeanor, and eye contact. Verbal signals (intentional or not) include: how the instructor greets students as they file in, the specific language used throughout the class, and level of enthusiasm. All these nonverbal signals tip off students as to expectations of their relationship to the instructor during the class session and afterwards.

Dress

While professional dress is rarely regulated in any significant manner within libraries, it is helpful to consider that how one dresses can be an indication of power and prestige on campus. When instructing a group of possibly intimidated undergraduate students, a "power suit" may further intimidate them and set you apart in unintended, nonverbal ways. First impressions are meaningful, and if students do not feel comfortable with

Table 5
Three Parts of Literacy

	Barriers to Information Literacy: Minority Student Learner	Barriers to Cultural Literacy: Instruction Librarian Learner
Competence	Vast majority of minority students arrive on campuses with the potential to succeed in college, but graduation rate disparity compared with white students suggests barriers to their success, including isolation and feeling disrespected.	Many librarians are not currently culturally literate enough to be successful cross-cultural communicators or teachers. We need to develop new skills. We may not be aware of the issues concerning communities of color, and may not be knowledgeable of the diversity of research interests that exist.
Confidence	On primarily white college campuses, some minority students lack necessary confidence to ask for help for fear of prejudice or ridicule. Many feel uncomfortable and isolated, like visitors, rather than valued partners on these campuses. The lack of minority staff within our libraries can also be an initial barrier.	Many librarians lack the confidence to teach across differences because of fear of offending others. They also lack opportunities to strengthen skills in the areas including cross-cultural communication, listening/feedback skills, presentation skills, and facilitation skills.
Acceptance	On primarily white campuses, many minority students feel isolated and unwelcome. They are reminded daily that they are different when they may be the only minority in many of their classes, when they eat in segregated cafeterias in the dorms, and when the curriculum does not reflect their cultures.	Many librarians fear not being accepted cross-culturally. Many wish to reach out and help, but fear rejection and offending others. It is, however, our responsibility as librarians to build relationships with minority communities both in and out of the classroom in order to break down these barriers.

their instructor, they are less likely to try to build important rapport.

Relationship Building

Because most library instructors only have fifty minutes within which to reach students, it is very difficult to build strong relationships. There are some techniques, however, that can help make the class a building block to a longer-term, helping relationship:

- Perhaps the most important and profound way to let students know that you care about their success is to tell them straight out. Start and end your classes by telling them that you care about their academic success (perhaps that's why you became a librarian?). If they know you care, they will be much more likely to come to you for help. This is an easy and effective way to bridge differences across race, gender, nationality, and physical ability. Their level of engagement during the class will rise if they feel some sort of connection with you.
- Display genuine interest in their paper topics: use their topics to illustrate your class. Ask them about their topics as they are filing into class, and ask them to volunteer their topics as you are teaching. The material will have added meaning for them, and will show them that you care.
- Share of yourself personally: tell personal anecdotes and stories about yourself and others to illustrate vital points during the class. Vivian Sykes, while a Ph.D. student at the University of Michigan School for Information, tracked the engagement level of students during library instruction sessions. She found that students' engagement levels rose dramatically when instructors were relating personal stories to their students (Sykes, 1993).
- Offer follow-up mechanisms to indicate that you wish to continue the instructor relationship after the one-shot lecture is over. Offer office hours, your own reference desk hours, or other one-on-one ways to follow up. Give them your phone number, e-mail address, or other contact information.

- Create learning communities inside your classroom, and follow up by offering opportunities to learn cooperatively afterwards. When we have multicultural classes, where all learning styles are present, it is necessary to engage in active and participatory learning and teaching. By engaging in cooperative learning, all styles of learning can be served. Reserve library space for follow-up study tables or small groups.

Peer Teachers in the Classroom

Many instruction librarians find their resources stretched to the limit. They are juggling greater demands on their time and scheduling more classes to be taught. Adding to these pressures is the growing need for diverse instruction to multicultural users on multicultural topics, coupled with the reality that most of our instruction teams are composed of primarily white librarians who may or may not be comfortable and able to meet these increasing demands. In order to diversify instructional staff, stretch the reach of overwhelmed instruction librarians, and reach students in a more meaningful way, librarians across the country have turned to using peer teaching in their classrooms.

Much has been written in the education literature about the overwhelming successes of peer instruction in all subject areas. Studies have documented that peer teaching and learning improves both the quality and quantity of learning in academic areas from mathematics to English literature to biology/medicine (Cushing and Kennedy, 1997; Ernst and Byra, 1998; Winston and Downing, 1998). Capitalizing on the idea that peer instruction helps to overcome issues of intimidation in the classroom, utilizing peer information counselors to help co-teach bibliographic instruction classes is one way to ease tensions, both cultural and otherwise, in the classroom.

At the University of Michigan, Peer Information Counselors (PIC) have assisted librarians in doing instruction since 1985. PIC students have assisted librarians with instruction in virtually every subject area, but are primarily asked to assist with classes that are multicultural in nature. Librarians at the University of Michigan have reported that when PIC students co-teach or assist in the classroom (both computerized and noncomputerized), there is a noticeable difference in the level of interaction between the students and the instructor during instructional sessions. Students feel freer to ask questions and get more assistance if they fall behind or need help.

PIC students serve many purposes when co-teaching. First, they are positive role models for other students, especially minority students, who can see that PIC students have mastered difficult and confusing information literacy skills. Second, PIC students, as is true with any coteachers, help reach students in a way one instructor alone cannot. Third, PIC students have the experience to know how best to present material so that it is meaningful to their peers; they are able to relate to them at their level. Fourth, PIC students connect and build relationships with the students, which often brings them back to the reference desk or office hours long after the class is over.

At Michigan, PIC students have been trained to conduct some elementary instruction sessions on their own. These sessions, while usually not course-integrated and always quite basic, nonetheless stretch the reach of the instruction staff. Examples of the groups these classes are targeted to include:

- minority student organizations—PIC students, often members of these organizations themselves, have taught sessions to student groups such as the Black Student Union and the Chicano Student Organization.
- student athlete support program—PIC students have conducted small-group training sessions for student athletes, who, due to schedule difficulties, often cannot attend regularly scheduled library information sessions.
- minority peer advisors—PIC students have worked in conjunction with campus minority peer advisors in the residence halls to conduct classes in the dorms to coincide with activities such as Chicano History Week and Black History Month.
- summer programs—in conjunction with the campus's minority affairs office, PIC students have conducted classes for various summer groups that often include minority students our campus is trying to recruit.

PIC students extend a warm welcome to the library, insure

that students know basic research and access techniques, and serve as role models and mentors to the students they reach through these sessions. The library benefits by reaching more students than is otherwise possible, partnering and developing relationships with many departments across campus, and contributing to the academic success of both the PIC students and the students they teach. The PIC program has even succeeded in recruiting some of its students to attend library school, thus making a further contribution to diversifying our profession. For more information on starting and managing a Peer Information Counseling program see Downing, MacAdam, and Nichols (1993), MacAdam and Nichols (1989), and Winston and Downing (1998).

ASSURING A MULTICULTURAL CLASSROOM: OUTREACH TO MULTICULTURAL CAMPUS UNITS AND PROFESSORS

In order to reach our increasingly diverse users, it is the responsibility of librarians to reach out to the campus and to ensure that all our users know they are welcome and encouraged to use our services. In order to do so effectively, keep these three considerations in mind:

1. Know your campus community! You can only serve your multicultural users effectively if you know who they are. Do some campus research on how many students of color there are at your institution. Get statistical breakdowns for all under-represented groups. Also, see if there are statistics on how many students are U.S. citizens. The issues and barriers for English-as-a-second-language students are different from those for U.S.-born students.

2. Collect data on what programs currently exist to support the retention of students of color. Create learning partnerships with those programs when possible, since these will provide entrées to many students of color. Connecting your instruction to existing programs will also help make it more meaningful. Some likely minority student support programs include:

- athletic program
- office of minority services
- campus housing
- minority-support units within individual schools and colleges.
3. Finally, explore which programs on campus are taking the lead in teaching multicultural content. You will want to tie in library instruction to these courses and faculty. You must make certain these students, faculty, and support staff know the library is interested in partnering with them, and that you have valuable services and collections that will help them succeed. Some likely academic units on campus include:
   - American culture programs
   - Women's studies
   - Latino studies programs
   - Black studies programs
   - Asian American studies programs
   - Native American studies programs.

Some campuses combine these programs under a general heading of American Culture. Some campuses have programs for one minority group, but not another. Know your campus offerings. Talk to your campus administrators who keep statistics on which programs students of color are engaged in, and target those programs.

RECRUITMENT AND COLLECTIONS

Recruitment to Our Profession

As you are engaging in your outreach and instructional activities, remember that we all can play (and have a responsibility to play) a role in the recruitment of more people of color into our profession. Whether it is an undergraduate student who has taken an interest in an instruction class, a library student assistant, or a paraprofessional within the library, these are all potential recruitment sources from which to encourage talented people to enter library school.

Collections

As we engage in our outreach and instructional activities, we must remember to have our collections reflect the diverse nature of users and their research interests. If our collections do not do so, then our instructional activities and other attempts to bridge differences across campus will fall far short of their potential impact (Diaz, 1994).

SUMMARY

Interracial teaching requires more of us as instructors. While not easy, the rewards of cross-cultural instruction far surpass the risks and work. It requires self-evaluation, flexibility, an openness to learning, reworking of learning frameworks and examples, as well as added emphasis on the affective side of learning.

The rewards of strong interracial instruction are many, both for all students (not just racial minorities) and for instructors. These rewards include more varied and interesting course materials, stronger opportunities for everyone to learn from one another, and stronger and more enriching cross-cultural relationships.

REFERENCES

Adams, Maurianne. 1992. "Cultural Inclusion in the American College Classroom." In *Teaching for Diversity*. San Francisco: Jossey-Bass.

ALISE. 1998. *1996–97 Library and Information Science Education Statistical Report*. Chicago: Association for Library and Information Science Education.

Anderson, James A., and Maurianne Adams. 1992. "Acknowledging the Learning Styles of Diverse Student Populations: Implications for Instructional Design." In *Teaching for Diversity*. San Francisco: Jossey-Bass.

Bowser, Benjamin P., Gale S. Auletta, and Terry Jones. 1994. "Communication, Communication, Communication!" In *Confronting Diversity Issues on Campus*. Newbury Park, Calif.: Sage.

Collett, Jonathan, and Basilio Serrano. 1992. "Stirring It Up: The Inclusive Classroom." In *Teaching for Diversity*. San Francisco: Jossey-Bass.

Cushing, Lisa Sharon, and Craig Kennedy. 1997. "Academic Effects of Providing Peer Support in General Education Classrooms on Students Without Disabilities." *Journal of Applied Behavior Analysis* 30 (Spring): 139–51.

Diaz, Joseph R. 1994. "Collection Development in Multicultural Studies." In *Cultural Diversity in Libraries*, by Donald E. Riggs and Patricia A. Tarin. New York: Neal-Schuman.

Downing, Karen, Barbara MacAdam, and Darlene Nichols. 1993. *Reaching a Multicultural Student Community*. Westport, Conn.: Greenwood.

Ernst, Mike, and Mark Byra. 1998. "Pairing Learners in the Reciprocal Style of Teaching: Influence on Student Skill, Knowledge, and Socialization." *Physical Educator* 55, no. 1 (September): 24–37.

Green, M. F. 1989. *Minorities on Campus: A Handbook for Enhancing Diversity*. Washington D.C.: American Council on Education.

Hall, Patrick Andrew. 1991. "The Role of Affectivity in Instructing People of Color: Some Implications for Bibliographic Instruction." *Library Trends* 39, no. 3 (Winter): 316–26.

Keefer, Jane. 1993. "The Hungry Rat Syndrome: Library Anxiety, Information Literacy, and the Academic Reference Process." *RQ* 32, no. 3 (Spring): 333–39.

MacAdam, Barbara, and Darlene Nichols. 1989. "Peer Information Counseling: An Academic Library Program for Minority Students." *The Journal of Academic Librarianship* 15, no. 4 (September): 204–209.

Northwest Regional Educational Laboratory. *Cross-Cultural Communication*. Available online at *www.nwrel.org/cnorse/booklets/ccc/index.html* [cited 1999, January 26].

Schmitz, Betty. 1992. "Creating Multicultural Classrooms: An Experience-Derived Faculty Development Program." In *Teaching for Diversity*. San Francisco: Jossey-Bass.

Steele, Claude. 1997. "A Threat in the Air: How Stereotypes Shape Intellectual Identity and Performance." *American Psychologist* 52 (June): 613–29.

Sykes, Vivian. 1993. "Incorporating Storytelling into Bibliographic Instruction." Unpublished paper. University of Michigan, Ann Arbor.

Taylor, Ronald A. 1995. "The Great Divide." *Black Issues in Higher Education* 12 (November 16): 22–25.

Tuckett, Harold W., and Carla J. Stoffle. 1984. "Learning Theory and the Self-Reliant Library User." *RQ* 24 (Fall): 58–66.

U.S. Department of Commerce, Bureau of the Census. *Computer Use in the United States: October 1993*. Available online at *www.census.gov/population/socdemo/computer/report93/comp1.txt* [cited 1999, October 27].

Winston, Mark, and Karen Downing. 1998. "Helping Students of Color Succeed: Implementing and Managing a Peer Information Counseling Program." *Leading Ideas* 3 (July): 2–5.

FURTHER READING

Bowen, Dorothy N. 1988. "Learning Style Based Bibliographic Instruction." *International Librarian Review* 20 (July): 405–13.

The Chronicle of Higher Education: Almanac Issue 1988. Vol. 45, no. 1 (August 28).

Diversity Officer, American Library Association. Referrals to multicultural resources within ALA, workshops and training sessions on multicultural services.

Diversity Officer, Association of Research Libraries, Washington, D.C. Workshops conducted on cross-cultural communication, management, and leadership issues.

Downing, Karen, and Joseph Diaz. 1993. "Instruction in a Multicultural/Multiracial Setting." In *Learning to Teach*. Chicago: Association of College and Research Libraries.

Drueke, Jeanetta. 1992. "Active Learning in the University Library Instruction Classroom." *Research Strategies* 10, no. 2 (Spring): 77–83.

Erikson, Frederick. 1979. "Talking Down: Some Cultural Sources of Miscommunication in Interracial Interviews." In *Nonverbal Behavior: Applications and Cross-Cultural Implications*. New York: Academic.

Gilton, Donna. 1994. "A World of Difference: Preparing for Information Literacy Instruction for Diverse Groups." *Multicultural Review* 3, no. 3 (September): 54–62.

Mellon, Constance A. 1988. "Attitudes: The Forgotten Dimension in Library Instruction." *Library Journal* 114 (September 1): 137–39.

de la Pena McCook, Kathleen, and Kate Lippincott. 1997. *Planning for a Diverse Workforce in Library and Information Science Professions*. Tampa: University of South Florida School of Library and Information Science Research Group.

Wlodkowski, Raymond, and Margery Ginsburg. 1995. *Diversity and Motivation: Culturally Responsive Teaching*. San Francisco: Jossey-Bass.

Library Instruction for Lesbian, Gay, Bisexual, and Transgendered College Students

Sara McDowell
Ryerson Polytechnic University

Lesbian, gay, bisexual, and transgendered (LGBT) students are taking their rightful place on today's campus. LGBT studies are increasingly attracting interest in academic circles among both LGBT and heterosexual scholars. But how well are library services meeting the needs of these user groups? This chapter provides an overview of the experience of LGBT students on college and university campuses, discusses how current academic library collections and services meet their needs, and outlines library instruction strategies that improve access to information on LGBT subjects for all students.

THE CAMPUS ENVIRONMENT

College is an important period in the identity development of LGBT students. While many lesbians and gay men come out in high school, others choose to come out in the new and different environment provided by college: "For the transgender student the time away at college is often the first chance to challenge the gender role assigned at birth and to decide how to integrate transgenderness into life as an adult" (Lees, 1998: 37).

How are LGBT students received on campus? While they have achieved greater visibility and acceptance in recent years, and while many campuses now have LGBT student organizations or support services, harassment and sometimes violence are still common. According to a survey of 1,464 lesbian, gay, and bisexual college and university students, "40 percent indicated that they do not feel completely safe on their campuses, with 57 percent saying that their schools do nothing in response to hate crimes. [O]verwhelmingly, most students believe homophobia to be a serious problem at their schools" (Sherrill and Hardesty, 1994: 10). Homophobia—the fear of same-sex desire— is commonly acted out as intolerance, hostility, harassment, or violence toward LGBT people.

In the academic curriculum, interest in LGBT subjects is growing. A number of colleges and universities now offer minors in LGBT studies, and many others offer related courses. Nevertheless, the general mood in many classrooms remains conservative (Duberman, 1997). It is not uncommon for graduate students to be discouraged from researching LGBT subjects because they are not considered legitimate topics of research and may not benefit students' careers. Though some college faculty and staff are able to pursue their careers as out lesbians, gay men, bisexuals, or transgendered people, a significant number remain closeted out of fear of discrimination in hiring and promotion. In addition, faculty who introduce LGBT themes into the classroom may be accused of forcing their sexuality or gender identity on students or of introducing irrelevant content.

The University of Minnesota's Select Committee on Lesbian, Gay, and Bisexual Concerns reported testimony from undergraduate and graduate students about their experience in the classroom. "Students told of occasions when faculty made derogatory jokes, minimized or denied the contributions of LGBT people, and denied, made light of, or dismissed as irrelevant the sexual orientation of artists, scientists, or historical figures. Students also reported incidents of professors making overtly hostile or demeaning comments, including some implying that violence against LGBT people is justified and deserved" (1993: 15). In this kind of environment, many students choose to remain closeted in the classroom, even if they are out to friends and roommates. One UCLA student commented, "Coming out in the classroom at UCLA is apparently a total act of bravery" (Gideonse, 1998).

John D'Emilio notes that "silence in the classroom and around the seminar table about homosexuality sends a loud and powerful message" (1992: 145); it tells both heterosexual and LGBT students that the experience, history, and cultural contributions of lesbians, gay men, bisexuals, and transgendered people are less valuable than those of heterosexuals, and that their needs are less important. It tells students that there is something disturbing and unmentionable about same-sex desire and transgender expression. This silence or denial of the legitimacy of LGBT subjects is an expression of heterosexism—the belief in the inherent superiority of heterosexuality, and the assumption that everyone is or should be heterosexual. The heterosexist classroom environment not only fails to challenge the climate of bigotry that exists on the campus but also provides ideological support for that bigotry and homophobia.

Heterosexism in the classroom has a negative impact on both heterosexual and LGBT students. The lack of free and open discussion about sexuality and gender expression denies heterosexual and LGBT students alike the opportunity to fully explore and examine their own experience. The stress, anger, frustration, and fear experienced by LGBT students as a result of heterosexism and homophobia take a toll on their emotional health and interfere with their academic success. Students may become depressed, turn to substance abuse, or even commit suicide (Chesnut, 1998). Sherrill and Hardesty found that nearly one out of nine lesbian, gay, or bisexual undergraduate students would leave school at some time during their careers "because of coming out issues and victimization subsequent to coming out" (1994: 11). Heterosexual students take the heterosexist attitudes that they learn at college with them into the workplace, making them less able to contribute to a cooperative and effective work environment or to serve a diverse clientele.

LIBRARY SERVICES

What role do libraries play in the college life of LGBT students? Autobiographies of lesbians, gay men, and bisexuals often touch on the role that reading plays in the coming-out process. Three studies on the information needs of lesbian and gay library users (Creelman and Harris, 1990; Joyce and Schrader, 1997; Whitt, 1993) conclude that the library was either the first or second most important source of information to people during their coming out, and continued to be a vital ongoing information source to them. However, all three authors reported dissatisfaction about library collections on the part of the users surveyed. Creelman and Harris comment that the "lack of relevant, practical information, and the often negative or male-centered images presented in the literature, frustrated a significant number of women who were interviewed" (1990: 40).

Indeed, many library collections have not kept up with the rapid growth in LGBT publishing in recent years. The 157 respondents to a survey of public and college libraries conducted for *Library Journal* in 1995 demonstrated "widespread, though not universal, inattention to gay book collections" (Bryant, 1995). Among the respondents, 50 percent of libraries had 30 titles or fewer, 26 percent had between 30 and 150 titles, and only 23 percent had more than 150 titles (Bryant, 1995). In comparison, the San Francisco Public Library's gay collection numbered 6,000 items at the time of the survey. Bryant's findings are supported by Christensen and Sweetland, who conclude in their study of the treatment of lesbian, gay, and bisexual titles in the review media and their selection by libraries that "few of even the best gay/lesbian/bisexual titles are being selected by librarians," (1995: 38).

Thus, not only the size but also the quality of collections needs to be examined. Library collections may contain a disproportionate amount of dated or biased material that does not adequately reflect the voice of these user groups. Collections may be biased in favor of gay male perspectives, with inadequate representation of lesbian, bisexual, or transgender viewpoints. Collections may also be biased in terms of race, ethnicity, religion, class, age, or ability.

Accessibility of periodicals is particularly problematic. A study of the availability of gay and lesbian journals in U.S. libraries, as well as their coverage in standard indexing and abstracting tools, reported that with "only twenty-two percent of recommended gay and lesbian journal titles [in *Katz's Magazines for Libraries*, 8th edition] indexed in standard indexing tools and only nineteen percent held by a reasonable number of libraries, access to a majority of gay and lesbian journal literature is difficult to achieve through standard library procedures. Thus researching a gay or lesbian topic becomes an arduous task"

(Kilpatrick, 1996: 80). Kilpatrick found that ethnic or youth-oriented journals and magazines were particularly under-represented in collections and indexing.

Problems with small collections are compounded by inadequate bibliographic access, which Gough and Greenblatt describe as "systemic bibliographic invisibility" (1992: 61). "Many library materials of interest to lesbian and gay library users are unnecessarily difficult to locate because of the outmoded, prejudicial, inadequate, or inappropriate terminology employed by such subject heading schemes as the Library of Congress Subject Headings (LCSH) and Sears Subject Headings" (61). As one example, Gough and Greenblatt point out that although *gay* was in general usage in the 1970s, it was not until 1987 that LCSH adopted the term *gay* instead of *homosexual*.

When LGBT library collections and access tools are inadequate, they contribute to the heterosexist message on campus, with detrimental effects on the well-being and academic success of LGBT students. More important, they hinder access to the information that LGBT students need to survive in college on both intellectual and personal levels. By providing appropriate access to information, academic libraries can play a role in dismantling heterosexism and homophobia on campus, and in creating a positive and healthy learning environment that meets the needs of all students. To fail to do so is to accept and perpetuate the current disadvantaged position of LGBT students.

LIBRARY INSTRUCTION

The limitations of library collections and bibliographic access need to be addressed in their own right. The focus of this paper, however, is on how to provide library instruction that is inclusive, is not heterosexist, and can meet the information needs of all students for LGBT materials.

The first step in developing an instructional program is to evaluate current services. The checklist in Table 6 can help in evaluating instructional services for LGBT students. Discussion about each area follows.

Before considering specific instructional strategies, however, it is important to look at ways of becoming more aware of LGBT

Table 6
Evaluation Checklist

_____ Do you feel confident responding to questions on LGBT topics? If not, what would you need in order to become more confident?

_____ Are you familiar with the current concerns and information needs of LGBT students on your campus?

_____ Are you aware of local LGBT resource centers and information sources to which you could refer library users?

_____ Does your library include LGBT resources in library displays or create specialized displays of LGBT materials?

_____ Does your library produce specialized LGBT finding aids, such as pathfinders, bibliographies, or Web directories, or include LGBT material in finding aids in other relevant disciplines?

_____ Does your library include LGBT content in library instruction workshops, or produce specialized LGBT workshops?

_____ Do you work collectively with LGBT library workers, students, and faculty to produce programs?

_____ Are students able to access information confidentially, without the mediation of a librarian? To what extent?

_____ Do your services reflect the diversity of the LGBT community in terms of sexuality, gender expression, race, ethnicity, religion, gender, class, and ability?

Source: This checklist was inspired by, and borrows from, Cal Gough and Ellen Greenblatt's "Test your Gay/Lesbian Service Quotient" (1992: 61).

culture and the local needs of your campus group. One method is to attend lectures and cultural events on campus or to get involved with faculty or student groups. Another is to read introductory texts or anthologies in your collection, or to scan campus newspapers and local or national magazines. Professional organizations and discussion groups can also be a source of support. For LGBT academic, college, or youth discussion groups, see Barnett and Sanlo (1998).

The American Library Association's Gay, Lesbian, Bisexual, and Transgendered Round Table produces a variety of publications, maintains a listserv, and operates a useful Website at _http://calvin.usc.edu/~trimmer/ala_hp.html_. Additional listservs of interest are GAY-LIBN and LEZBRIAN.[1] For further reading, you can consult the selected bibliography that follows this paper.[2]

Remember that you do not need to work alone. You can produce excellent work when you collaborate on programs with other campus groups, such as LGBT library workers, student, faculty, or community groups.[3]

One important factor to consider when developing LGBT instruction programs is the diversity of the LGBT community. Lesbian, gay, bisexual, and transgendered students all have different experiences and different needs. The community also reflects the full spectrum of society in terms of race, ethnicity, religion, social class, age, and ability. Your library users could include an African American transsexual woman, a gay Muslim international student, and a Native lesbian grandmother. It is also important to remember that LGBT people of color, and others outside of the dominant society, may have greater difficulty accessing appropriate information because of the biases in collections and access tools discussed earlier. This makes it particularly important to reflect the full diversity of the LGBT community in instructional activities.

Lisa J. Lees has studied the needs of transgendered students in particular. *Transgender* refers to the way that gender identity is experienced, rather than to sexual orientation. "Transgender persons are those who are not comfortable living within the confines of the social stereotypes of gender as applied to themselves" (Lees, 1998: 37). Lees points out that

> closeted transgender people in the student population are the largest set of transgender people on campus and the most difficult to contact. Although they may have a high need for information and a desire to be able to discuss transgender issues, they are likely to be afraid of taking any action that would mark them as transgender. You must reach this population in a way that makes information available and give them reason to believe they can safely ask for help. The best way to do this is to increase the general awareness of transgender issues on campus. (39)

This need for privacy and confidentiality is shared to a degree by lesbian, gay, and bisexual students. Students who feel unsafe in the campus environment may be reluctant to risk approaching library staff for fear of singling themselves out as

LGBT, or of receiving a homophobic reaction. The need for confidentiality should be considered in the design and delivery of instruction programs.

Instructional Strategies

LGBT students can benefit from a broad range of instructional strategies, including displays, pathfinders, and workshops. I will introduce each approach, with reference to my work at Trent University in the province of Ontario, Canada.

Displays

Library displays are invaluable in challenging the silence around LGBT issues and in contributing to an LGBT-positive environment on campus. They have great potential for educating users about the range of resources available in the library, in terms of both subject matter and media. They also function as an outreach method that helps to break down the feelings of mistrust that LGBT students may hold toward library staff. Displays also offer a wonderful opportunity for collaboration with student or faculty groups, because they draw on a variety of skills. A display can be timed to coincide with LGBT events on campus or with events such as National Gay and Lesbian Book Month in June. Bibliographies, bookmarks, or pathfinders can be produced as supplementary materials.

In addition to specialized displays, it is important to include LGBT content in general library displays or in displays on related subjects. For example, include information on LGBT history in displays on local history and recent acquisitions.

At Trent University, a display was created through the collaboration of a librarian and two student library workers. One goal was to educate library workers and challenge the heterosexism that existed in the library as a workplace. Another was to make the Trent University community aware of the vitality and diversity of the LGBT population and of the various resources available in the library and the broader community. It included book and video jackets from the library collections and personal collections of library staff; newsletters, magazines, flyers, and posters from local and regional groups; a banner featuring the names of famous LGBT persons in history; post cards and other features intended to add color and interest; and a central statement of purpose. For further suggestions about developing displays, see Gough (1990).

Bibliographies and Pathfinders

Bibliographies and pathfinders are excellent methods of providing instruction to LGBT students in a way that respects their need for independence and privacy. These tools also contribute to a more LGBT-positive atmosphere in the library, and are a good resource for library staff. A bibliography or pathfinder can provide an overview of the field, or focus on particular themes or media. Pathfinders can be distributed in the library, at appropriate locations on campus, or published in the student newspaper. Because of the value that LGBT students place on privacy and confidentiality, a Web-based format can be particularly effective. Ask LGBT campus or community organizations with homepages to create a link to the pathfinder.

At Trent, a pathfinder was posted on the library Website and published in a special annual edition of the student newspaper dedicated to LGBT issues; a student library worker did much of the original research. In addition to key reference works and Websites, it provides brief explanations of keyword- and Boolean-search techniques for finding LGBT materials in different media. There is additional detail on how to find LGBT biography and fiction, two types of material that are of interest to LGBT students but that may be difficult to identify. Trent University's pathfinder focuses on keyword searching, but another institution might want to include a list of appropriate subject headings.[4] An effort was made to adequately represent the full diversity of the community in the material covered and examples used.

While specialized research guides and pathfinders are valuable, it is vital to include LGBT content in general pathfinders or in pathfinders on related subjects. For example, in an English Literature research guide, include bio-bibliographical material on LGBT writers. For further examples of LGBT Web pathfinders and research guides, see the Website Library Q at *www.cudenver. edu/public/library/libq/books.html*.

Library Workshops

Library workshops provide an opportunity for intensive instruction and hands-on practice and support. A specialized LGBT library workshop can be part of a regular instruction schedule, tied in with LGBT-awareness events or other functions organized by students or faculty, or created for a particular course. Appropriate avenues may identify themselves through outreach activities. At Trent University Library, for example, a workshop is scheduled annually as part of BGLAD (Bisexual, Gay, and Lesbian Awareness Days) events organized by the Trent Queer Collective. A workshop has also been presented at a faculty conference on queer pedagogy held at Trent, which made it possible to introduce relevant resources at the Trent Library as well as to invite discussion about library services. Thus the faculty workshop served as an instructional opportunity, an outreach opportunity, and a learning opportunity for the librarian.

When designing an LGBT workshop, tailor the content to the needs of the particular course or group. In any workshop, discussion of keyword searching and Boolean operators will be valuable to teach methods of negotiating the wide range of terminology that students can expect to encounter when researching this subject. In my workshops, I ask the class to brainstorm different terms that express sexual orientation or gender identity. I write down student suggestions on an overhead, roughly organizing them with broader terms at the top and more specific terms at the bottom. Terms that you might expect to include for sexual orientation would be *sexuality, sexual orientation, queer, homosexual, gay, lesbian, bisexual,* and variations on *same-sex,* such as *same-sex relationships, same-sex desire,* and *same-sex rights* (Stewart, 1995). For gender identity or sexual identity, you might expect to include the terms *transgender, transsexual, trans, crossdresser, drag queen, drag king, butch, femme, FTM* (female to male), *MTF* (male to female), *androgyne,* and *intersex* (Feinberg, 1996; Nangeroni, 1996). The terms *gender dysphoria, transvestite, female impersonator, male impersonator,* and *hermaphrodite* can be controversial or derogatory, but may also be found in the library catalog or indexes. Of course there are possible variations of each word, such as *lesbian, lesbians,* and *lesbianism,* or *transgender* and *transgendered.*

Remember to include terminology specific to particular ethnic or cultural groups among your student body, bearing in mind that sexual and gender roles can vary from society to society and that terminology may not be directly transferable. At Trent University, there is a large aboriginal student population. The terms *two-spirit* or *two-spirited* are in current use by aboriginal people in some areas, but the Library of Congress Subject Headings (LCSH) uses *Indian gays* and *Indian lesbians*. The terms *third gender* and *fourth gender* refer to traditional gender roles in aboriginal societies, but LCSH uses *Berdaches* (Roscoe, 1998), which is considered derogatory by many aboriginal people. For terms in aboriginal languages, consult with local students or faculty.

As already noted, some of the LGBT vocabulary cited is controversial. The word *queer*, once considered derogatory, has now been reclaimed and is used frequently in academic discourse. In contrast, the term *homosexual*, once in general use, has developed a more negative connotation, reflecting the time when same-sex desire was considered an illness. The word *transvestite* is considered derogatory by many cross-dressers (Nangeroni, 1996). In order to search the library catalog and bibliographic databases where dated or derogatory vocabulary may still be prevalent, students need to experiment with terminology, even if it is offensive to them. This can cause anger and frustration. It is important to provide time to acknowledge and discuss the controversial or derogatory nature of the language, the ideologies behind the language, and what the use of such language reveals about library cataloging and indexing systems. This could be an opportunity to introduce a critical-thinking component to the workshop to deal more generally with the need for and approaches toward evaluating information sources. For groups who are marginalized, critical-thinking skills are survival tools.

Once the keywords have been introduced, it is important to discuss the concept of broader and narrower terms. For example, students should be aware that when looking for information on lesbians or bisexuals it may be necessary to use the broader terms *homosexual* or *gay*, which currently refers predominantly to gay men, but has also been used as an umbrella term for men and women in the past. Demonstrate how to use Boolean "or" to combine different terms for a more efficient search, as well as truncation symbols to accommodate variations, such as *(gay or gays or homosexual?)*.

Regardless of whether a library offers specialized LGBT workshops, it is important to include LGBT content in general library instruction, or in instruction in related areas. This ensures that all instruction is inclusive and reflects the diversity of the student body, and that all LGBT students are reached, even if they are not out and active in the LGBT community. Include LGBT examples in search strategy exercises. The *Trent University Library Orientation Programme* (Luyben et al., 1996), a self-study workbook for first-year students, includes the following examples in its explanation of the Boolean search operator "or":

> This technique is particularly useful for finding information on groups where terminology may have changed over the years, or may reflect ideological differences. For example:
> indian? or native? or aboriginal?
> homosexual? or lesbian? or gay or gays

Finally, the value of the Internet as a research and instructional medium for lesbian, gay, bisexual, and transgendered students should not be overlooked (Lees, 1998; Lucier, 1998). Not only is the Internet an invaluable means of accessing information to supplement limited collections, it is also an effective research medium for those students who desire independence and confidentiality. It is important both to teach LGBT students Internet skills in order to facilitate their research, and also to use the Internet to mount instructional materials. Advertise your regular Web research tutorials through LGBT student centers or newsletters. Make sure that your Website includes links to generic Web-searching tutorials for students who prefer to teach themselves. Include Internet searching in your general LGBT tutorials, or consider offering a specialized Internet tutorial on LGBT topics if there is sufficient demand. Put your LGBT pathfinder or other finding aids online. Consider creating an interactive LGBT library skills tutorial online.

CONCLUSION

A number of themes have persisted throughout this discussion. First is the need to reflect the diversity of the LGBT student community in all instructional strategies and materials. Another is the strong need for independence and confidentiality experienced by some LGBT students and the necessity of employing strategies that respect that need. Finally, there is the importance of including LGBT content and strategies throughout the library instruction program in order to reach all students, to raise awareness of LGBT issues, and to make sure that the library instruction program fully reflects the diversity of the student body.

> Transgender behavior has been sensationalized and stereotyped in movies and on talk shows to the point where it is difficult to hold a rational conversation on the topic with a member of the general public. (Lees, 1998: 38)

> Bisexuals have either been rendered invisible or parodied so thoroughly that misconceptions are all that most people know as working definitions of bisexuality. (O'Brien, 1998: 32)

Students who have lived under the shadow of such stereotypes and misinformation are entitled to a campus environment that encourages and enables the pursuit of truth. Academic libraries must not allow inadequate, heterosexist collections and services to hinder students. Rather, we must ensure that all students have equal access to the information that they need in order to make sense of their lives and to build a society based on equality and mutual respect.

NOTES

1. GAY-LIBN is a discussion group for gay, lesbian, and bisexual library workers and their friends. To subscribe, send the following message to listproc@usc.edu:
     subscribe GAY-LIBN your first name your last name
   LEZBRIAN is a discussion group for lesbian and bisexual women library workers. To subscribe, send the following message to listserv@listserv.acsu.buffalo.edu:
     subscribe LEZBRIAN your first name your last name

2. Cal Gough and Ellen Greenblatt have produced much valuable work. A new two-volume publication edited by Gough and Greenblatt is expected from McFarland in 2000.
3. I would like to thank Tami Albin and Aznan Abu Bakar for their hard work, and all my colleagues at Trent for their support and encouragement.

   For online directories of campus LGBT contacts or community centers, respectively, see *National Consortium of Directors of LGBT Resources in Higher Education,* available at *www.uic.edu/orgs/lgbt,* or *National Directory of Gay and Lesbian Community Centers,* at *www.gaycenter.org/natctr.* For Canadian information, consult: *Gaycanada.com* at *www.cglbrd.com.*
4. For a list of LGBT Library of Congress Subject Headings, see DeSantis (1999).

REFERENCES

Barnett, David C., and Ronni L. Sanlo. 1998. "The Lavender Web: LGBT Resources on the Internet." In *Working with Lesbian, Gay, Bisexual, and Transgender College Students: A Handbook for Faculty and Administrators,* edited by Ronni L. Sanlo. Westport, Conn.: Greenwood.

Bryant, Eric. 1995. "Pride and Prejudice." *Library Journal* 120, no. 11 (June 15): 37ff. Available online at EBSCOhost/Academic Search FullTEXT Elite/ 9506307609 [cited 1999, January 19].

Chesnut, Saralyn. 1998. "Queering the Curriculum or What's Walt Whitman Got to Do with It?" In *Working with Lesbian, Gay, Bisexual, and Transgender College Students: A Handbook for Faculty and Administrators,* edited by Ronni L. Sanlo. Westport, Conn.: Greenwood. Citing N. Evans and V A. Wall, eds. 1991. *Beyond Tolerance: Gays, Lesbians, and Bisexuals on Campus.* Alexandria, Va.: American College Personnel Association.

Christensen, Peter G., and James H. Sweetland. 1995. "Gay, Lesbian and Bisexual Titles: Their Treatment in the Review Media and Their Selection by Libraries." *Collection Building* 14, no. 2: 32–41.

Creelman, Janet A. E., and Roma M. Harris. 1990. "Coming Out: The Information Needs of Lesbians." *Collection Building* 10, no. 3–4: 37–41.

D'Emilio, John. 1992. *Making Trouble: Essays on Gay History, Politics, and the University.* New York: Routledge.

DeSantis, John. 1999. "Library of Congress Queer Subject Headings." *Library Q.* Available online at *www.cudenver.edu/public/library/libq/books.html* [cited 1999, January 20].

Duberman, Martin. 1997. "Teaching Our History." *Advocate* 744 (October 14): 99ff. Available online at EBSCOhost/Academic Search FullTEXT Elite/ 9710286369 [cited 1999, February 14].

Feinberg, Leslie. 1996. *Transgender Warriors: Making History from Joan of Arc to Dennis Rodman.* Boston: Beacon.

Fischer, Debra. 1995. "Young, Gay . . . and Ignored?" *Orana* 31 (November): 220–32.

The Gay, Lesbian, Bisexual, and Transgendered Round Table of the American Library Association. Available online at *http://calvin.usc.edu/~trimmer/ala_hp.html* [cited 1999, November 4].

Gaycanada.com. Available online at *www.cglbrd.com* [cited 1999, March 14].

Gideonse, Ted. 1998. "Visibility 101." *Advocate* 769 (September 29): 36ff. Available online at EBSCOhost/Academic Search FullTEXT Elite/1138042 [cited 1999, February 14].

Gough, Cal. 1990. "Library Exhibits of Gay and Lesbian Materials." In *Gay and Lesbian Library Service,* edited by Cal Gough and Ellen Greenblatt. Jefferson, N.C.: McFarland.

Gough, Cal, and Ellen Greenblatt. 1992. "Services to Gay and Lesbian Patrons: Examining the Myths." *Library Journal* 117, no. 1 (January): 59–63.

Joyce, Steven, and Alvin M. Schrader. 1997. "Hidden Perceptions: Edmonton Gay Males and the Edmonton Public Library." *Canadian Journal of Information and Library Science Revue* 22, no. 1 (April): 19–37.

Kilpatrick, Thomas L. 1996. "A Critical Look at the Availability of Gay and Lesbian Periodical Literature in Libraries and Standard Indexing Services." *Serials Review* 22 (Winter): 71–81.

Lees, Lisa J. (1998). "Transgender Students on Our Campuses." In *Working with Lesbian, Gay, Bisexual, and Transgender College Students: A Handbook for Faculty and Administrators,* edited by Ronni L. Sanlo. Westport, Conn.: Greenwood.

Lucier, Aaron F. 1998. "Technology: A Potential Ally for Lesbian, Gay, Bisexual, and Transgender Students." In *Working with Lesbian, Gay, Bisexual, and Transgender College Students: A Handbook for Faculty and Administrators,* edited by Ronni L. Sanlo. Westport, Conn.: Greenwood.

Luyben, Jean, Sara McDowell, Linda Matthews and Dianne Cmor. 1996. "Trent University Library, Library Orientation Programme." Peterborough, Ont.: Trent University Library.

Nangeroni, Nancy R. (1996). "Transgenderism: Transgressing Gender Norms." *GenderTalk.* Available online at *www.gendertalk.com/tgism/tgism.htm* [1999, February 11].

National Consortium of Directors of LGBT Resources in Higher Education. Available online at *www.uic.edu/orgs/lgbt* [cited 1999, March 14].

National Directory of Gay and Lesbian Community Centers. Available online at *www.gaycenter.org/natctr* [cited 1999, March 14].

O'Brien, Kirsten. 1998. "The People in Between: Understanding the Needs of Bisexual Students." In *Working with Lesbian, Gay, Bisexual, and Transgender College Students: A Handbook for Faculty and Administrators,* edited by Ronni L. Sanlo. Westport, Conn.: Greenwood.

Renn, Kristen A. 1998. Lesbian, Gay, Bisexual, and Transgender Students in the College Classroom. In *Working with Lesbian, Gay, Bisexual, and Transgender College Students: A Handbook for Faculty and Administrators,* edited by Ronni L. Sanlo. Westport, Conn.: Greenwood.

Roscoe, Will. 1998. *Changing Ones: Third and Fourth Genders in Native North America.* New York: St. Martin's.

Sherrill, Jan-Mitchell, and Craig A. Hardesty. 1994. *The Gay, Lesbian and Bisexual Students' Guide to Colleges, Universities, and Graduate Schools*. New York: New York University Press.

Stewart, William. 1995. *Cassell's Queer Companion*. London: Cassell.

University of Minnesota Select Committee on Lesbian, Gay, and Bisexual Concerns. 1993. *Breaking the Silence*. Minneapolis/St. Paul, Minn.: Author.

Whitt, Alisa J. 1993. "The Information Needs of Lesbians." *Library and Information Science Review* 15 (Summer): 275–88.

FURTHER READING

Gough, Cal, and Ellen Greenblatt, eds. 1990. *Gay and Lesbian Library Service*. Jefferson, N.C.: McFarland.

Gough, Cal, and Ellen Greenblatt.1994. "Gay and Lesbian Library Users: Overcoming Barriers to Service." In *Diversity and Multiculturalism in Libraries*, edited by Katherine Hoover Hill. Greenwich, Conn.: JAI.

Greenblatt, Ellen. (1999) "Books." *Library Q*. Available online at *www.cudenver.edu/public/library/libq/books.html*.

Kester, Norman G., ed. 1997. *Liberating Minds: The Stories and Professional Lives of Gay, Lesbian, and Bisexual Librarians and Their Advocates*. Jefferson, N.C.: McFarland.

Lutes, Michael A., and Michael S. Montgomery. 1998. "Out in the Stacks: Opening Academic Library Collections to Lesbian, Gay, Bisexual and Transgender Students." In *Working with Lesbian, Gay, Bisexual, and Transgender College Students: A Handbook for Faculty and Administrators*, edited by Ronni L. Sanlo. Westport, Conn.: Greenwood.

McNaron, Toni A. 1997. *Poisoned Ivy: Lesbian and Gay Academics Confronting Homophobia*. Philadelphia: Temple University Press.

Outcalt, Charles, Curtis F. Shepard, and Felice Yeskel. 1995. *LGBT Campus Organizing: A Comprehensive Manual*. Washington, D.C.: National Gay and Lesbian Task Force Policy Institute.

Rhoads, Robert A. 1994. *Coming Out in College: The Struggle for a Queer Identity*. Critical Studies in Education and Culture Series. Westport, Conn.: Bergin and Garvey.

Sanlo, Ronni L., ed. 1998. *Working with Lesbian, Gay, Bisexual, and Transgender College Students: A Handbook for Faculty and Administrators*. Westport, Conn.: Greenwood.

Part 3

FIRST-GENERATION COLLEGE STUDENTS AND AT-RISK STUDENTS

OVERVIEW

College students who are the first in their families to attend college have a number of characteristics in common with at-risk students—those who are at peril for academic underachievement or failure. Both categories of students tend to come from families with lower-than-average family incomes, both may face a lack of social support for their academic endeavors, and both attend the gamut of institutions: public and private, two-year and four-year colleges and universities. In both groups, there are wide variations in their familiarity with and effective use of libraries.

There are also a number of differences, however, between first-generation and at-risk students. First-generation students tend to be older and thus have traits in common with returning students (see Holmes's chapter in Part 4 of this volume), they are less likely to reside on campus, and they lack the special programs and developmental classes that provide support and structure for at-risk students.

These various factors have implications for user education. For example, students officially characterized as "at-risk" can be identified. Librarians can forge alliances with the administrators of programs that provide support for them, and can develop instructional programs that meet the particular needs of these students at their institutions. First-generation college students, however, are a hidden minority: without directly asking them, it is very difficult to identify these students; reaching them as a group is even more challenging. What these groups have in common, however, is that they have had less access to computer technology than their peers. They may need additional assistance in the basics of computing that underpin the use of the technology for research-related activities.

If instruction is provided outside of class time, pay special attention to scheduling sessions at times that nonresident first-generation students can attend. Since they are more likely to live off-campus than at-risk students, and because they often have jobs and family responsibilities on top of their academic careers, slotting instruction into their schedules can be a daunting task. Keep in mind, however, that the array of options that user-education librarians provide to answer the needs of these students will assist all students. One such option, detailed in Tyckoson's chapter, is to provide peer-mentoring programs, which are often attractive to a wide spectrum of students, including at-risk students.

The following two chapters provide background information on first-generation college students and at-risk students to help user education librarians better understand these groups and their needs. The chapters also provide a variety of suggestions for user education programs and instructional methods that will assist these students in becoming adept researchers, including:

- Encourage students to participate in institutional initiatives such as first-year experience programs and developmental-instruction programs.
- Offer some classes that teach basic computing skills; without them, students will be unable to use electronic research tools.
- Schedule classes and personalized research service appointments when students are available, including evenings and weekends.
- Create a classroom climate conductive to learning, where student participation is planned for and valued.
- Emphasize the significance of the material to be taught to the students' needs and lives.

Library Service for the First-Generation College Student

David A. Tyckoson
California State University, Fresno

For many students, college provides a direct route to the American Dream: getting a good education leads to getting a good job, which leads to getting a good home and a better lifestyle. However, the college experience can be a difficult one, especially for students from families for whom a college education has not been the norm. These so-called first-generation students often have a difficult time adjusting to the college experience. They cannot rely on the support and experiences of parents or other family members for guidance. Statistically, they are older than the traditional college student, have lower family income levels, are more frequently minorities and/or recent immigrants, and are more likely to drop out. In addition, first-generation college students generally have had less experience using libraries and often need instruction in the basic concepts as well as in research methods. This chapter brings together information obtained from the literature, statistical surveys, and interviews with first-generation students at California State University, Fresno (otherwise known as Fresno State University) to help librarians provide library and information services to first-generation students so as to improve their likelihood of academic success.

THE FIRST-GENERATION COLLEGE STUDENT

There is a group of students that we see every day but never notice. They are on every college campus. They can be in any college classroom. They major in everything from agriculture to business to education to theater. They cannot be identified by the color of their skin, nor can they be distinguished by the languages that they speak. Some are just out of high school, some are adults, and a few are senior citizens. They know that there are others like themselves on campus, yet they have a very difficult time finding each other. They do not have support groups. Most colleges have no special programs for them, yet they have some of the greatest difficulties adjusting to collegiate life. A hidden minority, they are first-generation college students. They are different from other students, and they need help.

For the majority of college students, the journey through the higher education system is an expected part of a continuing maturation process. These students follow in the footsteps of their parents and grandparents, often enrolling in the same institution that earlier generations of the family have previously attended. For these students, college life is an expectation—perhaps even a tradition. Whether these students appreciate (or even desire) the assistance, they are able to draw upon the experiences of other family members for help in making key academic and career decisions. For these students, college visits, dorm life, football games, term papers, and final exams are a standard component of their culture. Throughout universities and colleges across the nation, most students fall into this category.

For the so-called first-generation college students, however, this family-support network does not exist and the higher education experience is a foreign and possibly hostile environment. These students, the first in their immediate family to attend college, often have at least as many obstacles, aggravations, revelations, and temptations in their path to academic success as traditional students, but do not have any immediate family experience with higher education that might help them to overcome those obstacles. For first-generation students, college is a new, exciting, and often frightening experience; as a result, these students can have a difficult time adjusting to college and its academic expectations—and also to the information-seeking, critical-thinking, and synthesizing process that is central to academic research. Frequently feeling they are alone in the system, first-generation students often survive at the margins of academia. Attention to their problems by faculty, administrators, and librarians can make a big difference in whether they actually achieve their educational goals.

Characteristics of First-Generation College Students

First-generation college students come from every part of contemporary American society. They represent every race, age, ethnic group, and religion. First-generation students cannot be placed into the traditional categories into which we divide students, because they belong to all of those categories. First-generation students may be male or female, minority or majority, English-speaking or bilingual, under twenty or over fifty, academically gifted or on academic probation. They defy all of our traditional labels. Several studies, however, have revealed that there are some demographic characteristics that are common among them. Two studies in particular reveal a number of important differences between first-generation and other students (Nunez and Carroll, 1998; Terenzini, 1995).

Lower than Average Family Income

One of the most significant and dramatic statistical differences between first-generation and other students is average family income. One study indicates that the families of first-generation students have an average income level that is one-third below that of other students (Terenzini, 1995). The primary implication of this disparity is that first-generation students are almost always at an economic disadvantage over their more traditional counterparts and thus are susceptible to all of the problems associated with lower-income students. As a group, first-generation students have lower retention rates and take longer to complete their degrees. They are less likely to live on campus and more likely to have to work while attending school. This economic disadvantage is the key underlying factor for many of the problems that first-generation students encounter.

College Choice and Enrollment Status

First-generation students are much more likely to attend public institutions of higher education than other students (Nunez and Carroll, 1998: 35). Whereas 43 percent of all college students in the sample year were labeled first-generation students, only 25 percent of the students enrolling at private four-year colleges were so identified. Students whose parents had completed or attended college were three times more likely to select a private college than a first-generation student.

First-generation students were only slightly more likely to select a public four-year college, with 30 percent of new students enrolling in public four-year colleges, where first-generation students are outnumbered by other students by a factor of more than two to one. The institution of choice for most first-generation students is the two-year community college, where they make up over one-half of the total enrollment. An even higher enrollment pattern is seen in private, for-profit, two-year colleges. First-generation students comprise two-thirds of the enrollment in these schools, many of which concentrate on vocational and trade programs.

Enrollment and Residence Patterns

First-generation students are much more likely to attend college on a part-time basis than other students (Nunez and Carroll, 1998: 16): nearly 30 percent versus only 13 percent of other students. First-generation students are also less likely to reside on campus (only 16 percent) than are others (40 percent). Nearly half of all first-generation students live with parents or other family members. One-third of first-generation students work full-time while attending college, as compared to less than one-fourth of other students.

College choice and rate of attendance is strongly influenced by the lower average economic status of first-generation students. Although a few first-generation students receive academic or athletic scholarships to four-year institutions, most first-generation students must stretch their available financial resources in order to be able to attend college at all. To accomplish this goal, they often attend schools with the lowest possible cost, enroll part-time, and live at home. Though these decisions allow the student to obtain a college education, they also can serve to alienate the student from the mainstream of college life. While working toward a degree, the first-generation student is less connected to the institution as a whole than are other more traditional students.

Trends in Attendance

The high rate of enrollment of first-generation students in public two-year and four-year colleges is a direct result of the success of the public higher education movement in the United States. Beginning with the Morrill Act in 1862, access to higher education for all citizens has been a hallmark of American society. Aided by the GI Bill following World War II, millions of students enrolled in college who would not have otherwise considered higher education as a viable alternative. Almost one-third of all World War II veterans participated to some degree in this program, and most of them were first-generation college students. This huge increase in enrollment led to a boom in building and expansion of college campuses. The post-war growth in both the number and size of public institutions has enabled several million first-generation students to obtain a college education.

As states created large systems of public colleges, more and more first-generation students were able to enroll. Many states made a conscious effort to provide an institution of higher education geographically close and economically affordable for every resident, allowing anyone the opportunity to begin their academic career while commuting from home. Systems such as those in California, New York, and Ohio have indeed made higher education a part of many families' lives who otherwise would have been excluded. Today's trend towards distance education programs is an attempt to extend that outreach to the point where anyone with a computer and a phone line is able to participate in the higher education process. One of the potential benefits of distance education programs is their ability to reach all citizens, regardless of geographic limitations. If they can achieve this goal, first-generation students may have the most to gain of any potential student group.

Interviews with first-generation students at Fresno State University confirm these national trends. Fresno State University has a high proportion of first-generation students, many of whom live with the issues described above. For these students, two of the most important criteria used in selecting a college are economics and convenience.

RETENTION OF FIRST-GENERATION STUDENTS

First-generation students are less likely to obtain a degree or to remain in college than are other students; Nunez and Carroll (1998) found that over one-third of all first-generation students dropped out of school within five years of first enrolling, compared to less than one-fourth of other students. Retention rates are lowest for those students attending public two-year colleges, where only 55 percent will either have attained a degree or still be enrolled. Interestingly, those first-generation students who attend private, four-year colleges have the highest overall rate of retention. This may be an indication that private schools are making a better effort than public schools to provide a culture of support that meets the needs of first-generation students. However, since first-generation students are least likely to enroll in a private college, this group of first-generation students is a self-selected subset of all first-generation students and is not representative of the typical first-generation student.

No matter the type of institution attended or degree sought, first-generation students average a 10 percent lower completion rate than their counterparts (Nunez and Carroll, 1998). This ratio remains constant for all types of institutions and for all forms of enrollment. It is important to note that even when disregarding all other factors, students whose parents have attended college are 10 percent more likely to complete their degree than first-generation students. It is clear that first-generation students need added encouragement and support to remain in school and to complete their degree.

CLASS AND CULTURE

To understand first-generation students, we must understand the role of class and upward mobility in American society. For most first-generation students, class is the most defining factor—more so than gender, race, ethnicity, or other social labels. Almost by definition, first-generation students are the products of working-class or lower-middle-class backgrounds. Since parents and grandparents lacked a college education, they had no chance to become members of the professional or academic classes. Without the college degree, jobs in most middle- and upper-class occupations were out of reach. Although some families of first-generation students are highly successful in their fields, such as business, agriculture, or the trades, most remain members of the working class. Regardless of their occupation, the lack of a college degree causes them to hit an occupational and social ceiling through which they cannot break.

Most parents of first-generation students must accept these limits on their own occupational and social status, but they want their children to have better lives than themselves. The college degree is often seen as the ticket to that better life. Parents envision the degree enabling their children to become doctors, lawyers, teachers, managers, and other members of the professional class. Parents consider upward mobility through education a key component of the American Dream and one that they want to make available to their children. Most first-generation students grow up in an environment in which they are encouraged to achieve more than earlier generations, and this attitude shapes much of their academic experience.

Unfortunately, political and economic pressures often work against first-generation students. Following the strong postwar growth in public higher education in the 1950s and 1960s, there has been stabilization and even some contraction during the 1980s and 1990s. Costs have risen significantly, and it has become more difficult for lower-income students to find sufficient financial aid to attend college. Political pressure to deny funds for social programs has cut off some of the mechanisms that poorer families could use in the past to improve their status in society. Cutbacks in social, educational, and financial aid programs make it difficult for any family to support a first-generation student. Economic and social discrimination against recent immigrants and lower-income families discourages some students from ever pursuing their education.

Family Pride, Family Support, Family Conflict

To many first-generation students, the family is one of the most important factors in their lives. Since birth, the family has structured the educational, social, and economic aspects of their experiences. First-generation students who have grown up in a working-class environment view a college education as a way to move beyond the social and economic restrictions of their parents. Family members often see college enrollment by a child as a sign that future generations will live a better life, and parents and other members often make sacrifices in their own lives to make it happen. In some cases, an entire family will pool its resources to enable a single child to get a college education.

However, this family support can place a heavy burden on the student who is selected to enroll in college, a burden not felt by more traditional students. There is great pressure to succeed, especially when the parents and other family members have gone without some of their own desires to enable the student to attend. The family may try to live the college life vicariously through the student, making the progress of the student the topic of virtually every conversation with friends and relatives. Some view the success or failure of the student to be the success or failure of the entire family.

Family support can also turn into family conflict. Although many parents and families of first-generation students are very supportive, they also can become somewhat envious of the college student. Many parents would like their child to be just like themselves, only more highly educated. However, the college experience inevitably produces changes in the student, some of which may go against the wishes and desires of the family. The student who begins listening to a different kind of music, starts reading more books, and spends a great deal of time at the library may be viewed by siblings, parents, and noncollege peers as becoming too bookish, too snobby, or just too academic for the old family ways. The family may want the student to succeed, but it also wants the values of the student to remain unchanged by the process. This attitude places tremendous pressure on the student, who must balance the time required to succeed in coursework with time for family and workplace demands. This balance is difficult for all students, but is even greater for first-generation students, whose families do not understand the often enormous time requirements of college classes.

Cultural Conflicts

First-generation students frequently find themselves torn between several cultures. The student must fit within the culture of the parents, which places a high value on its ethnic heritage and social norms. But the student is also immersed in American popular culture, whose images as presented through advertising, the media, and music impose an imagined set of values based upon the concept of youth. Finally, there is the culture of the academy, which values investigation, discourse, and debate, including questioning those values espoused by family and the media. First-generation students have an even more difficult time than others moving among the three cultures, in large part because the family culture can have a very difficult time comprehending the academic culture. First-generation students can easily become alienated and feel that they are not really a part of any culture that they encounter in their lives (London, 1992).

Interviews with a small sample of students at Fresno State University confirm this. These students struggle with all three cultures; they feel they are not gaining ground in the academic one, yet at the same time feel they are losing touch with their family culture. Another factor arose in the Fresno study: As more than half of these students belong to families that are recent immigrants to the United States—most had one or more parents who were born outside the country or were themselves natives of other nations—ethnic ties to other cultures are extremely strong, as the family has had less time to become Americanized.

The large number of relatively recent immigrants accounts for the variation in demographics of first-generation students over time. Whereas early in the twentieth century the first-generation student was likely to be a European immigrant, today's first-generation students are probably Latin American or Asian. At present, first-generation students are twice as likely to be Hispanic than their more traditional peers (Terenzini, 1995). And as each immigrant group becomes integrated into American society, the number of second- and third-generation college students increases.

A Matter of Priorities

Those of us who have made a career in academia make a subtle yet important assumption about our students. This assumption underlies much of how we structure academic life, from class schedules to term papers to library assignments, and it demonstrates the inherent bias of our own academic culture. Yet this assumption is least true for the students on the margins, including many first-generation students. This assumption is the concept that college coursework is the highest priority in a student's life.

Faculty, administrators, and librarians are all guilty of this assumption. Because the academy is foremost in our lives, we naturally assume that all who participate place that same priority on higher education. For many students, however, college is not their first or even second priority. For many first-generation students, the immediate needs of earning an income and supporting a family come before getting an extended education, which, though desired, sometimes must be sacrificed in order to maintain a balance in the other vital facets of life.

First-generation students, for whom education can be at best the third priority, have a difficult time competing academically with students for whom the degree is the primary activity in their lives. This may account for the higher drop-out and stop-out levels among first-generation students. Interviews with first-generation students at Fresno State University confirm this. Many of the students are struggling to balance education, work, and family, and identify education as the first activity to be compromised when the need arises. The first-generation student may strongly desire to achieve the college degree, but is also willing to postpone or even cancel that desire when it interferes with family or employment.

LIBRARY SKILLS OF FIRST-GENERATION STUDENTS

First-generation students indicate the same level of prior library use as all other students as measured by the College Student Experiences Questionnaire (Terenzini, 1995: 27). This survey measures student exposure to the entire college experience, from the classroom to social life to the research process. Based upon these results, we should expect no difference in library performance between first-generation and other students.

Interviews with first-generation students, however, show that they tend to be closer to the extremes of the scale than are their more traditional counterparts. Some first-generation students have a very high level of library experience, having used the library weekly or monthly during their childhood. Due to economic factors, many had few books and educational materials in the home, and they used the library to expand their horizons and interests. These students have a high knowledge of library use and would score highly on any information competence scale. Most of these students are able to transfer their library and research skills to the college environment and can adapt easily to the academic library.

At the other extreme are first-generation students who have had little or no library exposure. These students come from schools and communities with poor or nonexistent libraries and may also have grown up in a family or cultural environment in which reading and research were not encouraged. For these students, the library is intimidating in its size and complexity, and its use is an unwelcome and daunting task. Though they may be very bright intellectually, they are not familiar with the library-research process and need a great deal of help. Thus, some sort of information-skills program is essential and has the potential to mean academic success or failure of these students.

WHAT CAN WE DO TO HELP FIRST-GENERATION STUDENTS?

The librarian obviously cannot eliminate all of the obstacles facing first-generation students; much of what happens to them is out of the control of the library or of any other single campus department. However, as librarians we can assist them in learning the information and research process. For first-generation students, such knowledge may be the difference between academic success and academic failure.

Identify First-Generation Students

First-generation students often feel alone in the classroom, with no special orientation programs or designated sections of courses just for these students. By simply asking a class how many students are the first in their family to attend college, we can help those students. Such a question lets them know that we are aware of the difficulties that they face and also allows students to identify each other and to form informal support groups.

Of course, were this the only question asked of the class, it would stand out as unusual and could be taken to be discriminatory. However, when combined with other demographic questions, it can be helpful. For example, covering other issues relevant to first-generation students—such as questions on how many students work full-time or part-time, have family who are alumni, live in a bilingual home, and commute to campus—can help the librarian tailor the instruction to meet the needs of the students in the classroom. Although the identification of first-generation students is not a profound concept and really does nothing inherently to improve their success rate, it does let them know that we are aware of their difficulties and may raise their willingness to consult with the librarian at a later time at the reference desk or in other similar environments.

Schedule Instruction Sessions during Evening and Weekend Hours

Most academic libraries offer a variety of instructional programs to their students, many of them tied to specific courses and scheduled to meet during the usual class time. However, it is also common to offer formal or informal drop-in sessions that instruct students about search strategies, specific databases or tools, information sources in specific subject fields, and other areas of interest. Subjects covered by these seminars include a variety of useful resources, from choosing a topic to using the catalog to searching the Web. Unfortunately, these workshops are frequently scheduled only during the 9–5, Monday–Friday, "regular" workday. These sessions may fit the scheduling needs of full-time traditional students (and the librarian), but are very difficult for working students to attend. From our experience at Fresno State University, the Saturday library-instruction programs are consistently the most heavily attended. By scheduling a number of different sessions back-to-back on Saturdays, we enable students to attend several of our classes in a single day. These classes are very popular with working students, many of whom are first-generation college students who cannot attend the weekday sessions.

Design Library Assignments that Do Not Discriminate

There are a number of ways that library assignments can inadvertently discriminate against first-generation students. For example, assignments that require students to spend large blocks of time physically in the library are more difficult for commuting and working students. While some time in the library is essential in learning the research process, assignments that simply repeat the same skills over and over do not add to the student's understanding but simply take up valuable time. Similarly, although assignments are generally intended to instruct students in the use of a specific library, assignments that may be completed in other libraries may be more convenient for some first-generation students. Alternatively, assignments that may be completed from home will also be more accommodating for many students.

Assignments that require students to spend money for copying, printing, or purchasing assignment packets can discriminate against lower-income students. Thus, requiring photocopies of articles that the student found during the literature search ensures that the student finishes the process but can become expensive if the student is using several lengthy journal articles. Also, keep in mind that even the subject content of library assignments can discourage first-generation students. Assignments that use a large amount of academic or bibliographic jargon will only confuse the student who has little familiarity with college-level research. In addition, the same subject bias that has been measured in standardized tests may also occur in library assignments and thus discriminate against lower-income students, many of whom are first-generation students. Cute examples with inside jokes about college life may be meaningless to the student who lives off campus and attends school part-time.

Therefore, when designing assignments, we must take these issues into account and remember that all students may not be equally prepared to understand them or have an equal opportunity to complete them.

Provide a "Family Friendly" Environment

As discussed above, many first-generation students must divide their time between school and family. These students greatly appreciate a library that allows non-student family members to participate along with the students. In this context, "family friendly" is not a moral or religious issue but an access issue. Many academic libraries, for example, discourage children from entering, so library policies that allow children to use the facility while a parent studies are greatly appreciated. At Fresno State University, we see children of students in the library every day and frequently have children attending an instruction session along with a parent. As long as the child is not disruptive to the class, the child is allowed to stay in the room while the session is in progress. Our library also has a children's literature collection that, though intended primarily for teachers working on curriculum planning, also receives heavy use by children of students and staff. In fact, the children's collection has the highest circulation rate per volume of any subject collection in the library. A long-term effect of allowing children in the library is that the children gain an appreciation for—and become comfortable in—the academic environment, which will benefit them when they get older and become second-generation college students.

Offer Personalized Research Services

Like other students who may require extra assistance in the research process, first-generation students can benefit from in-depth reference and research services. Academic libraries offer these services under a variety of names, such as "Research Consultants" and "Term Paper Advisory Services." These services are usually by appointment and allow the student to receive more attention and assistance from the librarian than is possible at the reference desk. To be effective, appointments must be available at times convenient to the student, and the students must be aware of the service and how it can help. These services do not replace traditional reference service but rather supplement it for those students needing in-depth help.

Establish Peer Mentoring Programs

Despite our efforts to provide research assistance, some students are still reluctant to consult a librarian. This hesitation can be amplified when there is a perception of strong cultural differences between the librarian and the student. In such situations, students respond best to guidance from other students. Peer mentors are used by some libraries as a means of providing basic research assistance to other students. In these programs, students who are trained in basic library and information skills are assigned to work with other groups of students. While these services are not specifically aimed at them, many of the students who receive help are indeed first-generation college students. For example, at Fresno State University we have developed a peer library-instruction program for migrant students. These students, almost all of whom are first-generation students, are the children of migrant farm workers and are considered to be one of the most at-risk groups on campus. The library peer-advising program is one way the University Migrant Services office helps to increase the academic retention and success rates for these students. Peer-advising programs for other groups of students can have the same effects.

Become a Part of the First-Year Experience

Many colleges have implemented first-year-experience programs to introduce students to the culture of academic life. These programs are designed for all students but have the greatest effect on those students least familiar with the college environment. First-year-experience programs help bring first-generation students up to speed in a variety of aspects of college life, including the research process. At Fresno State University, the program is called University One. Upon completion of this course, all students have been exposed to library-instruction sessions that cover basic skills such as using the OPAC, finding periodical articles and searching the Internet.

IMPACT OF LIBRARY INSTRUCTION

The impact of library instruction and information literacy programs on first-generation students can be quite profound. In some cases, the attainment of strong information skills makes the difference between academic success and failure. As with other students, information skills learned at the college library also transfer into their workplace and family lives. For first-generation students who have had little exposure to library research, an understanding of the research process can be a tremendous asset. A first-generation student interviewed at Fresno State University—a thirty-something African American male, married and the father of two young children—spoke to the value of the process: "People in my culture often say that we have no heroes. Hell, I know that we have lots of heroes. My father is a hero and my grandfather is a hero. After I took that library class, I learned the power to find out about others. Now when people tell me that, I take them to the library and show them what they can find." For this student, library instruction opened a new window into his own history. Although not every student will have such a strong reaction, many first-generation students will show a dramatic increase in information skills.

First-generation students face a myriad of educational, societal, and cultural obstacles in their paths to a college degree. They have many of the same needs and problems as members of other at-risk groups, along with the additional burden of being an invisible minority on most campuses. There are few special programs to help them succeed, and most faculty members are unaware of their existence. The librarian cannot overcome all of these hurdles, but, by being cognizant of them, librarians can help these students achieve the goal of a college education, a good job, and a better life. In a small way, what we do at the library can help first-generation students achieve the American Dream.

REFERENCES

London, Howard B. 1992. "Transformations: Cultural Challenges Faced by First-Generation Students." *New Directions for Community Colleges* 80 (Winter): 5–11.

Nunez, Anne-Marie, and C. Dennis Carroll. 1998. *First-Generation Students: Undergraduates Whose Parents Never Enrolled in Postsecondary Education.* Washington, D.C.: U.S. Department of Education, National Center for Education Statistics.

Terenzini, Patrick T., Leonard Springer, Patricia M. Yaeger, Ernest T. Pascarella, and Amaury Nora. 1995. *First-Generation College Students: Characteristics, Experiences, and Cognitive Development.* University Park, Penn.: National Center on Postsecondary Teaching, Learning, and Assessment. ERIC Document ED387004.

At-Risk Students

Trudi E. Jacobson
*University at Albany, State University
of New York*

At-risk students are those students who are at peril for academic underachievement or failure. "At-risk students may lack the requisite background knowledge, the learning and study skills, the social support, or the self-management strategies needed for succeeding in a postsecondary setting" (Weinstein, 1994: 375). While at-risk students exist at all colleges and universities, they are most easily identified at those institutions that provide remedial or developmental classes, in which students with similar needs are grouped for additional instruction in areas such as reading, writing, mathematics, or study skills. Developmental instruction, which may also be labeled as compensatory, basic skills, or remedial instruction, is "college instruction that is adjusted in content, style or pace to meet the education needs of high-risk students. The adjustment is meant to raise the probability that such students will succeed at college work" (Kulik and Kulik, 1991: 1).

A recent study of remediation in U.S. higher education found that 78 percent of institutions that enroll freshmen offered at least one remedial reading, writing, or mathematics course in the fall of that year. However, the percentage of colleges offering remedial instruction varied by type: all public two-year schools and 81 percent of public four-year institutions offered such courses, whereas 63 percent of private two- and four-year schools did (Lewis and Farris, 1996: 5). The percentages of students enrolled in these classes also varied by type of institution. In the fall of 1995, the overall average of first-time freshmen enrolled in at least one remedial course was 29 percent. At public two-year schools the figure was 41 percent, 26 percent at private two-year schools, 22 percent at public four-year schools, and 13 percent at private four-year schools (9–10). Of those institutions offering remedial instruction, 39 percent reported that enrollment had increased in the past five years, while only 14 percent reported a decrease (11).

Many user education librarians are asked to teach students in developmental classes about the library and its information resources. Librarians can have a positive effect on at-risk students' chance of success in their academic work if the class is well-geared to their needs. There were a number of articles in the 1980s about library instruction for students in developmental programs, but with the increasingly sophisticated electronic resources now available, and the recognition of a need for a repertoire of teaching methods, it is time to revisit the topic. What teaching techniques best meet the needs of at-risk students? How can an instruction session be structured to be most effective for these students? This chapter considers some of the learning characteristics of this population and suggests teaching strategies to meet their needs, concentrating on teaching at-risk students as a group rather than on how to identify them within a more general class. The techniques suggested here, however, are also applicable to user education sessions for a wide range of students.

ISSUES

A number of issues should be considered when developing instruction for the at-risk population. Though similar to those issues faced in developing instruction for any group of students, they assume particular importance when working with at-risk students. The librarian needs to take into account the effects that students' cognitive levels, psychological types, and feelings about the library have upon the instructional experience. Generational issues and the impact of technology are also pertinent.

Affective

At-risk students frequently have not had the academic preparation that other students have had, or have not developed the skills necessary to succeed academically at college. This may translate into an unfamiliarity with libraries, particularly libraries of the size and complexity found at academic institutions, to a negative or dismissive attitude toward libraries, or to a fear of libraries. Students may be overwhelmed by the work required of them in their classes and may consider effective use of the library as just one more roadblock on the way to academic success. Without overcoming negative feelings about libraries, students will not be able to perform the research expected of undergraduates. Librarians teaching user education sessions need to address the affective, or emotional, needs of at-risk students, as well as their cognitive, or intellectual, needs.

Developmental

Educators need to continually remind themselves that not all students in each class are at the same level of development. Perry defined stages or positions of cognitive development—dualism, multiplicity, relativism, and commitment to relativism—that are appropriate to all students (see Moore, 1994; Perry, 1981). Professors and librarians are most likely to encounter students at the first three stages. Students at the stage of dualism see things as right or wrong; students at the stage of multiplicity believe that things are right, wrong, or not yet known—in other words, all opinions are valid. Relativists see the world as context-bound and understand that they can look to themselves as a source of knowledge. It is in the transition from stage to stage that students develop cognitively. While Perry's early work did not provide guidance on how to use the scheme in the classroom to promote more complex thinking, a number of other researchers have related it to teaching and learning (Moore, 1994).

Daragan and Stevens examine what implications these developmental stages have for user education: "Dualistic students view the library as a confusing array of information. They lack the patience, resolve, or interest to find answers on their own, and insist that answers come from faculty. If forced to seek out information, these students look for the *one* source that provides the *one* answer. Once they find it, they quit" (Daragan and Stevens, 1996: 71). Dualistic students view anything written as correct, so they are incapable of evaluating sources. Students at the multiplicity stage feel all opinions are correct and can easily be overwhelmed by information—finding yet more material through the strategies librarians teach just adds to their information overload. It is only when students reach the stage of relativism that students see the need for information and come to realize that knowledge is not absolute. These students are willing to find information that represents different viewpoints (Daragan and Stevens, 1996).

To better understand the students they will be teaching, user education librarians should be aware of the developmental research. McNeer is very helpful in this regard. Her article explores several different models of cognitive development, including an alternative framework for women's pattern of knowing, and relates these models to library instruction (McNeer, 1991). Some of the exercises described in the Strategies for Instruction section below may help students shift their thinking in the areas addressed by our instruction. As Bateman says, "Disequilibrium . . . is a key to adult learning. Only when we fail to make sense of the world because we are applying the wrong blueprint will we grow by building new blueprints, new patterns for organizing learnings, new programs for our mental computer" (1990: 30). Keep in mind that the lecture format encourages passivity among students, particularly those who are less complex thinkers, and is not an effective method to challenge them. Less complex thinkers learn best with an elucidated structure, which can be achieved by providing an outline and rationale for the instruction session, definitions of unfamiliar terms, and very clear guidelines for activities. Another way to incorporate structure is to include examples from the experiences of the students. This category of thinker also finds hands-on experience even more important than do more complex thinkers (Moore, 1994: 53).

Psychological

Just as students are at different levels of cognitive development, they also have very different personality types that respond differently to various teaching methods. The Myers-Briggs Type Indicator (MBTI) is the best-known instrument for assessing individuals' psychological types. There are four bipolar scales involved, and test takers are rated on each of them: extraversion-introversion, sensing-intuition, thinking-feeling, and judging-perceiving. Each type group has corresponding preferences. While librarians certainly aren't going to administer this test to students in their classes, research stemming from the MBTI can be helpful in determining how to structure instruction sessions.

A two-year study at the University of Florida found that the majority of entering students needing remediation were sensing types (Lawrence, 1982). A later study of the impact of affective variables on the performance of at-risk students again found that they were more likely to fall into the sensing rather than the intuitive category on the MBTI, which indicates "a preference for hands-on experience. They also prefer learning through interaction and visual stimuli rather than the traditional modes of the lecture and the text" (Dwinell and Higbee, 1989: 4). Sensing types also prefer structure, such as an explicit statement of the topic of the class, concrete objectives, facts, concrete examples, and the ability to practice their skills (Carskadon, 1994: 74–75). Keeping this in mind, librarians may plan accordingly.

Generational

In his book *Growing Up Digital: The Rise of the Net Generation*, Tapscott defined the term "Net Generation" as "the generation of children who, in 1999, will be between the ages of two and twenty-two, not just those who are active on the Internet" (Tapscott, 1998: 3). He argues that this generation is very different from previous generations, and that these differences need to be taken into account when teaching N-Geners (children of the Net Generation). Traits that affect N-Geners as learners are: their use of digital media for learning and communicating (5); their desire to collaborate on projects (10); a desire to learn based on discovery and participation (127); and their rejection of one-way, "broadcast" learning, such as lectures and textbooks (129). Tapscott foresees these traits, combined with more intensive use of digital media, leading to numerous shifts in the learning environment. Of particular concern to librarians teaching at-risk students are:

- moving from teacher-centered to learner-centered education
- moving from absorbing material to learning how to navigate and how to learn
- moving from the teacher as transmitter to the teacher as facilitator (Tapscott, 1998: 142–48).

These concepts are hardly new to instruction librarians, but they do present numerous challenges to instruction efforts.

Technological

Technology and the broad range of electronic resources available to researchers have complicated what we need to teach students. Instruction librarians grapple with the need not only to teach the concepts that help students become effective researchers (for example, primary versus secondary literature, scholarly communication patterns) but also to help students become capable searchers on a variety of information systems, tools that change far more frequently than print resources ever did. Beyond the question of what to teach students in this age of technology, there is the issue of how best to teach the material. An added difficulty is that librarians cannot expect all students' technological skills to be at the same level since some students will have had far more access to computers than others.

> In the United States there is a direct relationship between family income and access to computers and the Net. This correlation also exists between the higher- and lower-income schools. Some observers argue that this is just a temporary problem, but our research shows that the digital divide is actually widening, not disappearing. As the new technology trickles into poorer neighborhoods and schools, the better-off children are leapfrogging others—getting not only better access, but a wider range of services, faster access, the best technology, and, most importantly, increasing motivation, skills, and knowledge. This not only exacerbates the fluency gap but also the gap in different economic classes' capacity to learn and to have successful lives. Have-nots become know-nots and do-nots. (Tapscott, 1998: 11)

This is a particularly important issue when teaching at-risk students, many of whom come from economically disadvantaged backgrounds. In our brief instruction sessions, user education librarians are attempting to level the playing field and to introduce all students to the benefits of technology for doing research and for learning.

STRATEGIES FOR INSTRUCTION

While library instruction is important for all students, especially in today's complex information environment, it is particularly so for at-risk students. The instruction needs to begin on a somewhat lower level than for traditional students, because it is not safe to assume that at-risk students are as familiar with libraries and their general organization. This potential lack of basic knowledge, combined with the common anxiety about the library, can cause at-risk students to avoid the library whenever possible. Enabling students to overcome their anxiety and avoidance will increase the chances that they will succeed in their academic work.

> It is important to suggest to the students the possibilities that a library offers—the variety of materials available for study and enjoyment, and the different types of people who use the library. It is also a goal of the session to show the librarian as helpful, communicative, and able to empathize with different needs and points of view. Finally, the session should give the student an idea of how to access information in some of the major types of library materials and, more importantly, introduce the concept that access in a library is logical and systematic. (Ramey, 1985: 126)

Given that many librarians only have an hour with each class of students, this becomes a tall order now that the types of information sources have grown exponentially. In addition, the Internet, one of the key resources as students see it, isn't at all logical or systematic, and its "messy" nature needs to be compared to the logical arrangement of more traditional research tools.

In order to address at-risk students' affective and developmental needs, do not try to teach as much material as with some other classes. However, this should not be seen as detrimental. In the first place, just covering the material does not mean that students will learn it. Oxman-Michelli observes, "If a teacher covers the material, does that mean that students have learned? Or does learning mean engaging the students? Usually, teachers should cut down on what they cover and find creative ways to engage students in the subject matter" (Benderson, 1990: 9). Second, a session that is crammed with facts and detailed strategies may very well lose the interest of the students you would like to have appreciate the library's value. It is important to keep the affective needs of students in mind. An instruction session for at-risk students will teach some research strategies, but just as important is demonstrating that librarians and the library are approachable. When you are developing the instruction session—as with all instruction sessions—use the classroom instructor as a very important resource, finding out not only what the students should learn about the library, but also about students' familiarity with libraries and characteristics of the group that will help with planning the class. Good rapport with the instructor will be beneficial if you want to use class time before or after the instruction session to prepare for or reinforce learning. A few of the activities described later in this chapter are most effective or possible only if they take place outside of the library instruction session.

Classroom Climate

To meet the affective needs of at-risk students, classroom climate is particularly important. The instruction librarian needs to set the stage for learning to occur. "You must be both manager and creator of *climate*—a steward of the attitudes and feelings, joys and anxieties, the sense of accomplishment, etc., which students and instructors share during class, with an eye toward making the time spent challenging and profitable" (Timpson and Bendel-Simso, 1996: 3). Although librarians may meet with a class only once, it is still possible to create a climate conducive to learning that is supportive and engaging. It requires that you know the needs of your students and that you prepare the lesson plan to address these needs. Consider also how you plan to structure the class and if it feels fresh to you. Nothing is more deadening, for both you and the students, than teaching the same material the same way class after class. Timpson addresses these issues: "I also want teaching to be fun for me. There is a vitally important infectiousness here which students at all levels identify as enthusiasm. Student morale affects my morale and vice versa. My desire to be effective energizes my preparation before class and my concentration during class. I do believe that a positive environment is energizing for everyone" (13).

Classroom Activities

One nonthreatening method that can be used to set the stage for further learning involves the students from the very beginning of class. Divide students into groups of two or three, and give each group one of the two following exercises. The first is, "Your high school library probably looked very different from this library. List five differences between the typical high school and college or university library." The second, originally used for a class that was developing a virtual museum on the Web, is, "Both libraries and museums are repositories of culture, but no one would mistake one for the other. List six differences between libraries and museums." Since students are working together on one of these two questions and have several minutes to do so, they don't feel put on the spot to come up with a response. Discussion among the students may initially be slow or off topic, but they soon focus on the exercise, particularly as the librarian walks through the classroom, checking on progress and encouraging groups. Students feel a sense of accomplishment in coming up with as many responses as they can. The librarian elicits their responses by calling on different groups to provide differences, writing each on the board. This exercise engages students, provides structure by allowing them to contribute their own experiences, starts the class off on a light note, and is nonthreatening. It has the added advantage of letting the librarian determine what students know (did they pick up on the fact that college libraries use a different classification scheme than high school libraries?). It takes approximately the first ten minutes of class, with advantages that far outweigh the time that it takes from more "meaty" instruction.

This brief exercise addresses the goal suggested by Ramey in her description of an instruction session developed for students in the Georgia State University Division of Developmental Studies: "to help the student develop his or her own orientation to the library in the broadest sense of that term as 'intellectual or emotional direction.' The purpose is to help the student develop a sense of where libraries fit into his or her life as a student and into the lives of others in the college and community" (Ramey, 1985: 126).

A simple activity that helps students become more comfortable with the new, large, and perhaps intimidating library that they will be using during their academic careers is to answer their questions about how the library works. Often librarians pitch class material just a notch too high. It is illuminating to see what questions are at the forefront of our students' minds. However, just asking students what questions they may have about the library at the beginning of class will, in most cases, fall flat. Instead, ask the course instructor to have each student, in the class period before the library session, jot down one question they have about the library—there is no need for students to write their names on their sheets. The instructor can provide you with the questions before the library instruction session. There will be many similar questions, often about basics such as library hours, loan periods, and availability of material types other than books. Some questions, however, will be more sophisticated: how are the books organized on the shelf, how does the computer catalog work, and what types of electronic databases are available. And in some cases, it will be obvious that students have invented a question just to fulfill the assignment, but most of the students do want answers. This method of obtaining questions bypasses student reluctance to talk in class and, most importantly, involves the entire class. The librarian can begin class by answering some of the more basic questions (or by asking the group if one of them knows the answer) and then refer to additional questions as they come up later in the instruction. Students become more engaged, knowing the librarian is responding to their own questions, just as students are most interested when examples used during class are directly related to their assignment or interests.

Concept mapping is another activity that can be used with

at-risk students. It appeals to sensing types who prefer to learn through visual stimuli and a structured approach, and offers visual aids that highlight the structure of resources, concepts, and relationships involved with the research process. The use of concept maps enhances student metacognition—thinking about how one thinks. "To teach and guide metacognition . . . instruction must be based on the thinking processes. Those processes must be made transparent to the learner through awareness of thinking, [and] monitoring when thinking has broken down" (Pruisner, 1995: 51). Instruction librarians can use concept mapping in a variety of ways. You can ask students to draw maps at the beginning or prior to the library-instruction session in order to assess their understanding, or after the instruction to check students' grasp of the material taught. Drawing concept maps takes time, however, so consider asking the course instructor to use class time before or after the library session for this purpose. When time is at a premium, librarian-drawn concept maps can be used to facilitate discussion or provide an overview during class; at the end of class they can act as a summary or restatement of the ideas taught (Sherratt and Schlabach, 1990). In these cases, students do not benefit from the active-learning, thinking-awareness advantages inherent in self-drawn concept maps, but the maps still act as visual tools and organizers.

A librarian and a journalism lecturer developed an instruction session for remedial English and studies skills students that was to provide them with "a foundation in conceptualizing the library and its organization of resources . . . as well as some practice in how to approach research needs" (Madland and Smith, 1988: 54). The instructors for these at-risk classes requested an instruction session that would not duplicate the material taught in the required freshman English class. The resulting class was composed of a variety of activities to keep students engaged: student volunteers using scripts to play the role of information seekers, discussions of question analysis and information formats, an explanation of organization in a library, and an exercise in ordering call numbers. The authors found that the varied pace and activities made the presentation more successful in terms of student participation than had any previous session.

While at-risk student classes may have particular needs during an instruction session, this should not be construed to mean that they should not be challenged. Timpson and Bendel-Simso point out that teachers tend to feel "faintly apologetic for an ambitious class plan. Haven't almost all of us, at one time or another, assured our students that the material 'really isn't all that difficult'? This sort of reassurance, however, can be misguided, since the message given is mixed." They suggest directly telling students that the class will require effort on their part, and see how many rise to the challenge and perhaps exceed expectations (Timpson and Bendel-Simso, 1996: 16–17).

A challenging exercise that can be used to involve students, show respect for their ideas, introduce key concepts, and act as a platform for the instruction to follow is to have them work in small groups to develop "the ideal information-seeking tool or system." Ask each group to report briefly on its invention, and then compare actual tools or systems to their creations. While students may be disappointed in reality, the vividness of the comparison will help them retain knowledge of the systems they do learn. An alternate exercise would be to have small groups describe what they think would be the best ways to be able to look for information in a particular type of tool (online catalog, electronic database, Web search engine). Students will identify many of the traditional access points but may also come up with some surprising new ones. Exercises such as these meet the learning preferences indicated by Tapscott (1998): a desire to collaborate and to learn through discovery rather than through lecture.

Be sure to make the structure of the class explicit to the students, as well as emphasize why the material being taught is significant to them. This might take place following an introductory activity or answering student questions about the library, or it might even launch the class.

Hands-On Instruction

Technology provides another means for students to become actively involved in an instruction session. Many librarians teach their classes in computer classrooms, where students can have a hands-on learning experience. A study of eighty-one students in four sections of a second-semester freshman English class at the University of Wisconsin–Whitewater found that "students

in the sections that received guided hands-on instruction performed better on the post-test than students who were taught
using lecture/demonstration" (Bren, Hillemann, and Topp,
1998: 45). While these were not classes composed of at-risk students, the results are comparable for them. Students in seven
developmental writing classes, taught over a three-year period,
found the hands-on approach to learning basic research skills
to be an important factor in increasing their self-confidence
(Koehler and Swanson, 1990: 70).

While it is easy to provide hands-on opportunities in a computer classroom, some thought must be given to how to structure the class. Most computer classrooms have enough computers to make it difficult for a single librarian both to teach and
observe how students are keeping up with the class material.
Students often find the temptation of having a computer in front
of them just too strong to resist and start surfing the Internet
or another system for topics of interest. A classroom rover can
assist the instructor by helping students stay on track and by
taking care of more time-consuming glitches such as computer
freezes. In addition, not all at-risk students are equally familiar
with computers, and some may need some additional attention
during class. When students need to share computers because
of an insufficient number in the classroom, consider pairing a
more experienced computer user with a novice, if it can be done
easily. Ask the student less familiar with computers to be the
keyboardist, and ask the more expert student specifically to help
the partner (if the student isn't directly asked, he or she may
just feel frustrated with the slower pace). If students are more
evenly matched while sharing terminals, have them switch as
keyboardists halfway through the class.

Tapscott (1998) writes that N-Geners value learner-centered
rather than teacher-centered education, and also prefer to learn
how to navigate and how to learn, rather than simply to absorb
material. The best way to organize a hands-on session for at-
risk students to meet these learning preferences is to provide
students with a chance for structured exploration right at the
beginning of the computer section of the class. For example,
whether teaching database search strategies or Internet search
strategies, ask students to enter what they think is a good strategy for a topic that you provide (related to material they are

learning in class). You can then ask each student to announce the strategy and the number of items it garnered. It is important to stress at the beginning of this exercise that the strategies are not going to be considered right or wrong, so that students don't feel anxious about doing the exercise correctly. The wide variety of results based on the particular strategy entered engages students' attention and makes very clear to them, through their own experience, that not all searches are created equal. This creates an atmosphere where students want to learn more and provides an opening to start discussing with them why they think certain things happened. This method produces students more committed to untangling what might have happened in certain searches and better able to develop concepts based on the results, than if the librarian had demonstrated the searches or if students had typed in canned searches.

Sagamore Design Model

Masie and Wolman (1989) describe the Sagamore Design Model for developing and analyzing computer training, designed by the National Training and Computers Project. The model has six activities that generally occur when adults are learning how to use computers and that can accelerate learning when included. The first activity is *the set*, which should create a sense of anticipation and motivation amongst learners. It also includes stating class objectives and placing the material in context. The search strategy activity described above functions as a part of the set. *Information transfer* is the second activity listed, in which the course material is taught. It should be broken into manageable segments, and the authors suggest that the same instructional style and medium should not be used for more than twenty minutes.

Checking for confusion is important throughout the class, but the instructor shouldn't rely on learners to ask questions. The instructor should "solicit questions actively, because some learners will feel timid about asking questions, and others may be so confused that they don't even know what to ask. This solicitation may mean asking specific learners to paraphrase what you've talked about, explain which areas they're most or least confident about, or describe how they might apply this information to a particular task" (Masie and Wolman, 1989: 79). They also recommend another very useful teaching technique—that the instructor lob student questions back to other students. "This helps them test their understanding of the material, reinforces their new knowledge, and boosts their confidence if they are successful" (Masie and Wolman, 1989: 80). It also takes some of the limelight off the instructor and focuses it on student-learning. *Guided practice* should follow each segment of information transfer, with direct instructions for students to follow, so that the instructor can determine if students have learned the material. Students can work on their own topics or problems during *unguided practice*, at least some of which should occur during class time. A final *checking for understanding* should occur before the next information segment is embarked upon.

The Sagamore model is ideal for use with at-risk students. The mixture of activities meets different learning styles, and students' affective needs are addressed. It also channels productively the student desire to "play" on the computer during hands-on classes. If you can assure students that they will have time to explore and work on their own topics before the end of the session, they are more willing to follow the class during the more structured segments. The Sagamore model also incorporates opportunities to assess how well students are learning and allows them to experiment. All of these features address issues raised by Sorensen in her article in teaching developmental studies students:

> Recognize that developmental students tend to be very hesitant about asking questions or in any way indicating that they do not understand the instructor.
>
> Recognize, too, that most faculty members were successful in school, and have learning styles that are probably very different from those of many students, especially high-risk students. Therefore, information should be presented in a variety of ways to meet the needs of all students.
>
> Create opportunities which allow students to experiment without fear of failure.
>
> Be aware that many developmental students have never before learned how to process or organize information (Sorensen, 1988: 165).

In a research study of learning styles, Lee and Meyer (1994) compared students enrolled in developmental studies reading and English programs to academic core education majors enrolled in introductory education courses. They found that developmental students were significantly more passive in their learning characteristics. Some of these characteristics included being less focused in attention to task, less experienced in problem solving, and less able to conceptualize different ways to solve a problem. The researchers suggested some possible remedies: pairing passive learners with more active ones, using instructional technology, and using graphic organizers. While librarians do not have the luxury of time that classroom faculty do, recognizing student learning issues will suggest teaching techniques and will explain situations librarians face in the classroom.

CONCLUSION

The issues raised in this chapter will be useful to bear in mind for librarians designing instruction for at-risk students. However, it is important not to try to do too much during one class. Keep the class objectives in mind, as well as the need to involve students actively in their learning. Don't attempt to change your teaching methods radically all at once. Institute one change at a time, starting with one with which you feel most comfortable. Realize that not all ideas work equally well, and that sometimes an activity that is exciting and productive with one group of students might fall flat with another. Try to analyze why this may have occurred and make adjustments, but don't be dissuaded from using the activity again with an appropriate class. Once you are comfortable with some of the new methods you are using, ask a colleague to observe one of your classes and provide feedback. Discuss classroom activities that you are considering with the course instructor, who knows the students well and may make helpful suggestions. Trying new teaching methods can be challenging but also very rewarding, both for you and the students. Remember that teacher-centered and lecture-centered classes encourage student passivity rather than development.

In conclusion, a number of concerns come to mind when grappling with the issue of at-risk students. In a time when the number of at-risk students is rising, the subject has not been discussed extensively in the user education literature. A number of articles on the topic appeared in the 1980s, but radical changes in libraries call for new takes on the topic. Our practices need to reflect today's students and the today's library. Research on the effectiveness of different teaching methods for at-risk students is called for. As we broach the subject, we need to connect with the teaching specialist outside the library and work together to develop effective pedagogical models. We also need to consider how the user education programs and information literacy credit courses that we are developing, whatever format they take, meet the needs of at-risk students.

REFERENCES

Bateman, Walter L. 1990. *Open to Question: The Art of Teaching and Learning by Inquiry*. San Francisco: Jossey-Bass.

Benderson, Albert. 1990. "Critical Thinking: Critical Issues." *Focus* 24.

Bren, Barbara, Beth Hillemann, and Victoria Topp. 1998. "Effectiveness of Hands-On Instruction of Electronic Resources." *Research Strategies* 16, no. 1: 41–51.

Carskadon, Thomas G. 1994. "Student Personality Factors: Psychological Type and the Myers-Briggs Type Indicator." In *Handbook of College Teaching: Theory and Applications*, edited by Keith W. Prichard and R. McLaran Sawyer. Westport, Conn.: Greenwood.

Daragan, Patricia, and Gwendolyn Stevens. 1996. "Developing Lifelong Learners: An Integrative and Developmental Approach to Information Literacy." *Research Strategies* 14, no. 2 (Spring): 68–81.

Dwinell, Patricia L., and Jeanne L. Higbee. 1989. "The Relationship of Affective Variables to Student Performance: Research Findings." Paper presented at the 13th Annual Conference of the National Association of Developmental Education. ERIC Document 304614.

Koehler, Boyd, and Kathryn Swanson. 1990. "Basic Writers and the Library: A Plan for Providing Meaningful Bibliographic Instruction." *Journal of Basic Writing* 9, no. 1 (Spring): 56–74.

Kulik, James A., and Chen-Lin C. Kulik. 1991. "Developmental Instruction: An Analysis of the Research" (Research Report, No. 1). Boone, N.C.: Appalachian State University, National Center for Developmental Education. Quoted in Claire E. Weinstein. 1994. "Students at Risk for Academic Failure: Learning to Learn Classes." In *Handbook of College Teaching: Theory and Applications*, edited by Keith W. Prichard and R. McLaran Sawyer. Westport, Conn.: Greenwood, 375.

Lawrence, Joyce V. 1982. "The MBTI: Interview with Mary McCaulley." *Journal of Developmental & Remedial Education* 6, no. 1 (Fall): 14–19.

Lee, Yung-bin B., and Martha J. Meyer. 1994. "Learning Style Differences between Developmental Studies and Academic Core College Students: Implications for Teaching." ERIC Document 374751.

Lewis, Laurie, and Elizabeth Farris. 1996. *Remedial Education at Higher Education Institutions in Fall 1995*. NCES 97–584. Bernie Greene, project officer. Washington, D.C.: U.S. Department of Education, National Center for Education Statistics. Also available online at *www.nces.ed.gov/pubs/97584.html* [cited 1999, September 1].

McNeer, Elizabeth J. 1991. "Learning Theories and Library Instruction." *Journal of Academic Librarianship* 17, no. 5 (November): 294–97.

Madland, Denise, and Marian A. Smith. 1988. "Computer-Assisted Instruction for Teaching Conceptual Library Skills to Remedial Students." *Research Strategies* 6, no. 2 (Spring): 52–64.

Masie, Elliott, and Rebekah Wolman. 1989. *The Computer Training Handbook: How to Teach People to Use Computers*. Ed. 3.1. Raquette Lake, N.Y.: National Training and Computer Project.

Moore, William S. 1994. "Student and Faculty Epistemology in the College Classroom: The Perry Schema of Intellectual and Ethical Development." In *Handbook of College Teaching: Theory and Applications*, edited by Keith W. Prichard and R. McLaran Sawyer. Westport, Conn.: Greenwood.

Perry, William G., Jr. 1981. "Cognitive and Ethical Growth: The Making of Meaning." In *The Modern American College*. San Francisco: Jossey-Bass.

Pruisner, Peggy A.P. 1995. "Graphic Learning Strategies for At-Risk College Students. In *Eyes on the Future: Converging Images, Ideas, and Instruction. Selected Readings from the [27th] Annual Conference of the International Visual Literacy Association*. Chicago, Illinois, October 18–22. ERIC Document 391483.

Ramey, Mary Ann. 1985. "Learning to Think about Libraries: Focusing on Attitudinal Change for Remedial Studies Students." *Research Strategies* 3, no. 3 (Summer): 125–30.

Sherratt, Christine S., and Martin L. Schlabach. 1990. "The Applications of Concept Mapping in Reference and Information Services." *RQ* 30, no. 1 (Fall): 60–69.

Sorensen, Virginia P. 1988. "Bibliographic Instruction in a Developmental Studies Program: A Paired Course Approach." *Research Strategies* 6, no. 4 (Fall): 161–67.

Tapscott, Don. 1998. *Growing Up Digital: The Rise of the Net Generation*. New York: McGraw-Hill.

Timpson, William M., and Paul Bendel-Simso. 1996. *Concepts and Choices for Teaching: Meeting the Challenges in Higher Education*. Madison, Wisc.: Magna.

Weinstein, Claire E. 1994. "Students at Risk for Academic Failure: Learning to Learn Classes." In *Handbook of College Teaching: Theory and Applications*, edited by Keith W. Prichard and R. McLaran Sawyer. Westport, Conn.: Greenwood.

Part 4

RE-ENTRY, GRADUATE, AND SEASONED STUDENTS

OVERVIEW

The students in all three of the following chapters can be considered in some manner to be returning students. "Re-entry" in John Holmes's chapter refers to students who have taken a break in their academic careers and are returning because of career shifts, a change in their personal lives, or an interest in a specific activity or subject. Students in this group can be difficult to identify, as the average age span for undergraduates has increased and no longer fits the 18-to-22-year-old norm of previous decades. In addition, re-entry students are unlikely to come to library instruction sessions in groups. Graduate students are also returning to campus, some after a lengthy absence, and the same is true for seasoned, or senior, students. These two groups are, however, much more likely to be easily identified and may well come to the library with a class.

These three segments of the student population share other common features: returning students often have a wealth of life experience, even if they have been out of school for only a few years. Children, a job, and other nonacademic commitments provide them with valuable perspectives. Frequently among the most motivated in a class, these students can make the connections between what happens in the classroom and its application to "real life." This in turn can increase the interest and interaction among other students in the class.

These nonacademic commitments, however, usually mean that the returning student is pressed for time, especially in the case of re-entry and graduate students. Fitting library instruction into the schedules of these two groups calls for some creative timing and programming. Evenings and weekends are often the only times these students have available to study and do research, which means those are the times to offer workshops and training. Fortunately for the teaching librarian, students attending these sessions have chosen to be there and want to learn the techniques and resources being demonstrated, much as the first-generation students discussed in Tyckoson's chapter.

One instruction method that applies to all these groups of returning students is that of the general orientation, from a quick tour of the library to a longer session involving actual training. Transfer student offices, individual departments, and the appropriate outreach programs on campus that cater to the seasoned student are all important contacts for the user education librarian. Teaching approaches do differ for these groups, however, as they have different goals; re-entry students need to learn to use the resources efficiently, and frequently from off-site; graduate students need to learn the depth of the resources available in their discipline; and seasoned students may have goals such as increasing their comfort level with technology. In all cases, once librarians have met with these students in a group setting, they can pave the way for return visits and individual assistance.

Key techniques to look for in the following three chapters include:

- Use campus resources to identify the target audience.
- Assist these users in nontraditional ways, whether that means guiding returning and graduate students through institutional bureaucracy, or finding out where a visiting Elderhostel group can park on campus.
- Teach with problem-based learning methods, making the session content most relevant to the audience.
- Format sessions to accommodate varying learning styles as well as physical and logistical needs.
- Provide flexible instruction, both in terms of time—nights and weekends—and access points, such as tutorials, online working groups, and individual consultations.

Just in Case, Just in Time, Just for You: User Education for the Re-Entry Student

John W. Holmes
University of Washington

People who do not educate themselves, and keep reeducating themselves, to participate in the new knowledge environment will be the peasants of the information society. And societies that do not give all *their people a chance at a relevant education, and also periodic opportunities to tune up their knowledge and their insights, will be left in the jetstream of history by those who do.*
—Harlan Cleveland, 1985

It was appropriate [in the thirties] to define education as a process of transmitting what is known only when the time-span of major cultural change was greater than the life-span of individuals. Under this condition, what people learn in their youth will remain valid and useful for the rest of their lives . . . [T]oday this time-span is considerably shorter than that of human life, and accordingly our training must prepare individuals to face a novelty of conditions. Education must therefore be defined as a lifelong process of continuing inquiry. And so the most important learning of all—for both children and adults—is learning how to learn, acquiring the skills for self-directed inquiry.—A. N. Whitehead, 1931

There is little doubt that lifelong learning will be a necessity for the next century and beyond. The economic transition from manufacturing and industry to a service- and information-based economy will place increasing amounts of money and time at

127

the disposal of more and more people. At the same time, the aging of the U.S. population is creating new attitudes toward the process of aging and stimulating an expansion of knowledge bases in many fields, including education and medicine. Some education scholars have suggested that traditional models for learning, based on primary learning populations under the age of twenty-one (pedagogy), may no longer be applicable to a student demographic composed of as many as 50 percent non-traditional students. Some have adopted new education models focusing on adult learners (andragogy) and on learning across the life span, though these models have yet to be tested through substantial research.

RE-ENTRY STUDENTS: REASONS FOR RETURNING

One of the fastest growing categories of non-traditional students includes those returning to formal education after several years' absence—re-entry students. These students are returning to higher education for a number of reasons, as outlined below.

Career Change

Rapid evolutionary advancement in technology, shifting economic patterns, and downsizing trends within industry and manufacturing have created a need for a more versatile and mobile labor force, making this a prime factor in many students' decisions to return to formal education. The "Information Age" requires facility with information and the technologies that store, manage, and communicate that information. Even many executives in the industrial sector find themselves seeking the security of these new competencies in order to move laterally into new fields.

Job Advancement or Security

The ability to gain promotion and maintain relevance in the labor pool is often contingent upon acquisition of new knowledge or skills. Many re-entry students are motivated by the desire to realize a potential not fully explored during earlier educational experience. Others have reached one set of potentials and would like to explore supervisory or management opportunities for which additional education or training may be necessary.

Understanding Life Situations

Many re-entry students come back to formal education in order to address the conflicts and experiences of everyday life with more confidence and greater self-awareness. The need to cope with life-changing events—marriage, death, family problems, unemployment, debt, aging—creates the stress that frequently results in a return to the classroom.

Learning for Its Own Sake

Many re-entry students indicate a desire to explore a specific discipline or pursue more information on a subject simply because it interests them. They have raised families, held long-term jobs, and taken on positions of increasing social and community responsibility. Their desire to pursue further formal learning is motivated by their love of a specific activity or subject, or a love for the *process* of learning itself.

CHARACTERISTICS

There is an indication that the growing number of adult learners re-entering institutions of higher education is causing educators to rethink curricula and teaching methods. Because re-entry students will be the most important new group of academic library users for at least the next ten to thirty years, they may end up changing not only the ways in which librarians teach information skills but also the direction in which education itself moves.

Their remarkable heterogeneity makes a complete definition of the re-entry student difficult or misleading. We can, however, say that they are, by and large, adults between the ages of twenty-four and sixty-five, generally working, many married and with children in school, and returning to higher education after an absence of two to forty-five years.

Knowles (1990), Knox (1977), Cross (1981), and Apps (1981), among others, have studied the situation of adult learners, each attempting to articulate conceptual frameworks from which to better understand them. While there is no agreement on workable theory, there is considerable agreement on the characteristics that make the population distinct.

Experience

Re-entry students have life experience that is broader and deeper than that of traditional students—experience gained through college, employment, family, and an increasing agenda of social responsibilities. They are older, but age is not necessarily the distinguishing feature of this difference. "Rather, age reflects certain life experiences, educational experiences (both formal and informal), sociocultural contexts, psychological beliefs, perceptual expectations, and a probable historical-generational effect" (Kasworm, 1990: 364). The adult learner "accumulates an expanding reservoir of experience that causes him to become an increasingly rich resource for learning" (Knowles, 1990: 56). Re-entry students have had the opportunity to test previous knowledge in real-life situations and prefer to draw upon their experience in their learning activities.

Increased Goal Orientation

Re-entry students are, for the most part, voluntary students; they have a heightened eagerness to receive instruction and an increased receptivity to the acquisition of new skills. It is not the expectation of their families that drives them back to school, or the fact that their friends are enrolled, or because they have nothing else to do. Their motivation to learn is normally an immediate need for acquired skill or knowledge—learning as a means to an end. The immediacy of their goals frequently allows less academically prepared re-entry students to outperform their younger peers. The relative lack of need for the bigger picture—the structure of knowledge within a discipline, for example—creates an intense focus on the immediate results of their inquiry, with less need for speculation on the possible future outcomes of learning. Re-entry students also tend to be less preoccupied with the search for personal identity than are traditional students, who are still assembling the pieces, so to speak, looking for new ways in which to express themselves. Most re-entry students have established stable identities and acquired status within their communities, and at most are looking for ways to further refine their personalities in new social and professional contexts.

INDEPENDENT LEARNERS

Like most adults, re-entry students are independent learners, focused on practical life problems and less likely to view faculty as authorities in any area beyond a single discipline. No longer immersed in the process of pedagogical dependency, their "self-concept moves from one of being a dependent personality toward one of being a self-directed human being. . . . [Their] readiness to learn becomes oriented increasingly to the developmental tasks of [their] social roles" (Knowles, 1990: 39). In addition, "[their] time perspective changes from one of postponed application of knowledge to immediacy of application, and, accordingly, [their] orientation toward learning shifts from one of subject-centeredness to one of problem-centeredness" (39). Re-entry students have internalized the motivation for their own personal learning. Most re-entry students have higher educational goals than other students do, "tend to be less interested in . . . survey courses [and] prefer single concept, single-theory courses that focus heavily on the application of the concept to relevant problems. This tendency increases with age" (Zemke and Zemke, 1984).

Experience with New Technologies

Many re-entry students have information and commonsense skills that outstrip their technological skills. Some have worked extensively in technology-based industries but have not, in the course of their work, connected the skills required of them daily with the greater body of knowledge in a scholarly discipline or with the more generalized, nonprofessional needs that attend their social and political roles. They have an increased need to see their already-acquired technical skills achieve successful applications in practical contexts.

Many have anxiety in their relationship with new technologies, often arising from awareness of the enormous proliferation and accelerated evolution of information technology over the past ten years. The reliance on the use of these technologies in many new educational activities may be the greatest individual source of anxiety the re-entry student faces. Combined with grave doubts about their ability to continue learning at

later stages in life, this factor may suggest potential low retention rates among adult learners.

Anxiety about Competition with Younger Students

The ubiquitous competition for academic success felt by most
traditional students does not generally engage re-entry students,
for whom grades hold less meaning. Instead, re-entry students
focus on both more immediate and more enduring learning outcomes. Their understanding of the "real" meaning of education
tends to be pragmatic in nature, and they are likely to feel distracted by competition for grades. Nonetheless, anxiety arises
from concerns over the passage of time, decay of study skills,
inexperience with new technologies, slower response and comprehension times, and other age-related factors.

Problems and Obstacles

Frequently, re-entry students evidence negative self-images,
unrealistic goals, social-familial problems, and excessive practical orientation. They are often part-time students attending
weekend and evening classes, and most have less time to devote to the activities that support their curriculum, including
library use. Many have child-care, job, and transportation issues
not shared by their traditional counterparts. The emotional support of their immediate families becomes a significant factor in
their decision to continue the pursuit of academic goals.

Physical Factors

Some researchers have also noted ways in which physical
changes affect adults' learning. As physical reaction time slows,
more time is required to incorporate new concepts into existing frameworks and experiences, which suggests the need for
adult learners to have greater control of the pace of their learning. Even such factors as room temperature and noise are more
likely to impact the efficacy of re-entry instruction, particularly
with those students in their middle years and beyond.

TRADITIONAL USER EDUCATION AND ITS GOALS

Traditional library user education programs reside within the teaching mission of the university or college. These programs attempt to provide a foundational approach to information skills instruction that assumes little or no prior knowledge or experience with the use of broad and deep information resources for research purposes. Students participating in these programs learn the fundamentals of information storage and retrieval as they apply to specific assignments, some of which are manufactured for that purpose alone. Most students take a course in their first year that introduces library and information use on a small scale, with relatively low faculty expectations concerning the use of the information. Later in their curriculum they learn more about the flow of information within their major discipline, its modes of discourse, and appropriate primary and secondary source material. In its entirety, the package of traditional library instruction is only a small piece of the total higher education picture. It is preparatory, but not necessarily practical.

Re-entry students have been functioning as citizens and professionals for some years before returning to school. Already more experienced with information (though not necessarily more competent at using that information to create academic products, especially in light of the enormous increase in information publication and broadcast over the past ten years) they are more focused on immediate uses for the information they find. This is not abstract knowledge to be stored for later use, but practical information to be used for solving problems.

Instruction Strategies for Librarians Teaching Re-Entry Students

It is common knowledge among library instructors that information skills needed for lifelong learning cannot be imparted in a single fifty-minute workshop—or even in two or three of them scattered over four or five years. Librarians who want to reach re-entry students need to design a learning program that begins with active partnerships with faculty who teach these students. Opportunities and activities for relevant learning of effective information use have to be provided and coordinated with that faculty before an academic semester or quarter begins. Courses should be designed to present students with opportunities to solve problems that are personally meaningful. The teacher as facilitator will need to replace the teacher as sage, as subject- and discipline-based learning gives way to student-centered, problem-based learning. Librarians need to locate themselves within this new configuration, linking information skills with course syllabi and preparing themselves to address the individual needs of self-directed learners in pursuit of solutions to real-world problems.

The research in adult learning suggests that diversity of cognitive and learning styles tends to increase with age, which means libraries need to offer a greater diversity of learning experiences and activities. While selected literature in librarianship has reflected a growing interest in learning theory and instructional techniques, only in the last twenty years or so have librarians across the professional spectrum incorporated these principles into active programs. The relatively narrow focus and conditional success of user education for traditional student populations over many years is a strong argument against creating a separate learning experience for the adult re-entry student. Instead, it makes a strong case for a broader menu of instructional strategies—an array of options integrating all learning styles and addressing any information-seeking situation.

Four central assumptions about adult students and their implications for instruction include:

1. Adults are motivated to learn as they experience needs and interests that learning will satisfy; therefore, these are the appropriate starting points for organizing learning activities.
2. Adults' orientation to learning is life-centered; therefore, the appropriate units for organizing learning are life-situations, not subjects.
3. Experience is the richest resource for adults' learning; therefore, the core methodology of adult education is the analysis of experience.

4. Adults have a deep need to be self-directing; therefore, the role of the teacher is to engage in a process of mutual inquiry with them rather than to transmit his or her knowledge to them and then evaluate their conformity to it. (Knowles 1990: 31)

Complicating these issues is the fact that, in their teaching roles, librarians normally have less classroom contact time with students than faculty traditionally have. While many librarians now occasionally teach full-term courses on information skills and technology, most still teach the traditional fifty-minute or one-hour, one-shot lecture/workshop. Therefore, much of the literature on adult education appears difficult for librarians to put into practice. Many strategies for effective adult learning take time to unfold, but librarians may take guidance from the following strategies.

Inventory All the Learning Resources Within and Adjacent to the Institution

By encouraging learning outcomes that go beyond course objectives, librarians may empower the re-entry student on a broader scale. "[Instruction] should teach adult learners (a) how to retrieve information from all levels of the institution and (b) how to translate the specialized vocabulary of higher education into meaningful language" (MacKinnon-Slaney, 1994: 273). This observation suggests a holistic approach to library instruction, one that draws equally upon the traditional focus on formal library information sources and the process involved in solving more broadly based information needs. Instruction for re-entry students needs to be student-centered, life- and situation-based, beginning and ending in the experiences of the student, and connected to their real and immediate needs.

Create Relevant and Meaningful Instruction

The librarian must see that all instruction is practical. Make examples and cases important to the experience of the individual student. Keeping in mind the increased significance of time to re-entry students, instruction units should be prepared carefully to address specific and immediate needs. The librarian should be prepared to be *re*active in the classroom and office and *pro*active in seeking out re-entry students and discovering their individual needs. Adults want to know why learning a particular skill or concept is going to be useful or have meaning to them. Knowles (1990) suggests the usefulness of self-assessment instruments in assisting adult learners to discover the direction and depth of their own learning. User education librarians would also do well to keep instructions and learning tasks simple and straightforward. Adult learners have come to value accuracy over speed in the performance of assigned tasks, and clarity will assist in this.

Create Instructional Methods for as Wide a Variety of Learning and Personal Styles as Possible

Because their life experiences have been, in most cases, more diverse than those of traditional students, re-entry students are a more heterogeneous group. This requires the librarian to employ a broader menu of individualized learning tools and strategies. A single lecture, or even simple interactive approaches to instruction, do not begin to cover the range of learning options of a modest-sized group of adult re-entry students. These students are more likely to require an active hand in the creation of their own learning activities and the pace at which they are accomplished. This translates to the librarian-instructor making available to the student the resources necessary to solve as wide a variety of information challenges as possible. Use should be made of a variety of materials, with multiple opportunities for both activity and reflection.

Design Problem-Based Workshops

Students, faculty, and librarian may arrange a workshop that gives students a chance to work through information problems based on the research required for a specific course. Students may work in groups or individually to solve these information problems, which may be case studies or "real world" situations arising from community and/or campus issues and events. Whenever possible, cases should be integrated as fully as possible with the real-life challenges faced by the students and their environment. The ability to do extended problem-solving using information and the technologies that store, manage, and communicate it is a vital competency for the next millennium. It is best nurtured within activities that allow students to complete the problem-solving process under controlled conditions, rather than by simply performing the disparate tasks that comprise it. The integration of content and process is a key to the potential of problem-based learning.

Here is an example of this approach: Students are presented with a poorly structured problem or scenario. They should not have enough previous knowledge to solve the problem. They have to gather necessary information or learn new concepts, principles, or skills as they engage in the problem-solving process. The librarian then asks the students to list what they know about the scenario, including any data presented in the problem and any previous knowledge about the situation. The students must then, individually or in groups, articulate an exact statement of the problem based on what they know. This statement may have to be modified and refocused as new information is folded in. Typical problem statements may reflect discrepancies in event narratives, inconsistencies or anomalies, or the natural language statement of a client of professional services. The students then identify the information needed to fill in gaps. The goal of this activity is to guide searches that may take place online, in the library, and in other information resources. Finally, students explore and evaluate the information resources available and generate possible solutions and analyze them. Solutions may be presented orally or in writing.

Offer Consultations around the Calendar and Clock

Since most adult re-entry students attend classes in the evening and on weekends and have less time to devote to library research than traditional students, librarians need to be flexible in scheduling instruction for these students. Being prepared to make appointments for one-on-one consultations on weekends and in the evenings before and after classes is a step in this direction. Whenever possible, librarians should make an effort to form partnerships with re-entry students. These partnerships may take the form of research consultantships, technology tutoring, and advising and referral, among other models, and can be especially helpful in identifying potential learning problems and successfully involving the full range of information resources in solving them.

Supervise Independent Studies

Explore the possibility of working with re-entry students on an independent study related to their major disciplines or fields of study in which they are particularly interested. Some institutions provide cognates or courses "linked" to disciplinary courses. These adjunct units allow students to explore information, technology, writing, or other issues in relation to the content of the main course. Librarians should be willing to offer these types of experiences as independent studies when already existing courses are not available. Segregating the re-entry student from more traditional classmates also allows the librarian to address singular objectives in ways appropriate to a situation.

Independent studies also allow the student to play a more active role in designing her or his own learning objectives and self-assessment criteria. This strategy more fully engages the self-directed learner and brings into play the internal motivational factors that facilitate learning—and it ensures the relevance of the instruction.

Offer Weekend Workshops

Be prepared to offer weekend workshops on information and technology topics on a sign-up basis. These might cover such topics as publication cycles within specific disciplines, research case studies, and database workshops. The librarian must be willing to contact appropriate campus groups such as evening degree, distance education, extension, and continuing education programs, to identify re-entry students and market these opportunities.

Create Videos Covering Special Topics

Tours and orientations can be offered in video format, either through the World Wide Web or as a videotape that can be checked out for home viewing. Many such tools have already been created by libraries for new users and visitors. Videos for re-entry students may be tailored to match assignments, specific skills, or other situations. Workshops for re-entry groups might be videotaped for use by individuals or groups with similar interests or concerns.

Create Interactive Tutorials

Interactive, often Web-based, tutorials that are accessible from home or office can be used to introduce specific skills. Librarians should be willing to work with individual students to customize tutorials for specific purposes. Students can work through the problems in each tutorial and report to the librarian and/or faculty with questions and progress. The greater the number of these tutorials a librarian-instructor has on hand, the more prepared she or he is to address the broadest range of learning styles. They also prove most useful to the re-entry student whose ability to travel to the library for instruction is limited.

Create Networked Groups or Learning Communities, Online and in Person

The librarian and teaching faculty may arrange for an electronic discussion group for a course, for clusters of classmates working on similar projects, or for re-entry students who have requested the service through special programs or campus initiatives. The group can discuss information problems shared by specific subgroups or pose particular questions. Students may take more control over their learning by sharing information and resources and teaching each other with the guidance of the librarian and instructor. Groups may be given projects, topics to discuss, problems to solve, self-assessment activities, teaching assignments, or other tasks, as appropriate. The collaborative nature of these types of activities can stimulate confidence and create strong social connections.

Communicate and Collaborate with Faculty and Administration

The librarian must create and maintain collaborative partnerships with faculty who teach re-entry students and with appropriate campus units who provide and coordinate support for re-entry populations. The collaboration begins with a syllabus that integrates information skills into its objectives. It is then contingent upon the librarian to schedule workshops, consultations, and other strategies to help students deal with their research. Many faculty who regularly teach re-entry students omit independent library research from their syllabi for the very reasons that make these students distinctive—less time for academic activities, anxiety about information technologies, and a relative inability to access library materials and systems.

Design Instruction in Adult-to-Adult Collaborative Modes

It is important to interact with re-entry students as adults; the key to the instructor's role is the ability to act as a pathfinder, or facilitator, rather than as an authority. "In the adult class the student's experience counts for as much as the teacher's knowledge" (Lindeman, 1926: 166). The focus must remain on the student's need to solve a relevant problem, not the transmission of knowledge. Time should be taken early in a workshop or other learning situation to elicit expectations from re-entry students and give them an opportunity to reflect upon and articulate their learning objectives.

Be Concerned with the Success of the Student

Re-entry students are likely to take failure more personally than traditional students are. It is important for the librarian to take a deep interest in the success of re-entry students, delving into their specific and immediate needs for information, and providing supportive feedback when that information connects positively with needs.

Attend to Physical and Psychological Comfort

"The learning environment must be physically and psychologically comfortable; long lectures, periods of interminable sitting, and the absence of practice opportunities" should be avoided (Zemke and Zemke, 1984). In addition, re-entry students are more likely to lose self-esteem at moments when they are asked to take risks in a learning situation. This population has a memory of previous negative experiences in the classroom, including authoritarian teachers, and is burdened with distractions outside the classroom that impact their educational experiences. They are likely to take fewer risks than traditional students and to select less innovative or complex learning tasks, especially when choosing a project or doing library research— for example, using print resources or writing a traditional term paper rather than doing a PowerPoint presentation or building a Web site. They may also opt *not* to seek help when using the library.

Teach Self-Awareness and Reflective Learning Skills

Successful teachers are able to draw upon the inner resources of their students and to relate the skills being addressed to fields other than their own. The process of reflection, making crucial connections between internal and external processes, should be a significant part of instruction. Re-entry students are often seeking

> an increase in the ability to perceive and hold complexity, to tolerate ambiguity, to experience one's own and others' feelings more richly, to see oneself and others in a broader context, and to make wholehearted commitments in a complex, tentative and interdependent world ... a developmental shift from relatively tacit, unexamined ways of knowing and a sense of self as a passive receiver toward a more critically reflective stance on their culture and a more active notion of themselves as learners. (Daloz, 1990: 206)

Find Visible Ways of Valuing Each Individual Student

"If there is one fundamental difference between teaching traditional college-age students and returning students, it is the need to take into account the older student's work and life experience as a beginning place for learning" (Apps, 1981: 147). Adults must be able to integrate new concepts with existing beliefs and knowledge in order to use and retain the information effectively. Listening carefully to individual students and finding means for them to apply their experience and knowledge to the learning process is part of effective facilitation. Make sure that re-entry students understand that there may be many "right" ways of doing something.

CONCLUSION

The most successful library instruction program for re-entry students appears to be one that is equally effective for all groups within a library's user community. The strategies suggested in this chapter will make any library user education program stronger, regardless of the environment within which it functions or the specific user community whose needs it is designed to satisfy. More and more evidence informs us that student- or user-centered learning is the most effective means of engaging and motivating students—and most effective, as well, in making such learning both practical and lifelong. In order to provide the most useful instruction to the greatest number, programs must offer an expanded menu of learning options that address the heterogeneous learning styles of adult learners—those who are re-entering formal education as well as those who are *becoming* adults during their first college or university experience.

Effective instruction programs for re-entry students facilitate the integration of new knowledge and accumulated experience; place greater emphasis on using information for problem solving in self-directed and self-paced learning activities, leading to greater potential contributions to lifelong learning; provide comfortable and noncompetitive environments for instruction; promote collaborative group activities that support effective partnerships in work and social settings; clarify learning goals and their underlying purposes; and provide point-of-need instruction and support that reflects a student population with substantial responsibilities outside of their academic commitments.

REFERENCES

Apps, Jerold W. 1981. *The Adult Learner on Campus: A Guide for Instructors and Administrators*. Chicago: Follett.

Cleveland, Harlan. 1985. *The Knowledge Executive: Leadership in an Information Society*. New York: Truman Talley Books, Dutton.

Cross, K. Patricia. 1981. *Adults as Learners*. San Francisco: Jossey-Bass.

Daloz, Laurent A. Parks. 1990. "Mentorship." In *Adult Learning Methods*, edited by Michael W. Galbraith. Malabar, Fla.: Robert E. Krieger.

Kasworm, Carol F. 1990. "Adult Undergraduates in Higher Education: A Review of Past Research Perspectives." *Review of Educational Research* 60, no. 3: 345–72.

Knowles, Malcolm. 1990. *The Adult Learner: A Neglected Species*. Houston: Gulf.

Knox, Alan Boyd. 1977. *Adult Development and Learning*. San Francisco: Jossey-Bass.

Lindeman, Eduard C. 1926. *The Meaning of Adult Education*. New York: New Republic.

MacKinnon-Slaney, Fiona. 1994. "The Adult Persistence in Learning Model: A Road Map to Counseling Services for Adult Learners." *Journal of Counseling and Development* 72, no. 3 (January): 268–75.

Whitehead, A. N. 1931. "Introduction." In *Business Adrift*, by Wallace B. Donham. New York: McGraw-Hill.

Zemke, Ron and Zemke, Susan. 1984. "30 Things We Know for Sure about Adult Learning." *Innovation Abstracts* 6, no. 8 (March 9). Available online at *www.hcc.hawaii.edu/intranet/committees/FacDevCom/guidebk/teachtip/adults-3.htm* [cited 1999, July 15].

FURTHER READING

Andrews, Theodore E., Robert W. Houston, and Brenda L. Bryant. 1981. *Adult Learners (A Research Study)*. Washington, D.C.: Association of Teacher Educators.

Carr, David. 1983. "Adult Learning and Library Helping." *Library Trends* (spring): 569–83.

———. 1989. "The Situation of the Adult Learner in the Library." In *Reaching and Teaching Diverse Library User Groups*, edited by Teresa B. Mensching. Ann Arbor, Mich.: Pierian.

Hammond, Carol. 1994. "Nontraditional Students and the Library: Opinions, Preferences, and Behaviors." *College & Research Libraries* 55, no. 4 (July): 323–41.

Hu, Michael. 1985. "Determining the Needs and Attitudes of Non-Traditional Students." *College and University* 60, no. 3 (Spring): 201–209.

Iovacchini, Eric V., Linda M. Hall, and Dennis D. Hengstler. 1985. "Going Back to College: Some Differences between Adult Students and Traditional Students." *College and University* 61, no. 1 (Fall): 43–54.

Kegan, Robert. 1982. *The Evolving Self*. Cambridge: Harvard University Press.
———. 1994. *In Over Our Heads: The Mental Demands of Modern Life*. Cambridge: Harvard University Press.
Kennedy, Mary Ellen. 1984. "Bibliographic Instruction in the Academic Library: Looking at the Adult Student." In *Library Instruction and Reference Services*, edited by Bill Katz and Ruth A. Fraley. New York: Haworth.
Leverence, Mari Ellen. 1997. "A Study of Nontraditional Students' Perceptions of Their Library Research Skills." *The Reference Librarian*, no. 58: 143–61.
Malloch, Douglas C., and David C. Montgomery. 1996. "Variation in Characteristics Among Adult Students." *Continuing Higher Education Review* 60 (Spring): 42–53.
Sheridan, Jean. 1986. "Andragogy: A New Concept for Academic Librarians." *Research Strategies* 4, no. 4 (Fall): 156–67.
———. 1990. "The Reflective Librarian: Some Observations on Bibliographic Instruction in the Academic Library." *Journal of Academic Librarianship* 16, no. 1: 22–26.
Smith, Robert M., and Associates. 1990. *Learning to Learn Across the Lifespan*. San Francisco: Jossey-Bass.
Steffen, Susan Swords. 1989. "Designing Bibliographic Instruction Programs for Adult Students: The Schaffner Library Experience." *Information Reports and Bibliographies* 18, no. 6: 14–18.
Taylor, Kathleen, and Catherine Marienau, eds. 1995. *Learning Environments for Women's Adult Development: Bridges Toward Change*. San Francisco: Jossey-Bass.
Tomaiuolo, Nicholas G. 1990. "Reconsidering Bibliographic Instruction for Adult Reentry Students: Emphasizing the Practical." *Reference Services Review* 18, no. 1 (Spring): 49–54.

User Education for Graduate Students: Never a Given, and Not Always Received

Helene C. Williams
University of Washington

Students entering graduate school are expected to know how to do library research. This assumption stems from logical reasoning, for how could someone possibly have survived this long in the educational system without being able to effectively navigate in the library and in the larger world of information? Unfortunately, this assumption is false. Increasingly, reference and subject librarians encounter graduate students who have either never had to do an in-depth research paper, or who are studying in a content area new to them. We cannot rely on students having had library instruction at the undergraduate level, and subject specialists often must provide both the process (such as how to use an index, where to find the journals) and the content (such as what are the specific resources in this field) instruction to this user group. In many instruction programs, graduate students are a forgotten, or invisible, community. This chapter provides an overview of the literature in this area, as well as the theory behind and methods involved in graduate-level user education.

CHANGING DEMOGRAPHICS

The increased need for user education for graduate students originates from several factors. First, there are simply far more graduate students than ever before. Graduate enrollments increased from 955,000 in 1969 to 1,743,000 in 1995 (U.S. Department of Education, 1999: 211). The largest jump in enrollment has been fairly recent, with a 26 percent rise between 1985 and 1996 (187). At the same time, there has been a dramatic shift in the number of women in graduate programs: the number of full-time women in graduate programs rose 66 percent between 1985 and 1996, whereas the number of men enrolled increased by 23 percent (187). None of these statistics take into account the burgeoning number of international students and the increase in minority enrollments, which are also factors in the changing demographics of the graduate student population.

As the numbers have been changing, so too have the tools used for work and study. While people increasingly use computers on the job, this does not necessarily translate into information literacy in the course of graduate school. According to the *Digest of Education Statistics*, in 1997 78.7 percent of workers holding master's degrees used computers on the job, as did 74.6 percent of Ph.D. or professionally degreed workers (U.S. Department of Education, 1999: 481). Access to home computers for graduate students was 75.3 percent, though only 67.2 percent actually used them (482).

Another factor to consider in terms of technology is the overall discrepancy between men's and women's comfort levels with using computers. Many studies, including those by Brosnan (1998), Brunner and Bennett (1998), Corston and Colman (1996), and Shashaani (1997), discuss the relationships between gender and technology; Jiao and Onwuegbuzie (1998) specifically address the issue of gender and library anxiety.

These demographic factors, along with the long-held belief that graduate students are indeed self-sufficient when it comes to library research, influence the need for and directions taken by library instruction programs. As noted by Shapiro and Hill (1979), many are quite skilled in data collection and analysis in laboratory experiments, but they are not equally well-trained in using the research tools of a library. Even those who have received library research training as undergraduates more often than not also need instruction, given the ongoing changes in access and technology.

FACULTY ASSUMPTIONS

There is a large gap between the faculty's assumptions regarding library skills and what the students actually know. According to 91 percent of faculty respondents to a 1981 survey, they "assume that graduate students basically know how to use the library" (Dreifuss, 1981: 122). This gap is echoed in other studies, including those by Collins (1988), Pickert and Chwalek (1984), and Tucker (1984). This longstanding belief is also reflected in an early survey, from which Griffin concludes that communication between faculty and librarians, plus programming that teaches not just the "what there is and how to find it" skills but also the reasons why, is the direction to follow for library instruction for graduate students (Griffin and Clarke, 1972: 471).

The lack of preparedness of graduate students for dissertation-level research should not be underestimated; as Simpson says, "Contrary to popular student belief, a dissertation is not an unconscionably long term paper" (Simpson, 1986: 113). Students who approach graduate research with this attitude will most likely not engage in the problem-solving, multidimensional synthesis necessary for success in their field. Students who have received some library use training, on the other hand, tend to use more sophisticated finding tools and have developed more scholarly research skills (Reynolds, 1987).

Interestingly, a connection exists between the level of faculty publishing and their opinions of graduate student research skills: "It appears that faculty from more productive departments believe graduate students are less likely to be able to use library resources for research" (Boosinger, 1990: 477). Faculty in such departments may deal with a larger number of graduate students, and these faculty are also more likely to be familiar with library resources. Faculty from less-productive departments may themselves not be as familiar with library resources, which in turn affects their sense of what their graduate students know or need to know. Persuading the latter group that library instruction is necessary is likely to be much more difficult than the former.

Faculty who are aware of the lack of skills in graduate students bemoan the fact, using concepts familiar to all instruction librarians; according to Klemm, "We don't need to train walking encyclopedias. . . . We need to train people to *use* knowledge" (Klemm, 1987/88: 17). Outside of the library literature, however, very little recognition exists that there is a role for the library here, in either undergraduate or graduate instruction—a conclusion echoed by Jacobson and Vallely (1992) as well as Bailey (1985). Two exceptions include studies in the fields of geography and history. Geography professors Nancy and George Bain (1985) acknowledge that students need systematic exposure to library research, and created a workbook that is used by both undergraduates and beginning graduate students to fill that need. History professor Robert Swierenga says that it is common for students to be taught to read a subject, such as history, but not how to do research in that subject. "Students lack the requisite knowledge of the very reference tools that are specifically designed to aid them in their task. We expect plumbers or carpenters to know when and how to use the tools of their trade, but we do not give students the same apprenticeship in the use of library tools" (Swierenga, 1984: 392). His solution is an infusion of library instruction in a graduate historical-methodology course, an idea echoed by Simpson. Far more prevalent, however, are articles like Klemm's, which discuss facets such as process-based learning, critical thinking skills, and even core courses tailored to individual needs, but which do not make the connection as to how some of these skills may be incorporated into the graduate curriculum. Even treatises on an entire discipline, such as Lunsford, Moglen, and Slevin's (1989) collection of essays on doctoral studies in English, make no mention of library instruction—though there is much discussion of the lack of critical thinking skills in graduate students. Therefore, one of our goals as subject specialists and user education librarians should be to make sure that these faculty and departments are aware of us and what we can offer.

Klemm notes, "Scholarship and analysis skills are best taught by one who has them" (Klemm, 1987/88: 19). We as librarians often know that faculty in our areas are not as up-to-date or as comfortable with information technology as we are, and therefore we have an obligation to make our skills known to them; we are also obligated to do so in ways that do not threaten the nebulous "territory" surrounding individual faculty and departments. If graduate students are limited "to the tools and techniques which these professors themselves learned as graduate students," they become faculty who "simply perpetuate the process and the preconceptions" of library research and resources (Miller, 1989: 248). Other faculty list skills they would like to see graduate students attain to be more marketworthy. Goellnicht (1993) discusses providing them with teaching opportunities, seminars on grant writing and vita preparation, and travel funds for research, but he includes nothing about the potential use of librarians or library resources to achieve these goals. In a discussion of professional competencies in graduate education, Smart and Hagedorn model several educational strategies. The conclusion they reach for graduate students in all disciplines is that research competencies "would benefit from an emphasis on convergent strategies where greater attention is devoted to finding practical uses for ideas and theories, solving problems, and making decisions based on finding solutions to questions or problems" (Smart and Hagedorn, 1994: 255). Again, these reflect not just disciplinary skills, but broader information literacy concepts that can be addressed through user education.

THE GOAL: FLUENCY WITH INFORMATION TECHNOLOGY, FOR USERS AND LIBRARIANS

Among the many technology-driven changes that have occurred in the last twenty years, one of the largest is the move to end-user online searching. User education literature contains much about librarians doing mediated searching; Clayton and Nordstrom (1987), Collins (1988), Duffill (1985), Holler, Ruscella, and Scharf (1991), and Hoover and Clayton (1989) all discussed instruction for graduate students in the context of the librarian doing the actual online searching. In some cases, users were trained to perform their own searches, but the focus was usually on one database specific to a discipline, such as ERIC for education students. Not all that long ago, users needing online searches would meet with someone whose job it was to do these searches in multiple disciplines—and often without assistance from the subject specialist, who did not have, or perhaps did not want, training in online databases. Much of the existing literature on

graduate-level user education, which was written in the mid-
to late-1980s, reflects this separation, treating the subject specialist independently from the online searcher. This technological, as well as generational, gap obviously does not correspond
to the current state of libraries, information technology, and user
access; there is an opportunity and a need for newer research
in this area.

Users at all levels are not the only ones affected by the burgeoning availability of online resources; subject librarians are
now "online specialists" and have an increased responsibility
to teach the appropriate searching techniques. This can be a for-
midable challenge, as graduate students and faculty have increased desktop access to databases and the Internet as a whole,
yet they do not have the training to evaluate the resources they
are using and the quality of the results obtained.

Although good online searching skills are important to the
success of graduate students' research, the larger picture of information literacy must be kept in mind. As research forms a
substantial part of the career of the graduate student-turned-
faculty, we are obligated to train this next generation of faculty
researchers who would be, as Rosenberg notes, "library-literate
at more than one research location" (Rosenberg, 1984: 389).
There is some discussion about whether this is even possible,
however. There is the "argument that teaching search strategy
can result in long-term retention and can produce library users
who apply this experience to become self-sufficient, self-reliant
library and information users" (Kirkendall, 1989: 81); in contrast,
the claim put forward by Feinberg is that librarians "should
stick to teaching those things that are within our expertise, and
we should aim our teaching to meet the immediate library research needs of our students" (Feinberg, 1989: 85). Since technology, and the world of information, is in such a state of constant change, he asks, how can we know what skills will be useful to the lifelong learner ten or fifteen years from now?

The concepts of information literacy provide a partial answer to that question: We can teach students to identify information needs as well as methods for obtaining and assessing
that information. A recent report by the National Research
Council's Committee on Information Technology Literacy proposes the concept of information fluency, a deeper level of un-

derstanding and ability in terms of information technology. Originally charged with creating "literacy" requirements, the Committee chose "fluency" as more apt, as "the notion of 'fluency' captures best . . . connotations of the ability to reformulate knowledge, to express oneself creatively and appropriately, and to produce and generate information (rather than simply to comprehend it)" (National Research Council, 1999: 1–5). Although aimed specifically at the use of information technology, the Committee's breakdown of the three types of knowledge necessary for FITness (fluency with information technology), applies to disciplinary fluency as well:

- Intellectual capabilities, or one's ability to apply technology in complex situations, are also described as "life skills."
- Fundamental concepts are the "book learning" portion of fluency.
- Contemporary skills are those necessary to accomplish tasks, and they change as technology products do (National Research Council, 1999).

Since FITness is aimed at students only in the context of information technology, an additional piece needs to be added to the picture to fulfill both Feinberg's desire that we meet the immediate research needs of students as well as the larger goal of fluency within a discipline. During this period of transition from print to electronic resources, it is important to introduce graduate students to print sources in their discipline, including local and/or rare resources; in most cases, these have not yet, and may never be, replaced by online alternatives. Many students are unaware that these print sources exist, as are some newer librarians. With the advent of end-user online searching and FITness initiatives, the mediating role of librarians has changed; it still exists, and remains a vital part of the research process.

With these concepts in mind, then, how do we best deal with the graduate student population? As can be seen from the literature, there is a gap in many user education programs; in some cases, graduate students are dealt with like undergraduates, and in others they are treated like faculty (Ackerson, 1996). Other programs do not deal with graduate students at all and instead focus on the better-defined user groups, as noted by Lipow

(1976). Undergraduates and faculty have distinctly different needs, whereas graduate students tend to operate in both the student and classroom instructor modes. To further complicate matters, graduate students are often distance students rather than on-campus users, and their access needs differ from those working in the library or from an on-campus wired facility.

The remainder of this chapter discusses strategies for tackling these challenges. In order to create a successful program, it is important to remember the goals of user education for graduate students. Foremost among these goals is that we are not aiming to make mini-librarians out of the graduate students; this is echoed by Shapiro, who, in a graduate user education course, provided "budding social sciences researchers with an opportunity to explore intensively the intricacies of the search process itself" as opposed to offering a traditional social sciences reference course (Shapiro and Hill, 1979: 76). Indeed, as Lowry notes, the goal "is not only to teach students about the traditional library resources and services upon which successful research depends, but also to orient them to the changing world of electronic information and to begin to prepare them for a future in which an understanding and mastery of new techniques and resources will be essential" (Lowry, 1990: 23).

There are other factors to keep in mind in addition to the general fluency concepts discussed above. Kazlauskas's article on the feasibility of course-integrated user education for graduate students concludes that this user group needs more instruction than is possible with the course-integrated method: "Graduate students need specific bibliographic instruction that can be generalized to any academic library but is individualized to their specific research needs" (Kazlauskas, 1987: 10). This statement is echoed by others including Gratch and York (1991), who admit that the most labor-intensive instruction, one-to-one, is also the most effective. It should be noted that a search of the literature to update Kazlauskas's findings reveals little regarding user education specifically for graduate students since the late 1980s, so again, there is a need for more current research on this subject.

Other concepts regarding graduate education as a whole, however, are available. According to Jiao and Onwuegbuzie (1998), graduate students have high expectations of themselves, as well as of faculty and librarians; these expectations tend to increase their anxiety levels. In addition, as they begin their research, these students are more likely to realize that the more they know, the more they realize there is to know about resources and technology. This reinforces the correlation between the activities in a productive department and faculty requirements of graduate students. Students also expect to work in groups in a process-based environment. Along with these expectations come anxieties, including:

- interpersonal anxiety, including being anxious about asking for assistance
- perceived library incompetence, including feeling overwhelmed
- location anxiety, including not knowing where things are
- mechanical anxiety, relating to using computers and other equipment such as copy machines and microform readers
- resource anxiety, meaning discomfort with a library's lack of resources (Onwuegbuzie, 1997).

Allaying these anxieties through effective user education goes far toward creating the information-fluent researchers advocated by the National Research Council.

GRADUATE STUDENTS' NEEDS

A 1976 study at the University of Michigan asked Ph.D. alumni about the most important objectives of their dissertations, producing results that are not dissimilar to those we might expect today:

- to acquire broad research skills
- to organize and communicate research findings
- to develop the capability of making future contributions to knowledge
- to identify important problems
- to develop high-level problem-solving skills (Dunlap, 1976).

The research skills necessary for producing a dissertation obviously translate into elements of lifelong learning, information literacy, and fluency within a discipline. Combining these educational objectives with the demographics of graduate students—who are older, returning students, often enrolled part-time, who need access from home or work, twenty-four hours a day—we can start to put together elements of a user education program for this population.

In addition to defining the audience demographics, it is important to establish objectives for the program. What needs to be accomplished for the program to be deemed successful? What skills do the graduate students need to have to achieve their goals? What resources—be they electronic, print, or human—exist to meet the demands of a graduate-level user education program? Investigating the many different options for instruction activities helps determine answers to these and other questions.

Just as most programs have several types of user education activities for undergraduates, so too is there a need for more than one level of programming for graduate students. However, it is also important to recognize that graduate-level user education is not simply "BI-plus."[1] The needs of graduate students do parallel those of undergraduates to some extent, but it is important to determine and address the differences as well. One of the first needs to address is that of making sure faculty and students know the user education program exists. Parrish (1989) conducted a needs analysis at Bowling Green State University and found a lack of awareness of services available to graduate students; publicizing these services could well cut down on some of the types of anxiety discovered by Onwuegbuzie (1997). It is important, as Michalak notes in his essay on the role of subject specialists in the graduate community, that "the student becomes aware that there is a librarian connected with the academic department to assist at the proper time" (Michalak, 1976: 258).

In terms of resources, the research of Duffill (1985) and Bradigan, Kroll, and Sims (1987) reminds us that graduate students need to look at much more specialized materials than do undergraduates, and that they do not always need extended explanations as to how sources work, as undergraduates often do. More important at this stage is the need for hands-on experience with resources, both print and electronic. Other issues to be addressed included the varied learning styles in a graduate classroom (Onwuegbuzie, 1998). According to several researchers, graduate students prefer active learning, and students at the University of West Florida who expressed dissatisfaction with instruction sessions did so because of the noninteractive methodology used (Franklin and Toifel, 1994). Instead of the traditional show-and-tell approach, students preferred participatory, hands-on sessions. Each class has its own dynamic, however, and some students may prefer to absorb information by listening rather than doing, and some disciplines lend themselves more to individual research than group work. The librarian needs to take this into account when preparing for the session by incorporating several different activities and by presenting material in more than one way.

One other element that is perhaps the most crucial is that instruction programs—for graduate students or other populations—must pay attention to the human element. This includes both the human resources available at the library as well as those involved in instruction across campus. Collaboration is necessary for advances in scholarship, and there has been at least one proposal for reviving the scholar/librarian model, in which "human interaction is a reality check" (Christensen, 1994: 204). Although this proposal was aimed at undergraduate term paper clinic programs, it is applicable to interactions with graduate students and faculty as well.

LEVELS OF USER EDUCATION

Once objectives have been established for a graduate user education program, the multi-level programming can begin. In many cases, one or more of these levels of activity will already be in place and may need little modification. If the human element is the cornerstone of an instruction program, then it makes sense that the first step in building the program will be to establish contact, both with the faculty and the graduate students.

Of import here is the question of exactly *who* will be the contact from the library. In most settings, there is a user education coordinator who fields the bulk of the instruction requests, which come mainly from the high-use departments such as English and history, and from lower-division courses with multiple sections all following essentially the same assignment. However, subject specialists are the more logical contacts at the upper-division and graduate levels, because of their background in the discipline and their existing liaison activities. Some authors have recognized the consulting and teaching roles of subject specialists, perhaps best summed up by Hay, who says that "bibliographic instruction is another area where subject bibliographers can do a superior job compared to non-subject trained librarians" (Hay, 1990: 14).

There are several liaison activities mentioned in the literature to help librarians establish contact with a department as well as to determine instruction needs. Some are formal, such as the syllabus study conducted by Rambler (1982), a faculty survey as discussed by Schloman, Lilly, and Hu (1989), or the actual assignment of a librarian to a department. Twenty years after Michalak's discussion of subject specialists working with faculty and graduate students, we see liaison roles expanding. Activities mentioned by Benson in his examination of ways to become familiar with faculty and graduate student research needs and interests include:

- interviewing faculty about their research projects
- reading faculty and graduate student publications
- attending classes and lectures (Benson, 1995).

Meeting faculty and students on their "turf" not only makes for better-informed liaisons but also helps integrate our services with user needs. In today's fast-paced electronic world there is the added opportunity of meeting faculty in their offices and demonstrating new databases and interfaces, as this often translates to a recognition of the need for user education sessions for their students. The support to be gained through faculty contact is, as Benson notes, "indispensable if we are to make the contacts with the graduate students we desire" (Benson, 1995: 63).

One-Shots: Orientation at Entrance

The first contact with graduate students is usually through departmental orientations. One of the main purposes of a general orientation is to make the students aware of the library services and resources geared toward their needs; though this can be done in the library or off-site, it is important that graduate students know the locations or access points of these services and resources. The need for geographic, site-specific orientation may be viewed by these students as beneath them, but the much-maligned "library tour" often has the effect of lessening location anxiety, thus addressing another of Onwuegbuzie's anxiety issues (1997). Tours also introduce those new to the system to "hidden" collections and, as noted by Griffin and Clarke, "local variations in filing or shelving that often confuse students, librarians, and faculty alike" (Griffin and Clarke, 1972: 467).

Another method of initial contact involves working through the institution's administration and organizations, such as the University of Arizona program described by Cox and Johnson (1992). This program provides a general introduction to graduate research, services, and resources, and is discipline-based, rather than department-based, reaching students in departments that would not otherwise have provided for a library orientation. As for what can be achieved in this type of setting, Piette and Dance's (1993) statistical evaluation of large orientation sessions aimed at incoming graduate students in many disciplines concludes that teaching students how to access information, rather than specific subject areas, is more effective. They argue that Kazlauskas's point about user education needing to be subject specific is no longer true; however, this author maintains that experience and the literature show a program of instruction for graduate students needs to have both the general and specific components.

Beyond Orientation: Getting into the Classroom

General Workshops

The next level beyond the one-shot orientation session is the workshop aimed at graduate students in a discipline but not tied to any specific department. Bradigan, Kroll, and Sims describe a workshop program offered at the Ohio State University Libraries in the mid-1980s as one piece of an instruction program for graduate students. The goals of the workshops were "to increase graduate students' awareness of library resources, and to help them identify the appropriate tools and steps for their own research projects" (Bradigan, Kroll, and Sims, 1987: 336). By leading students through the research process using a sample interdisciplinary topic, the librarians showed how these steps were applicable to the students' own projects. These workshops were not part of the graduate curriculum but could easily be incorporated into orientations held by specific departments, thus achieving programmatic implementation. In this case, the workshop program was run by two librarians: one a subject specialist, and one from the user education office. Other workshops not tied to a specific discipline can cover services, such as the sessions offered at the University of Arkansas. Gupta, Salisbury, and Bailey (1995) describe a project on the issue of access versus ownership, and the required workshops graduate students must take before using the document delivery service.

Course-Related Instruction

Department- or discipline-based sessions allow the introduction of more specific subject-related resources, and one of the most-discussed approaches is the research methods course taught by departmental faculty that incorporates one or more library sessions. Clayton and Nordstrom (1987) describe a six-credit, two-semester methods course, which has one library session. In this education research seminar, students are introduced to the basic resources in educational research, including ERIC. In this case, the goal appears to be to help students become more articulate in asking for assistance, rather than to become more independent researchers. Madland (1985) also describes a single library session tied to a methods course; students in this course are from all disciplines, however, so general examples are used for the session and then students are invited to sign up for individual consultations. Simpson (1986) discusses a criminal justice methods course that requires four to six hours of user education, during which general methods, primary sources, and statistical and archival sources are covered.

Robert Swierenga (1984) has also incorporated a two-hour library session into a graduate historical research methods course at Kent State. The hands-on session with the subject specialist is followed up by an assignment requiring the students to evaluate several of the sources. From the faculty member's point of view, it is more important for students to describe the process rather than the results, which is a point often made by librarians as well. He also notes that not only students benefit from team-teaching: "their professors even learn a thing or two" (Swierenga, 1984: 396).

Integrating user education into courses other than department-based, research methods classes includes many of the same strategies as for undergraduate user education programs. The subject specialist's training comes in useful here, as he or she can approach faculty with suggested resources for their courses. Reading the course descriptions for a department and knowing which courses are offered each quarter or semester is one method for planning ahead in case more support is needed in terms of staff or space allocation for user education sessions.

Taking the one-shot one step further, Pickert and Chwalek (1984) describe a program at Catholic University, in which a general introductory session is held with students in the research methods course. Once students progress to the seminar-level courses, they have another session based on pathfinders. When students begin to work on their dissertation research, they then have more individual consultations on research strategies and specific resources.

An effective way to find out what course-related instruction is occurring at similar institutions, or how librarians are collaborating with faculty, is to query an appropriate listserv. BI-L, the library instruction list, is one starting point. Searching the archives or querying subject-specific lists may yield more information. For example, the Association of College & Research Libraries (ACRL) English and American Literature Section (EALS) recently discussed the involvement of English subject specialists in research-methods courses. More information on subject-based sections of ACRL can be found at *www.ala.org/acrl/secthp.html*.

Workbooks and Tutorials

Other activities that are similar to one-shot sessions include workbooks and tutorials. As mentioned earlier, Bain and Bain (1985) created a workbook aimed at upper-division undergraduates and beginning graduate students in geography. The workbook covers the usual range of resources, from books to periodicals to government documents; it was a collaborative effort between librarians and faculty, and built on the basic orientation provided in other segments of the user education program, such as the tour. This particular workbook was designed to be completed over a two-week period. Other workbook examples, such as the one for social work students described by Doelker and Toifel (1984), focus not only on library skills but also on encouraging a positive attitude about libraries and those who work there. The evaluation measure used in this case includes counting the number of references cited in student papers.

Handouts

For years, a staple of every instruction program has been the handout, and many library literature racks still contain the annotated bibliographies of research tools in various fields. Even at the beginning of plans for automation at the University of Michigan libraries in the mid-1970s, handouts were liberally used in response to graduate student needs (Dunlap, 1976). The question now is: What replaces the handout in the online world of desktop access? In response, libraries are putting their handouts online, more often in the form of tutorials and interactive modules. Bender et al. (1997) recommend tutorials as one element of a user education program for science and engineering graduate students. Tutorials can serve some of the functions of one-shot sessions, especially with distance learners—whether that distance be across the country or across campus—and other non-traditional users, as graduate students tend to be. Another advantage of the online tutorial is that it may deflect territorial tensions that arise between librarians and faculty. If students are aware of the tutorial and the librarian is not able to present a classroom session (for whatever reason), the assistance is still offered and in a more neutral, less imposing, manner.

Beyond the Classroom

Consultations

Maintaining contact with graduate students is the next level of activity in a graduate user education program. This can be accomplished informally at the end of orientation or one-shot sessions simply by inviting students to stop by the reference desk and ask for you when they have questions. Students who come to the reference desk with a specialized question are often unaware that there is a librarian in "their" area; referrals to the appropriate librarian can be made on the spot if the specialist is available. You can also keep subject specialists' business cards at the reference desk to hand out when suitable, especially when faculty approach the desk to ask about setting up "a library tour"; often they are also unaware of the more effective instruction services offered. Formal meetings can also be initiated. Kazlauskas (1987) cites the one-on-one consultation as being the most effective, though Ackerson (1996) takes these conferences one step further, proposing a model for thesis and dissertation-level searching by graduate students in the sciences based on the organization of scientific literature. Bailey (1985) also advocates partnerships between librarians, students, and faculty/advisors at the thesis level, with the short-term benefit of providing immediate assistance and the long-term effect of building strong researchers.

Bowling Green State University set up a formal consultation program, called the Personalized Research Consultation Service (PERCS). As described by Gratch and York (1991), this service teaches graduate students information-seeking skills through meetings tailored to an individual's subject, with a broader goal of making known the resources and services of the library. The potential issue of librarians infringing on faculty territory was dealt with by getting input from faculty at the start. For a program such as this, Gratch and York recommend that librarians develop a working relationship with the graduate college, not just individual departments; this could create more funding as well as increase communication about the service. Public relations and subject librarian training are also elements of the program. PERCS is aimed at thesis-level students, and provides more substantive assistance than a general orientation. More information about the current iteration of the PERCS program can be found at *www.bgsu.edu/colleges/library/infosrv/lue/ consult.html*.

Office Hours

Office hours may be viewed as one aspect of a consultation program, as they provide students with a fixed time to meet with a librarian. Both the drop-in or appointment methods work in this case. You might want to consider holding office hours in the academic department, which offers several advantages over the library:

- If office, or as is true in many cases, cubicle, space in the library is shared, meeting students in the department provides more privacy.
- By working in the department, the librarian can see what is (or is not) working in terms of remote access.
- It has been this author's experience that a different clientele tends to come to the academic department than to the library, and thus contacts can be made that otherwise would not happen.

Setting up the logistics of space in a department does not have to be difficult. The office of a faculty member on leave can be used, or (in the author's case) a faculty member could share an office one day a week by working out a schedule at the beginning of each quarter. Simply spending time in the department creates an awareness on the part of students and faculty that "the librarian" can assist—not only with user education matters but with collection development issues as well.

Issues of Territory

As the connections between librarians, graduate students, and faculty increase, we need to remain aware of potential areas of tension, from both faculty and librarians. As noted by Simpson, "libraries are not always as receptive to the kind of library/ scholar involvement" suggested here (Simpson, 1986: 122). Librarians may be reluctant to take on what they feel amounts to additional work, although the results of a successful program include better-trained students. Faculty, too, have spoken about librarians more actively entering the classroom and teaching arenas, and not always in a positive manner; Bender et al. (1997) recommend staying away from faculty "turf," as do Bailey (1985) and Dreifuss (1981). Dreifuss's suggestion of having students ask their faculty for library instruction rather than having the librarian approach the faculty can work to diffuse uncomfortable situations. Although it may be ideal for subject specialists to have working space in academic departments, consultations can take place either in the department or the library. Thanks to technology, the decrease in the physical boundaries of the library provides one more reason for the librarian to go to departments to demonstrate databases and other resources that can be accessed on the desktop. A training session for a faculty member can thus become an opportunity to offer instruction for an entire class.

Credit Courses

The one level of activity that best provides librarians the time and resources to teach graduate students research skills is, of course, the research methods course. Incorporating one or more library sessions into a department-taught methods course may be all that is deemed necessary by some classroom faculty, as discussed earlier. However, a librarian-taught, for-credit course affirms the library's role in the education of graduate students and can be a vital element in the partnership with faculty to achieve that goal.

There are several proponents of for-credit, graduate research methods courses. An early supporter was Michalak:

> Librarians can best perform the instructional function in coordination with academic departments by the development of formal courses of instruction in the bibliographical and research resources of a specific discipline. Ideally, these courses will be for credit in the student's major department particularly as the department then views the training in bibliographical and research resources as part of the methodological training of graduate students. This affects the seriousness with which students will approach the subject matter. (Michalak, 1976: 260)

Michalak notes that this instruction is applicable to undergraduates as well. However, it is this author's experience that graduate students ask for, and need, a level of instruction different from that of the undergraduate. One commonality between both groups is that they need the research *process* segment of the course, although the actual sources used may differ.

Other graduate credit courses in research methods are offered in a number of formats. Adams and Morris (1985) discuss a case study at William Paterson College, which in 1980–1981 piloted a library research course through a graduate education class; it ran for sixteen weeks, with ten of those sessions being team taught by a professor and one or more librarians. The course outline mirrors classes being offered today—including the evaluation of sources—so again, the process hasn't changed, but the access to the resources certainly has. In all of these examples, the cost of the instruction is high in terms of staff time, especially in the case of team teaching; the Paterson College program was later modified to include an introductory lecture with three more specific sessions covering reference sources, indexes, abstracts, curriculum materials, government publications, and statistical sources.

Another graduate credit course program taught by librarians was long offered at the University of Michigan; the development of these term-long courses began in the mid-1970s, and stopped only recently because of faculty turnover. According to Dunlap, providing term-long courses in research methods tailored to a specific discipline "has had the greatest impact on the training of graduate students and . . . will have the most far-reaching ramifications for the future" (Dunlap, 1976: 250). At Columbia University, a credit course called Research in the Humanities has been offered through the Graduate School of Arts and Sciences since the late 1980s; the evaluation and process goals for the course include the use of both traditional and electronic resources. In addition, the course description notes that "conceptual and theoretical issues attending the integration of technology into research in the humanities and history [are also] explored" (Columbia University). The Research G4000 course is linked to a number of departments; for example the course description can be seen on the French and Romance Philology page, at *www.cc.columbia.edu/cu/gsas/bulletin/frrpcata.html*.

The development of such courses differs at each institution. In some cases, research methods courses already exist and may be taught by departmental faculty, with or without collaboration with a subject librarian. In departments or disciplines where no such courses are offered, however, a proactive librarian can propose such a course, as seen in the following case.

The University of Washington's English Department had

sporadically offered a research methods course over the years. With faculty turnover and the increased focus on critical theory rather than textual research, the course was retired in the early 1980s. However, it was obvious to librarians, and increasingly to the graduate students and faculty of the department, that the need for such a course still existed. With the advent of new technology and multiple methods to access resources both traditional and electronic, no current faculty member felt qualified to take on the challenge of teaching a revived research methods course. With the support of the English Department Library and Technology Committee, which is comprised of a small group of English faculty who help disseminate information on new library resources and who advise in library-related matters of interest to the department, the author proposed teaching an updated version of the research methods course. The current online portion of the course is available at *faculty.washington.edu/helenew/engl592.html.*

The process of instituting a "new" course can be arduous, even in systems smaller than those of the University of Washington. No matter the size of the institution, the following steps need to be considered:

1. Curriculum committees in the department and perhaps even in the college must be consulted.
2. A syllabus, course objectives, and lesson plans must be prepared and approved by the proper groups.
3. Teaching space must be allocated, whether by the library or campus scheduling.
4. There is also the matter of payment: will the librarian teaching this course be compensated monetarily? Will there be release time for preparation and grading?

The goals of the academic program or discipline serve as useful parameters when building the curriculum for a research methods course. Reading departmental course descriptions and college bulletins can provide some information, but it is also important to involve the faculty of the departments or disciplines for which the research methods course is being offered. Meeting on an informal basis over coffee, or more formally through faculty meetings or library advisory council sessions, all enhance the librarian/faculty partnership that is necessary for these courses and, indeed, all levels of user education to be most effective. Curriculum discussions can range from the general—in this case, faculty wanted students to gain research skills in the humanities, which does cover a lot of territory—to the specific, such as whether sessions on HTML or analytical bibliography are best presented in a methods course.

As noted above, teaching a term-long course is a labor-intensive proposition, even if release time or other support is available. However, the time spent in proposing and creating the course, or in partnering with faculty to teach the course, provides long-term benefits to all parties. Faculty get the opportunity to update their own research skills while not being "shown up" by their own students, and graduate students receive instruction in the most effective ways to access resources, be they print or electronic. Librarians can often provide a more objective or perhaps broader view of a discipline than faculty, whose research is typically focused on one specific area. Librarians also use a wider array of resources aimed at different audiences in their day-to-day duties, and can integrate these into the instruction.

No matter how large the personal reward for teaching, however, it is important that the course—as well as all elements of a user education program—be evaluated. This assists in updating the curriculum as well as in assessing user needs; just as important is the use of evaluation in further marketing of the course or program element. If groups across campus, from students to faculty to deans, know about the efficacy of user education programs, they are likely to support them. When evaluating a term-long course, it is important to distinguish between what skills the students learned versus their rating of the course's difficulty. As D'Aniello notes, "When successful this type of course is invariably labor intensive for both instructors and students" (D'Aniello, 1984: 404). For example, nearly all of the evaluations of the University of Washington course listed it as consuming more time than the credit hours warranted, but nearly all of the respondents also commented that the course was worth the effort and should be required.

CONCLUSION

User education programs for graduate students differ between institutions, depending on the type of graduate degrees offered and the resources available. However, the one factor that can be relied upon to remain stable is the need for such programming. To build a successful program, the following elements are necessary:

- audience analysis, both for demographics and user needs
- goals of the program: what do you want to accomplish through this program, and what do students want it to do for them?
- elements of the program: what activities will meet the goals of the students and the librarians?
- marketing of the program, through formal and informal channels
- assessment, which can take several forms, such as anecdotal information from individuals, credit-course evaluations, and faculty evaluations of changes in student competencies
- training for library staff involved in the program; for example, subject specialists may need to update their teaching skills
- support, both from the library and institution as well as from the faculty.

The definition of a successful program, like its elements, varies, but needs to be based on meeting the initial goals. One potential negative of meeting those goals is that the volume of instruction can increase to a level that cannot be reasonably met. Thus, it is vital that the programmatic goals incorporate the needs and abilities of the user education librarians and subject specialists themselves to avoid becoming, as Benson says, "victims of our own success" (Benson, 1995: 67). A consideration that may help those wary about starting new instruction programs is that, while the initial workload may increase, there is the benefit of students asking better, more in-depth questions because of the training. Also keep in mind that a program does not need to have all the levels of instruction discussed in this chapter. In the best of all possible worlds there would be enough resources to incorporate all the ideas and projects presented here, but a combination of opportunities for process-oriented training, such as one-shot sessions or longer, for-credit courses, plus individual or small-group consultations will meet the majority of needs voiced by graduate students and faculty.

Perhaps the best way to look at user education programming for graduate students is as a cycle. If we train graduate students well, ensuring that they have the research skills they need for success in their field, when they then enter the classroom as a teaching assistant or a faculty member they will know the value of user education and will be more likely to utilize it in their classes and in their work with future graduate students. This long-term benefit serves as a powerful motivator for creating a strong user education program for the graduate students of today.

NOTES

1. BI stands for bibliographic instruction; the concept is that user education aimed at graduate students has a somewhat different purpose than for undergraduates. The programming should not simply be a mirror of the BI done for undergraduates, with a few added bonuses (more sessions, over a longer period of time)—it should reflect instead the depth and scope of graduate education as a whole.

REFERENCES

Ackerson, Linda G. 1996. "Basing Reference Service on Scientific Communication: Toward a More Effective Model for Science Graduate Students." *RQ* 36, no. 2 (Winter): 248–60.

Adams, Mignon, and Jacquelyn M. Morris. 1985. *Teaching Library Skills for Academic Credit.* Phoenix: Oryx.

Bailey, Bill. 1985. "Thesis Practicum and the Librarian's Role." *Journal of Academic Librarianship* 11, no. 2 (May): 79–81.

Bain, Nancy R., and George W. Bain. 1985. "Teaching Library Resources in Geography." *Journal of Geography* 84, no. 3 (May/June): 126–28.

Bender, Laura J., Robert C. Chang, Patricia Morris, and Chris Sugnet. 1997. "A Science-Engineering Library's Needs Assessment Survey: Method and Learnings." *Science and Technology Libraries* 17, no. 1: 19–34.

Benson, Larry D. 1995. "Scholarly Research and Reference Service in the Automated Environment." *Reference Librarian* 48: 57–69.

Boosinger, Marcia L. 1990. "Associations between Faculty Publishing Output and Opinions Regarding Student Library Skills." *College & Research Libraries* 51, no. 5 (September): 471–81.

Bradigan, Pamela S., Susan M. Kroll, and Sally R. Sims. 1987. "Graduate Student Bibliographic Instruction at a Large University: A Workshop Approach." *RQ* 26, no. 3 (Spring): 335–40.

Brosnan, Mark J. 1998. "The Impact of Psychological Gender, Gender-Related Perception, Significant Others, and the Introducer of Technology upon Computer Anxiety in Students." *Journal of Educational Computing Research* 18, no. 1: 63–78.

Brunner, Cornelia, and Dorothy Bennett. 1998. "Technology Perceptions by Gender." *Education Digest* 63, no. 6 (February): 56–58.

Christensen, Peter G. 1994. "Using English Department Library Liaisons in a Term Paper Clinic: Reviving the Scholar/Librarian Model." *Research Strategies* 12, no. 4 (Fall): 196–208.

Clayton, Victoria, and Virginia Nordstrom. 1987. "Bibliographic Instruction for Graduate Students in an Educational Research Seminar." *Education Libraries* 12, no. 2 (Spring): 51, 53.

Collins, Mary Ellen. 1988. "Teaching Research in Children's Literature to Graduate Education Students Using ERIC." *Research Strategies* 6, no. 3 (Summer): 127–32.

Columbia University. 1999. *Graduate School of Arts and Sciences 1999–2001 Bulletin*. Available online at *www.cc.columbia.edu/cu/gsas/bulletin/frrpcata.html* [cited October 29].

Corston, Rod, and Andrew M. Colman. 1996. "Gender and Social Facilitation Effects on Computer Competence and Attitudes toward Computers." *Journal of Educational Computing Research* 14, no. 2: 171–83.

Cox, Jennifer, and Ralph Johnson. 1992. "Transfer Students in the Library: The Forgotten Population." *Research Strategies* 10, no. 2 (Spring): 88–91.

D'Aniello, Charles. 1984. "An Historical Bibliography and Methods Course: The SUNY at Buffalo Experience." *History Teacher* 17, no. 3 (May): 396–404.

Doelker, Richard E., and Peggy Toifel. 1984. "The Development of a Self-Guided, Library-Based Materials and Methods Manual for Social Work Research." *Behavioral and Social Sciences Librarian* 3, no. 4 (Summer): 81–93.

Dreifuss, Richard A. 1981. "Library Instruction and Graduate Students: More Work for George." *RQ* 21, no. 2 (Winter): 121–23.

Duffill, Carole. 1985. "Strategies for User Education for Graduate Students." *IATUL Proceedings* 17: 163–70.

Dunlap, Connie R. 1976. "Library Services to the Graduate Community: The University of Michigan." *College and Research Libraries* 37, no. 3 (May): 247–51.

Feinberg, Richard. 1989. "Shorting-Out on Long-Term Goals: A Different Perspective on Bibliographic Instruction and Information Literacy." In *Coping with Information Illiteracy: Bibliographic Instruction for the Information Age. Papers Presented at the Seventeenth National LOEX Library Instruction*

Conference, edited by Glenn E. Mensching Jr. and Teresa E. Mensching. Ann Arbor, Mich.: Pierian.

Franklin, Godfrey, and Ronald C. Toifel. 1994. "The Effects of BI on Library Knowledge and Skills among Education Students." *Research Strategies* 12, no. 4 (Fall): 224–37.

Goellnicht, Donald C. 1993. "From Novitiate Culture to Market Economy: The Professionalization of Graduate Students." *English Studies in Canada* 19, no. 4 (December): 471–84.

Gratch, Bonnie G., and Charlene C. York. 1991. "Personalized Research Consultation Service for Graduate Students: Building a Program Based on Research Findings." *Research Strategies* 9, no. 1 (Winter): 4–15.

Griffin, Lloyd W., and Jack A. Clarke. 1972. "Orientation and Instruction of Graduate Students in the Use of the Library: A Survey." *College & Research Libraries* 3, no. 6 (November): 467–72.

Gupta, Usha, Lutishoor Salisbury, and Alberta Bailey. 1995. "SuperService: Reshaping Information Services for Graduate Students." *Research Strategies* 13, no. 4 (Fall): 209–18.

Hay, Fred J. 1990. "The Subject Specialist in the Academic Library: A Review Article." *Journal of Academic Librarianship* 16, no. 1 (March): 11–17.

Holler, Suzanne E., Phyllis L. Ruscella, and Meg K. Scharf. 1991. "We Mean Business: A BI Session for Business Case Analysis Students." *Research Strategies* 9, no. 2 (Spring): 95–100.

Hoover, Danise G., and Victoria Clayton. 1989. "Graduate Bibliographic Instruction in ERIC on CD-ROM." *Behavioral and Social Sciences Librarian* 8, nos. 1/2: 1–12.

Jacobson, Trudi E., and John R. Vallely. 1992. "A Half-Built Bridge: The Unfinished Work of Bibliographic Instruction." *Journal of Academic Librarianship* 17, no. 6 (January): 359–63.

Jiao, Qun G., and Anthony J. Onwuegbuzie. 1998. "Perfectionism and Library Anxiety among Graduate Students." *Journal of Academic Librarianship* 24, no. 5 (September): 365–71.

Kazlauskas, Diane W. 1987. "Bibliographic Instruction at the Graduate Level: A Study of Methods." ERIC Document 311932.

Kirkendall, Carolyn. 1989. "Competencies for Short-Term or Lifelong Learning? Coping with Information Illiteracy: Bibliographic Instruction for the Information Age." In *Coping with Information Illiteracy: Bibliographic Instruction for the Information Age. Papers Presented at the Seventeenth National LOEX Library Instruction Conference,* edited by Glenn E. Mensching Jr. and Teresa E. Mensching. Ann Arbor, Mich.: Pierian.

Klemm, W. R. 1987/88. "Ten Ways to Improve Graduate Teaching." *The College Board Review* 146 (Winter):16–19; 26–29.

Lipow, Anne Grodzins. 1976. "Library Services to the Graduate Community: The University of California, Berkeley." *College & Research Libraries* 37, no. 3 (May): 252–56.

Lowry, Anita Kay. 1990. "Beyond BI: Information Literacy in the Electronic Age." *Research Strategies* 8, no. 1 (Winter): 22–27.

Lunsford, Andrea, Helene Moglen, and James F. Slevin. 1989. *The Future of*

Doctoral Studies in English. New York: Modern Language Association.

Madland, Denise. 1985. "Library Instruction for Graduate Students." *College Teaching* 33, no. 4 (Fall): 163–64.

Michalak, Thomas J. 1976. "Library Services to the Graduate Community: The Role of the Subject Specialist Librarian." *College and Research Libraries* 37, no. 3 (May): 257–65.

Miller, William. 1989. "General Education, Graduate Education, and Instruction in the Use of Libraries." *The Reference Librarian* 24: 245–55.

National Research Council. Committee on Information Technology Literacy, Computer Science and Telecommunications Board, Commission on Physical Sciences, Mathematics and Applications. 1999. *Being Fluent with Information Technology.* Prepublication copy. Available online at *www.nap.edu/ readingroom/books/BeFIT* [cited 1999, September 26].

Onwuegbuzie, Anthony J. 1997. "Writing a Research Proposal: The Role of Library Anxiety, Statistics Anxiety, and Composition Anxiety." *Library and Information Science Research* 19, no. 1: 5–33.

———. 1998. "The Relationship between Library Anxiety and Learning Styles Among Graduate Students: Implications for Library Instruction." *Library and Information Science Research* 20, no. 3: 235–49.

Parrish, Marilyn. 1989. "Academic Community Analysis: Discovering Research Needs of Graduate Students at Bowling Green State University." *C&RL News* 50, no. 8 (September): 644–46.

Pickert, Sarah M., and Adele B. Chwalek. 1984. "Integrating Bibliographic Research Skills into a Graduate Program in Education." *Catholic Library World* 55, no. 9 (April): 392–94.

Piette, Mary I., and Betty Dance. 1993. "A Statistical Evaluation of a Library Orientation Program for Graduate Students." *Research Strategies* 11, no. 3 (Summer): 164–73.

Rambler, Linda K. 1982. "Syllabus Study: Key to a Responsive Academic Library." *Journal of Academic Librarianship* 8, no. 3 (July): 155–59.

Reynolds, Judy. 1987. "Master's Candidates' Research Skills." *Research Strategies* 5, no. 2 (Spring): 78–89.

Rosenberg, Jane A. 1984. "New Ways to Find Books: Searching, Locating, and Information Delivery." *History Teacher* 17, no. 3 (May): 387–90.

Schloman, Barbara F., Roy S. Lilly, and Wendy Hu. 1989. "Targeting Liaison Activities: Use of a Faculty Survey in an Academic Research Library." *RQ* 28, no. 4 (Summer): 496–505.

Shapiro, Beth J., and Richard Child Hill. 1979. "Teaching Sociology Graduate Students Bibliographic Methods for Document Research." *Journal of Academic Librarianship* 5, no. 2 (May): 75–78.

Shashaani, Lily. 1997. "Gender Differences in Computer Attitudes and Use among College Students." *Journal of Educational Computing Research* 16, no. 1: 37–51.

Simpson, Antony E. 1986. "Hurdling the Dissertation Barrier: The Library and the Needs of the A.B.D." *Behavioral and Social Sciences Librarian* 6, nos. 1/ 2 (Fall/Winter): 111–29.

Smart, John C., and Linda S. Hagedorn. 1994. "Enhancing Professional Competencies in Graduate Education." *Review of Higher Education* 17, no. 3 (Spring): 241–57.

Swierenga, Robert P. 1984. "Bibliographical Instruction in Historical Methods Courses: Kent State University." *History Teacher* 17, no. 3 (May): 391–96.

Tucker, Melvin J. 1984. "Historians and Using Tomorrow's Research Library: Research, Teaching and Training: Introduction." *History Teacher* 17, no. 3 (May): 385–87.

U.S. Department of Education. National Center for Education Statistics. 1999. *Digest of Education Statistics, 1998*, NCES 1999–036. Thomas D. Snyder, project director. Washington, D.C. Also available online at *www.nces.edu. gov/pubs99/digest98* [cited 1999, November 18].

Seasoned Students

Katy Lenn
University of Oregon

The age distribution in the United States is slated for big changes, as the 65-and-older segment is about to swell to unprecedented levels. This burgeoning group will impact institutions of higher education in many ways. Other than the fact that so many are either already members of that age group or on their way, what effect does this have on librarians?

This chapter illustrates the older adult demographic, examines its impact on higher education and academic libraries, and provides practical strategies for teaching older students.

THE DEMOGRAPHICS

Fueled by aging baby boomers, the older adult demographic is undergoing radical changes. Figures from the U.S. Administration on Aging attest to this transformation:

> The 75 million people born in the United States between 1946 and 1964 constitute the baby boom generation. In 1994, baby boomers represented nearly one-third of the U.S. population. Within the next 13 to 34 years, these people will enter the 65-years-and-older age category. As the baby boomers begin to age, the United States will see an unparalleled increase in the absolute number of elderly persons. While one in eight Americans was 65 years of age or older in 1994, in a little more than 30 years, about one in five is expected to be in this age group. (U.S. Administration on Aging, 1997a)

The availability of better health care is also affecting the population numbers. The average life expectancy for someone born in 1900 was 47, whereas today it is 75. "The number of persons aged 85 and older has more than doubled since 1965 and has grown by 40% since 1980" (U.S. Administration on Aging, 1997a).

The reverberations of this demographic shift are already being felt by higher education.

The Education Demographics

Coupled with the increasing number of those 65 and older is the changing nature of what constitutes the later years. Older adults are certainly not the passive group they once were. Changing attitudes about older people, revisions to retirement legislation, and a desire to "keep their hand in it" have some older adults choosing employment far past what was previously viewed as retirement age.

For others, the term "retirement" has undergone a transformation. Statistics show that the average retirement age in the United States dropped from 64 in 1965 to 62 in 1995. In addition, these younger retirees have found that with increased physical well-being and financial security they can accomplish much more than their parents did at the same age.

Travel, educational activities, and volunteering have replaced a more sedentary view of retirement for this new breed of retiree. Most realize they need to make their retirement years quality years, since at age 65, with changes in longevity, they have ten to twenty years left to live.

Many older adults express the need to stay mentally and physically active in retirement and acknowledge the role that education plays in their lifestyle. The National Center for Education Statistics found that in 1995, 17.6 percent of the 65+ adults and 31.1 percent of those aged 55–64 had participated in some type of educational activity within the last twelve months (National Center for Education Statistics, 1998). Other surveys reported that "enrollment for college students age 65 and older grew 27 percent from 1991 to 1995, and the Education Dept. says some 81,000 people over the age of 65 are part- or full-time students. Another 356,000 students are age 50 to 64" (Berman, 1998: 106).

As remarkable as these figures may be, they are only part

of the older adult education picture. Most statistical analyses reflect enrollment in formal education. Enrollment figures for informal programs are even higher, as shown by enrollment and program numbers for three national programs: in 1999 the Elderhostel organization had more than 270,000 students taking part in 10,000 programs (Elderhostel, 1999b); more than 250 Institutes for Learning in Retirement have been established throughout the United States, Canada, and Mexico (Elderhostel, 1999c); and OASIS (not an acronym), a national senior organization, has over 333,000 members (OASIS, 1999).

Finally, the demographic age shift is not the only factor to impact future programming in higher education. One of the single best predictors of participation in educational activities is previous educational involvement, and the educational attainment level in the United States is on the rise. "In 1990, nearly half (47 percent) of the elderly had not completed high school. Assuming that the educational profile of the 25 to 54 year old population in 1990 will represent the elderly population in 2030, more than 4 of every 5 elderly (83 percent) in 2030 would have completed high school or more" (U. S. Bureau of the Census, 1996).

The convergence of all these variables—greater numbers of older adults, increased activity among older adults, and a rise in previous educational experiences—all converge to create a new and challenging market for higher education.

WHAT DOES HIGHER EDUCATION OFFER?

Although the demographic transformation and the changing concept of retirement are relatively new, higher education has already been affected. So how is it responding to this growing student population? For many institutions, serving this age group is more a goodwill gesture than a revenue-generating venture. Some institutions, especially state-supported institutions, view services to this age group as part of a civic mission. It is also an excellent public relations tool: many institutions are not oblivious to the political power this group wields, since 67 percent of adults aged 65 and older vote. At the fund-raising and development level, enthusiastic students can become enthusiastic donors.

Older adults participate in a variety of higher education opportunities starting at the most basic level, that is, registering for general curriculum, for-credit courses. The motivation may be work-related, to achieve a degree, or for self-fulfillment. Many institutions also allow older adults the option of auditing classes at reduced or waived tuition. The advent of easy access to distance education may prove to be a forum that older adults will adapt to readily, especially for those who have difficulty leaving home due to health problems or who are geographically isolated.

Many institutions also offer specially designed programs for older students only that are popular for several reasons: scheduling is flexible (many courses/workshops do not require the commitment of a full term of classes), some are taught by peers, fees are less than standard tuition, the organizational structure gives members the power to direct offerings, and some students feel more at ease in classes composed of peers. Two of the most prominent programs affiliated with higher education are Elderhostel and Learning in Retirement.

The Elderhostel program, founded in 1975, allows individuals over the age of 54 to travel and participate in learning opportunities around the world. Courses are often offered on university and college campuses where meals and inexpensive housing are included in the tuition (the average is $390 per person) and university faculty teach the five- to six-day courses. Institutes for Learning in Retirement (ILR) and Learning in Retirement (LIR) programs affiliated with colleges and universities are fee-based membership organizations that actively involve their members in the planning and teaching of courses and events.

In keeping with the changing view of retirement, many older adults are looking for retirement housing that includes more than easy access to a golf course. Over 100 campuses have already established retirement centers that offer convenient access to the institution's educational, sporting, and entertainment opportunities—and, in some cases, health-care facilities. These popular communities, similar to condominium complexes coupled with assisted care, are filled soon after they open, often by alumni.

Finally, higher education can also connect with older adults beyond the institution's walls. Faculty can reach out to non-affiliated educational groups in the community such as local individual groups or well-organized national groups like OASIS that are geared to older adults. This type of outreach becomes a win-win situation, as it provides groups with guest lecturers and faculty members with community service opportunities.

LIBRARY CONNECTION

Libraries will encounter older students as they move through regular curriculum courses and use the services of the reference desk. But librarians can also take a proactive role and seek out these students. The first step is to identify campus organizations, such as continuing education departments, that serve this population. This step is essential since some programs, such as ILR's, are designed to rely heavily on their own membership for instructors who may overlook the library as a possible area for instruction and therefore fail to reach out to the library as a collaborative partner. Let your university's speakers' bureau or public relations department know about areas of expertise within the library and give them names of library staff willing to speak to groups. These departments maintain lists of on-campus experts and are usually the first point of contact when outside groups request speakers. To carry the proactive model to its fullest extent, ask about older adult groups that have contacted the department in the past and follow up by speaking directly to the program administrators at these organizations.

It is doubtful that these opportunities will offer librarians monetary compensation. Payment often takes the forms of an attentive class and appreciative responses from grateful students.

Content of Library Courses

Material already taught by the library is the best and easiest route to follow when developing content for older adult classes. Classes using computer technology may require a slower pace, but no assumptions should be made about this age group's experience with modern technology.

Prior to class, instructors should know what library privileges are available to these students and the answers to typical off-campus access questions. The content and time frame may need to be adjusted to fit the format the program routinely follows. An advantage of teaching these specialized courses is that they do not require long-term commitments, as most are usually offered as workshops or short courses and do not involve grading assignments, administering tests, and assigning grades.

Typical library offerings that translate nicely to older adult classes include:

- history of technology
- library research
- Internet courses
- preservation.

At the University of Oregon, ILR workshops on Internet searching and using the UO Library collections and services are presented in two-hour slots. Others have adopted the same content to fit the Elderhostel six-day format:

Michener Library Via The Internet: High Tech Research
(University of Northern Colorado)
Discover vast array of information, history and organization of World Wide Web. Discuss copyright, access, quality, censorship, and Internet privacy information. Hands-on, in-depth exploration of library resources. Divide and conquer cyberspace! (Elderhostel, 1999a)

The Fast Track To The Information Highway:
Your Key To Lifelong Learning
(University of Illinois/Urbana-Champaign)
This is a basic internet course, but participants MUST have a working knowledge of computers, preferably at least Windows 95. Emphasis on how to make the internet work for you. Information on selecting an internet provider and recommended plug-ins. In this hands-on course, learn how to transfer files, search databases/library catalogs, and use some of the most popular features of the internet: e-mail, discussion groups, electronic newspapers/magazines and shopping. Learn to search the worldwide web for infor-

mation on topics, such as investments, travel, best buys, genealogy/other people-searches to name a few. Technological advances, security issues, netiquette, technology ethics and policy issues will be discussed. (Elderhostel, 1999d)

Creating "new content" courses is easy for this student group. These courses allow the instructor content flexibility without the usual constraints of fitting regular curriculum requirements and timeframes. The broad interest level of older adults allows for the creation of courses based on the interests of library faculty or that highlight a special feature or collection in the library. These special topic courses may prove to be more popular with older students than they would in the institution's general curriculum. This University of Colorado Elderhostel course provides an example:

Archiving A Literary Giant: James Michener's Gift
(University of Northern Colorado)
Library administration and James Michener expert reveal Michener Special Collection, his life, his writing, his relationship with UNC, using technology to preserve history, and archival process of published and unpublished papers. (Elderhostel, 1999a)

Before contacting an organization, solidify the course content with goals and objectives in mind, yet maintain the ability to be flexible based on the group's needs. Access to facilities and the impact this has on instruction also need to be considered. For instance, offering instruction off-campus using computer and projection equipment will require special arrangements. Limited access to classrooms with computers may impede the ability to offer hands-on instruction. If an on-campus course is planned, parking may be an issue and the aggravation and expense may be a deterrent to enrollment.

INSTRUCTIONAL IMPLICATIONS

Adult learning theory is evolving, and there is not a thorough consensus on many issues involving how adults learn. The following are a number of general considerations regarding the motivation, intelligence/memory, and physical needs of older adults. The instructional recommendations that follow are based on standard guidelines and the author's experiences.

Motivation and Emotional Issues: Love of Lifelong Learning

It is doubtful that an instructor could teach a more motivated group than older adults. After all, they are the lifelong learners it is hoped all younger students will become; for them, learning is not a means to an end but part of the journey. Older students indicate different motivations for participation in educational activities from younger students (Courtney, 1989). Rarely are they driven by the external forces that motivate younger students, such as earning a degree that leads to employment. Older students may take a course to develop a new skill, such as learning to search the Internet or to conduct library research. Others take courses to increase their knowledge about a subject. For others, the motivation to participate is social, a mechanism to connect with people. A number of educational programs directed at older adults include social activities as part of the general programming. Some older students prefer to take courses with peers, but others seek out intergenerational opportunities to connect to a younger generation. Course content can be a deciding factor when choosing between older adult-only classes and intergenerational classes.

Older students add a new dimension to a classroom. They are less passive than most 18–20-year-old students and enjoy sharing their lifetime of experience and opinions. Instructors often report that lectures are transformed into dialogues. For instance, a history class discussing World War II is transformed with the personal recollections of students who lived through the experience. An intergenerational setting brings a different view of the learning process to the younger students, and the older students' enthusiasm for learning can be a powerful influence. These more active students add a great deal with their insights, but instructors must be sensitive to the fact that too many comments can derail a course's flow. Instructors should not be afraid to stop a drawn-out conversation but can and should offer the option to continue the discussion after class or in another forum, such as a class listserv. Students with many questions should be asked to make a note of them and offered the opportunity to discuss them with the instructor after class.

If a student's goal is to learn a new skill, especially a technical skill, the older adult may be more likely to enroll in an older adult-only course. Many students report increased anxiety if enrolled in a course with younger students who appear to be technically advanced. Instructors should be keenly aware of anxiety among students. It may be more noticeable in intergenerational classes, but it also happens in older adult-only classes where there is a large disparity of skills. When this happens, a break in the class offers a chance for the instructor to talk with and demonstrate concepts to the students experiencing a problem without drawing attention to them and delaying the class for basic instruction.

Older adults generally prefer to be directly involved in the planning of their educational activities and have a strong desire for certainty—that is, knowing that a class will meet their needs. Generally, the type of classes taught and the format used in higher education may not allow for student input before the first meeting. Instructors can address these concerns by providing a thorough description of the course (including course content), the availability of hands-on opportunities, and the level of computer experience necessary. Course objectives should be clearly stated at the start of class, and students should be queried about specific questions they anticipate the class content will answer. These questions can then be noted and addressed during the course.

Intelligence and Cognitive Changes

In the study of aging, one of the most misunderstood areas is its effect on intelligence. Though life experiences complicate an accurate across-the-board comparison of older and younger intelligences, most researchers agree that intelligence does not decline as sharply as popular theory proposes. Because studies comparing older and younger individuals can be inconclusive, longitudinal studies are important. One of the most extensive studies, the Seattle Longitudinal Study begun in 1956 by Warner Shaie and continuing today, reevaluates its subjects at seven-year intervals. The nature of the study allows researchers to track changes in abilities across the years. Shaie found that, "although by age 60 virtually every subject had declined on one ability, few individuals showed global decline. Virtually no one showed universal decline on all abilities monitored, even by the 80s" (Shaie, 1996: 273).

Many comparisons of younger and older intelligences involve the concept of fluid and crystallized intelligence, and studies have found a significant difference between age groups. Fluid intelligence is "associated with maximum information-processing speed," that is, the speed of retrieving information. Crystallized intelligence is defined as "acquired information and intellectual skills," the accumulated knowledge and the ability to apply new knowledge to old knowledge. Crystallized intelligence actually increases with age, whereas fluid intelligence declines. When gains and losses of these two intelligence types are calculated, older adults actually show a net gain (Eysenck, 1991: 3; Barber and Kozoll, 1994: 9; Horn, 1970).

In the older adult classroom, this would suggest that instructors should minimize the need to exercise fluid intelligence. In other words, avoid situations that require students to memorize and recall information quickly, and give participants time to practice new concepts and ideas. Work to use the strength of the crystallized knowledge by connecting new information to existing knowledge, by using similes and metaphors to explain complicated concepts. For example, the concept of e-mail, usernames, and domains is easier to understand when presented in the context of a post office as domain and username as a post office box.

Memory loss, like intelligence, is another area where the aging research is not conclusive. Many adults feel their memory decreases with age, calling the lapses "senior moments"; however, studies show that younger adults can be just as forgetful. The difference between the two groups appears to be that older adults are more sensitive to the problem (Sugar and McDonald, 1992).

Many older adults have developed strategies for dealing with faulty memory, such as taking notes. Older students may be anxious, however, to write down more of what is said in class than their younger counterparts. To minimize the need for copious note-taking, instructors can provide handouts with salient lecture information. Studies also show that older adults may have more trouble eliminating irrelevant material when doing complicated tasks (Plude and Hoyer, 1986), and so information presented should be clear and concise with little extraneous information.

Memory and intelligence are affected by a number of factors; two of the biggest impacting older adults are recent experience and health. In some memory studies, younger adults, usually college students, excel not because of better memories but simply because of their recent test-taking experience. Even within an older adult-only classroom, there may be a wide span among students, as some may be more immersed in the educational environment while others may be a little rusty. Health and nutrition also play a major role in the functioning of older adults and their ability to concentrate and learn. Since the motivation level of these students is high, be aware that signs of inattention or disinterest could be a indication that a student may not be feeling well.

Physical Setting

The physical needs of older students will have more impact on the teaching environment than the needs of the average younger student.

Noise Factors

It is a fact of life that hearing diminishes with age. Factories, logging operations, and military service are the types of general life experiences that affect hearing loss.

In the classroom, the usual noises take on added importance—slight annoyances become major distractions. Instructors should take note of ambient noise in the teaching environment, with computers and projectors the major culprits. Problems can often be minimized by relocating equipment: computer CPUs, for example, will generate far less noise if placed on the floor rather than on tabletops used by students. Many of these adjustments will benefit all students, not just the older ones.

To allow those who want to minimize their hearing difficulty by adjusting their placement in the classroom, announcements at the beginning of class should include where the instructor will be standing, whether a microphone will be used, and where noise-generating equipment will be located.

Standard instructional techniques take on increased importance—the need to enunciate, to repeat questions or comments that come from far corners of the room, to ask if everyone heard comments from the center of the room, and to avoid talking while facing the blackboard. Printed material is important not only for the visual learner but also for those who may miss verbal content. Instructors also need to know where to obtain assistive listening devices if requested by a student.

Visual Factors

Degradation of eyesight is also common as individuals age. Visuals used in class, such as overheads, slide shows, and Web projections, should be large and clear. Simple white backgrounds with good contrasting colors work best, and it is wise to avoid the temptation to use flashy computer-generated slide shows with dark backgrounds and light print.

For handouts, use simple fonts such as Arial and a slightly larger point size (12 to 14 point). Incorporating sensory cues such as color coding, italics, bold printing, underlining, and indentation makes it easier for students to follow along and pick up salient points.

Lighting should find a happy medium that allows low light for computer projection but still allows students to see handouts. Lighting also becomes a factor if people will be moving around the room—lighting needs to be adequate to avoid tripping.

Pacing Factors

No one likes to sit for long periods of time, and as the body ages sitting becomes more uncomfortable. Breaks should be incorporated into the class. Most older adults will feel comfortable getting up and leaving the classroom as needed, but an announcement at the beginning of class that this practice is acceptable will allay anyone's fear of insulting the instructor.

Mobility Factors

Each year approximately 40 percent of the U.S. population over the age of 65 experiences a fall due to loss of balance (Work, 1989). As movement can become restricted or difficult for older students, aisles should be kept clear and free of cords and wires. Have adjustable tables available for those students who use wheelchairs. Classes that require a great deal of walking should include that information in the course description, and the instructor should repeat it at the beginning of class. While planning the course, the instructor needs to verify that all stops on the tour are accessible and note where elevators are located along the route. If the group must be separated for the use of stairs and elevators, inform the two groups of rendezvous points.

If the course is geared at the entry-level computer user, instructors should plan on additional time to practice the eye/hand coordination necessary to use a computer mouse.

Logistics Factors

As coming to campus may not be a regular event for these students, extra information prior to class can minimize anxiety about the new location. Information should include parking locations, parking meter information, locations of handicapped spaces and accessible entrances, and local bus information. The University of Oregon LIR classes are scheduled for one hour, forty-five minutes so that students parked in two-hour meter parking spaces are not distracted at the end of class by the possibility of receiving a parking ticket.

Notify other staff of courses being held in the library so they can direct wayward students. Students will arrive early, sometimes by as much as forty-five minutes, so if possible have the classroom available and unlocked long before the class starting time.

CONCLUSION

The unprecedented increase in the older adult population has many ramifications across most sociopolitical aspects of life in the United States. Higher education and libraries will not only be affected but will want to court this new student group. The public relations benefits derived from assisting this group are already being felt by higher education. As the potential group of older students grows, so do the opportunities for librarians to reach out and teach them. While more time and effort are required in reaching, planning for, and teaching this group, the rewards are remarkable. These students use phrases like "treasure the opportunity" and "go home delighted" when referring to their instructional experiences. These are the people who "never wanted to leave the classroom" and describe themselves as those that "attend classes not because we have to, but because we want to" (University of Oregon, 1999). Working with these students is truly an extraordinary instructional opportunity.

REFERENCES

Barber, Cheryl A., and Charles E. Kozoll. 1994. *Teaching Older Adults : A Guide for Instructors*. Champaign: University of Illinois at Urbana-Champaign.

Berman, Dennis. 1998. "Late-blooming Scholars." *Business Week* 3587 (July 20): 106.

Courtney, Bradley C. 1989. "Helping Older Adults Learn." In *Handbook of Adult and Continuing Education*, edited by Sharan B. Merriam and Phyllis M. Cunningham. Scott Foresman/AAACE Adult Educator Series. Washington, D.C.: American Association for Adult and Continuing Education.

Elderhostel, Inc. 1999a. COLORADO—*Spring 99 (Apr–Jun) Elderhostel Catalog*. Available online at *www.elderhostel.org/catalog/states/06sp.html* [cited 1999, September 18].

———. 1999b. *Elderhostel Adult Education Senior Travel Opportunities*. Available online at *www.elderhostel.org* [cited 1999, March 29].

———.1999c. *Elderhostel—Institute Network*. Available online at *www.elderhostel.org/ehin* [cited 1999, March 29].

———. 1999d. *ILLINOIS—Spring 99 (Apr–Jun) Elderhostel Catalog*. Available online at *www.elderhostel.org/catalog/states/13sp.html* [cited 1999, September 18].

Eysenck, Michael W., ed. 1991. *The Blackwell Dictionary of Cognitive Psychology*. Cambridge: Blackwell.

Horn, John. 1970. "Organization of Data on Life-span Development of Human Abilities." In *Life-Span Developmental Psychology: Research and Theory*, edited by L. R. Goulet and Paul B. Baltes. New York: Academic.

National Center for Education Statistics. 1998. *Condition of Education 1998/Table 13–1: Adult Participation Rates*. Available online at *http://nces.ed.gov/pubs98/condition98/c9813d01.html* [cited 1999, September 25].

OASIS. 1999. *Welcome to OASIS*. Available online at *www.oasisnet.org/index.html* [cited 1999, March 30].

Plude, Dana Jeffrey, and William J. Hoyer. 1986. "Age and the Selectivity of Visual Information Processing." *Psychology and Aging* 1 (March): 4–10.

Schaie, K. Warner. 1996. "Intellectual Development in Adulthood." In *Handbook of the Psychology of Aging*. 4th ed., edited by James E. Birren and K. Warner Schaie. San Diego: Academic.

Sugar, Judith A., and Joan D. McDonald. 1992. "Memory, Learning, and Attention." In *Handbook of Mental Health and Aging*. 2d ed., edited by James E. Birren, R. Bruce Sloan, and Gene D. Cohen. San Diego: Academic.

U. S. Administration on Aging. 1997a. *Growth of America's Older Population*. Available online at *www.aoa.dhhs.gov/aoa/stats/growth97.html* [cited 1999, March 22].

———.1997b. *Profile of Older Americans: 1996*. Available online at *www.aoa.dhhs.gov/aoa/pages/profil96.htm* [cited 1999, March 22].

U. S. Bureau of the Census. 1996. *65+ in the United States*. Available online at *www.census.gov/prod/1/pop/p23-190/p23-190.pdf* [cited 1999, February 25].

University of Oregon. Learning in Retirement. 1999. *LIR General Information*. Available online at *http://lir.uoregon.edu/Q_A.html* [cited 1999, September 30].

Work, Janis. 1989. "Strength Training: A Bridge to Independence for the Elderly." *Physician and Sportsmedicine* 17, no. 11 (November): 134–38.

FURTHER READING

Birren, James E., R. Bruce Sloane, and Gene D. Cohen. 1992. *Handbook of Mental Health and Aging*. 2d ed. San Diego: Academic.

Fischer, Richard B., Mark L. Blazey, and Henry T. Lipman. 1992. *Students of the Third Age*. American Council on Education/Macmillan Series on Higher Education. New York: American Council on Education.

Fisher, James C., and Mary Alice Wolf. 1998. *Using Learning to Meet the Challenges of Older Adulthood*. New Directions for Adult and Continuing Education, no. 77. San Francisco: Jossey-Bass.

John, Martha Tyler. 1988. *Geragogy: A Theory for Teaching the Elderly*. New York: Haworth.

Lamdin, Lois S., and Mary Fugate. 1997. *Elderlearning: New Frontier in an Aging Society*. American Council on Education/Oryx Press Series on Higher Education. Phoenix, Ariz.: Oryx.

Merriam, Sharan B. 1998. *Learning in Adulthood: A Comprehensive Guide*. 2d ed. San Francisco: Jossey-Bass.

Merriam, Sharan B, and Phyllis M Cunningham. 1989. *Handbook of Adult and Continuing Education*. San Francisco: Jossey-Bass.

Sinnott, Jan D. 1994. *Interdisciplinary Handbook of Adult Lifespan Learning*. Westport, Conn.: Greenwood.

Young, Kenneth E. 1996. "Rediscovering the Joy of Learning." *AAHE Bulletin December 1996*. Available online at *www.aahe.org/bulletin/Bulletin*.

Part 5

THE NEEDS OF DISTANCE LEARNERS

OVERVIEW

The distance learner population is growing, and increasingly libraries are providing instruction to these students. Members of this population are often adult or returning students, who face many of the same issues mentioned in Part 4 of this book. They may lack library research skills, and they may have had little or no exposure to electronic databases and the Internet. Their availability or location frequently precludes their participating in traditional library instruction sessions. Yet these students have to produce the same types of research-based projects and papers that on-campus students do.

Just as there are numerous methods for teaching on-campus students, there are many ways to teach distance learners. Some of the methods apply to the student groups discussed in other chapters, such as e-mail, Web-based tutorials and guides, and individualized instruction, but distance teaching techniques also include some methods not normally used in the traditional classroom:

- TV transmission
- videoconferencing
- audioconferencing.

The technologies used in a distance learning program profoundly affect the form that the library instruction takes, and librarians may not have a voice in the format(s) selected. Beyond issues common to all user education programs, such as strategic planning, budgeting, staffing, institution and library missions, technology and promotion and marketing, working with the distance learning administrative office is a key component of a successful program, as noted in the next chapter by Heller-Ross and Kiple.

Heller-Ross and Kiple provide a definition of distance learners, overviews of three different programs, and an analysis of the issues faced on these three campuses. Brown and Holmes detail another model entirely, a program-based instructional unit that is the result of close collaboration between a faculty member and a librarian. User education librarians will find the following two chapters rich sources of ideas for teaching distance learners as well as for some methods that might be incorporated into existing on-campus programs.

As explored further in the following chapters, developing successful instruction for distance learners means the librarian must:

- Work closely with administrative offices responsible for distance learning on campus, as well as with the faculty teaching distance learning courses.
- Understand the importance of strategic planning, budgeting, and staffing for instructional programs.
- Adapt the program and individual sessions based on careful monitoring and analysis of changes in student skill levels as well as on their access to computers.
- Become adept in the learning technologies used in your distance education program and understand that these technologies will shape the way material is presented.
- Use adult learning theories to inform the development of programs and sessions.

Information Literacy for Interactive Distance Learners

Holly Heller-Ross
Plattsburgh State University of New York,

Julia Kiple
Carleton College

Imagine providing information literacy instruction to over 3,000 students at more than 100 locations in Maine each semester. Or delivering instructional services and materials to over 7,000 students from Florida, the Caribbean, and across the United States each year. Think about offering information literacy classes and research guides to approximately 500 students across 9 counties of rural upstate New York. These challenges are only part of information literacy for interactive distance learners, an exciting field of academic librarianship.

More and more institutions are exploring distance learning options as technological innovations, changing demographics, and financial incentives inspire academic administrators to look beyond traditional teaching methods and traditional young-adult students. According to *Peterson's Distance Learning 1997*, more than 700 accredited North American Institutions are offering distance learning programs (Koha, 1996). A 1996 survey of the Association of Research Libraries (ARL) members determined that 46 (62 percent) of the 74 responding libraries were participating in distance learning programs. Of these 46 respondents, 43 were offering library support services to the distance learning faculty and students (Snyder, Logue, and Preece, 1996).

As defined by the American Library Association (ALA) in

the *American Library Association Presidential Committee on Information Literacy: Final Report*, "to be information literate, a person must be able to recognize when information is needed and have the ability to locate, evaluate, and use effectively the needed information" (ALA, 1989). A *distance learning program* is "an organized program of postsecondary course work or independent study which is undertaken away from the main and branch campuses of the parent institution" according to the 1998 draft *Canadian Guidelines for Off-Campus Library Services* (Slade, 1998). This same document defines *distributed learning* as "an instructional model that allows instructor, students, and content to be located in different, non-centralized locations so that instruction and learning occur independent of time and place. The distributed learning model can be used in combination with traditional classroom-based courses, with traditional distance learning courses, or it can be used to create wholly virtual classrooms." *Distant learners* are defined as "students enrolled in a distance or distributed learning program or completing formal course work off-campus."

The Association of College and Research Libraries (ACRL) *Guidelines for Distance Learning Library Services*, last revised in July 1998, outlines the association's philosophy, guidelines, and definitions for distance learning. According to this document:

> *Distance learning library services* refers to those library services in support of college, university, or other postsecondary courses and programs offered away from a main campus, or in the absence of a traditional campus, and regardless of where credit is given. These courses may be taught in traditional or non-traditional formats or media, may or may not require physical facilities, and may or may not involve live interaction of teachers and students. The phrase is inclusive of courses in all post-secondary programs designated as: extension, extended, off-campus, extended campus, distance, distributed, open, flexible, franchising, virtual, synchronous, or asynchronous. (ACRL, 1998)

This chapter highlights several programs that have developed very different information literacy instruction approaches.

These programs can serve as models, starting points for discussions, or sparks for a new vision of instruction for distance learning. The University of Maine System Network for Education and Technology Services (UNET) uses the approach of providing extensive electronic resources, consulting with instructional faculty, working to collaboratively design course research assignments, and hiring distance site bibliographic instructors to work directly with distance learners. Nova Southeastern University (NSU) has lending agreements with two major research libraries, provides access to online research tools and document-delivery services, and delivers instruction to distance students attending summer institutes and on-campus orientations, or through site visits and Internet conferencing programs. Plattsburgh State University of New York (Plattsburgh) provides a full range of library instructional services for its interactive video and Internet courses through librarian site visits, a one-credit distance learning library-research course, print and Internet research guides, and in-class demonstrations and research tips. These three programs are detailed below, with examples and analysis of institutional responses to the critical issues facing instructional librarians in distance learning.

Other distance learning instruction librarians and program directors from across the United States responded to a 1998 electronic survey with information about their instructional philosophies, successes and failures, program evaluations, outcome measures, and future directions. The survey results are described and analyzed in the final section of this chapter.

DISTANCE LEARNING AND INFORMATION LITERACY

Distance learning students, like all students, must prepare for an electronic information age. Information literacy has become an unwritten requirement for the completion of a college education and successful competition in our information-driven economy. Many courses require students to demonstrate competency in electronic library and information research, electronic mail communication with faculty and classmates, electronic access to their academic records and registration, and proficiency in Internet and World Wide Web (WWW) research.

The challenge of distance learning library support comes

from the fact that, until very recently, most library collections (books, journals, and media) were selected for on-campus use, and most library services (instructional classes, print reserve services, research indexes or databases, and physical library tours) were designed for on-campus programs. These collections and services are often not well-suited to the needs of distance learning students.

Distance learning students require access to a wide range of library services, from reference assistance and bibliographic instruction to interlibrary loan, course reserves, circulation, and information network connections. Information literacy and library instruction programs are essential components of academic support for distance or distributed learning. Many colleges and universities have adapted their traditional bibliographic instruction programs to serve their new distance learning students. This adaptation requires significant work on the part of librarians and other teaching faculty because the range of information resources available to distance learners is often varied, hands-on instruction is not necessarily an option, and both instructor and student may need to learn new technologies.

Student Demographics

Distance learners are often part-time, adult or returning students, students in professions where continuing education leads to career opportunities or additional licensure (nursing and allied health, education, engineering, business), and students looking for degrees not offered by their local institutions. Many masters and doctoral students enroll in distance learning programs as a way to complete their degrees without leaving their jobs or moving their families. A new and growing group of distance learners are technologically proficient younger students who prefer the time-shifting, no-travel-or-dorm-room independence of interactive video, interactive television, or Internet courses. Some distance learning formats offer significant advantages to working adults, disabled or otherwise homebound students, students in rural and remote areas, students in the military or other jobs where assignments require frequent relocations, and incarcerated students. The profile of distance learners is shifting as the U.S. economy changes to require continuing education, more non-traditional students enroll in colleges and universities, telecommunication possibilities expand, and higher education redefines its mission.

Information literacy is a critical issue in our fast-paced social, economic, and political environment. In an electronic environment, students can find more information in a week than they would previously have been able to dig up in a month. Faculty expect students to easily sift through this mass of information in pursuit of meaningful research. Librarians have traditionally offered tours, training sessions, and research instruction to assist students with locating and using library resources.

Distance learning programs are designed and heavily marketed for adult and returning students. These students, however, frequently lack library research skills, may never have used an academic library, or may never have used computerized research databases. Their work hours and research hours may make participation in traditional library tours or research sessions impossible. Yet these same students must produce college-level papers and research projects. As librarians from the Western Michigan University Libraries stated in 1996, "They may be more dramatically confronted with the need to learn new technologies than younger students, and their lack of computer skills may be one more barrier in an intimidating academic environment" (Jayne, Arnold, and Vander Meer, 1998: 200). Clearly, efforts to provide instruction and research technology training are critical. One study at Northwestern University (Steffen & Marshall, 1993) showed that library research database instruction resulted in increased student database use and that students used a wider variety of resources. This would indicate that some basic library instruction is a minimal requirement.

Information Literacy Programming

An extensive range of information literacy programming is offered to distance learners, with many differing services offered by different institutions. Credit-bearing library and Internet research courses, WWW pages, video and Internet tutorials and tours, course-related (one-shot) instructional sessions in content courses, and individualized instruction at the request of distance learners can all be found at various institutions. One example of a comprehensive information literacy program has three main components: Introduction to Library and Information Research LIB101 (a one-credit, required course); on-request, course-related instruction focused on research concepts and tools tailored to course requirements; and computer literacy or network instruction focused on concepts and tools in electronic research and file management. Instruction formats are usually closely connected to the technology and format of the other academic course offerings, and, again, every possible format is currently in use somewhere.

Standards and Guidelines

There are established standards and guidelines for both library services for distance learning and for the provision of information literacy instruction. One of the most important statements comes from the 1998 ACRL *Guidelines for Distance Learning Library Services*: "The originating institution is responsible, through its chief administrative officers and governance organizations, for funding and appropriately meeting the information needs of its distance learning programs in support of their teaching, learning, and research. This support should provide ready and equivalent library service and learning resources to all its students, regardless of location" (ACRL, 1998). In addition, institutional accrediting bodies (such as the Commission on Higher Education Middle States Association and the National League of Nursing), state boards of education, and academic faculty governing bodies also set standards and criteria for library services and quality of instruction. Two recent articles provide overviews and analysis of existing guidelines and evaluation criteria (Lebowitz, 1997; Dasher-Alston and Patton, 1998).

ACRL also publishes guidelines for information literacy, including the 1997 *Guidelines for Instruction Programs in Academic Libraries*. This document states:

> Libraries work together with other members of the education community to participate in and realize the educational mission of the institution by teaching the identification, structure, intellectual access, and physical access

of information, information sources, and information systems through the design and development of instruction programs and services. Planning for the systematic delivery of instructional services should be incorporated throughout the library's activities, including the library's comprehensive planning and budgeting process.

There are important issues for librarians to settle before setting out to provide instructional services for distance learners. Broad questions about institutional mission, profiles of the intended distance learners, anticipated distance learning course offerings, and technological professional development must be answered before librarians can even begin to shape a program. Focused questions about the role of the library and the instruction librarians, overall library support services for the distance learning program, and questions about instructional objectives and pedagogy are equally essential in the early stages of the discussions. Some of the answers can only come from the individual educational institution; some ideas about what the answers mean for instruction may come from the experiences of other librarians.

REPRESENTATIVE PROGRAMS

Research and instructional needs of distance and on-campus learners have much more in common than is apparent at a first glance, as do the instructional programs described in this chapter. They all strive to meet the needs of their users, fulfill the educational missions of their institutions, and follow the guidelines set out by the library associations and accrediting agencies. Their similar goals highlight how the differences in approaches taken demonstrate the many alternatives for consideration. The different approaches are not permanently linked to the programs, nor is one any better than the others. They have developed from the practical experiences and philosophical ideas of the librarians who shaped them and represent different institutional profiles in terms of size and types of degrees offered. The institutions we examine here have all explored several distance learning technologies to reach their students and have come up with their own forms of collaboration between librarians and other faculty. They range in scale from international to statewide to regional programs.

University of Maine (UNET)

The University of Maine System Network for Education and Technology Services (UNET) provides support for distance learning courses offered by the seven campuses of the University of Maine. The university is state supported and is accredited by the New England Association of Schools and Colleges. The statewide network began offering distance learning courses in 1989 from the University of Maine at Augusta campus. Courses are delivered using television transmission, videoconferencing, audioconferencing, correspondence, and both synchronous and asynchronous computer conferencing.

UNET was formed in 1997 by the merger of the University System's computing and data processing services (CAPS) and distance learning technologies and services (Educational Network of Maine) to form a single point of contact for distance learning services. Although interactive television is the most heavily used technology in course delivery, with approximately ninety course offerings each semester, recent years have seen significant development of computer conferencing courses, with fifty-eight online courses running in the spring of 1999.

The Off-Campus Library Services office coordinates the provision of student and faculty information resources, research instruction services, copyright clearances for faculty, and training for distance site and UNET staff (Lowe, 1998). Students are provided with access to library catalogs, research indexes and databases, free document delivery of books and articles, and telephone and Internet reference assistance. Information literacy has been incorporated into many course curricula, with librarians providing in-class instruction as well as prepared guides and Internet pages. Librarians teach a portion of the Introduction to the College Experience course, which is required for students in the General Studies Program and is highly recommended by advisors to returning adult students (Lowe, 1995; Lowe, 1999).

Nova Southeastern University

Nova Southeastern University (NSU) in Fort Lauderdale, Florida, adopted distance learning early, offering courses since the 1970s. The university operates as an independent nonprofit educational institution, and is accredited by the Southern Association of Colleges and Schools. NSU's 7,000 distance learning students are enrolled in master's and doctoral degree programs, as well as several graduate certificate programs. The university offers computer and videoconferencing courses at over 150 distance sites (or clusters) throughout Florida, the United States, the Caribbean, and around the world (Tunon and Pival, 1997; Tunon, 1998).

Library support for distance learning is provided by the Distance Library Services Office in the Einstein Library. The head of Distance Library Services coordinates an extensive program of reference, document delivery, interlibrary loan, and instructional services for distance learning faculty and students. Librarians respond to student research needs by preparing and distributing research handouts, working with faculty to integrate instruction into course outlines, and by offering instruction sessions in several distance learning formats. The library has also established lending agreements with two major research libraries so that students can request materials directly from additional library collections, thereby saving the time needed for interlibrary loan through NSU.

Distance library services continue to grow and expand with NSU's distance learning academic program, and as technological advances have made increased library access possible. Services in the early 1990s consisted primarily of mediated database searching and document delivery, but have now expanded to include Internet access to research databases, research instruction, and course-integrated instruction.

Plattsburgh State University

Plattsburgh State University is located in the northeast corner of New York State, about twenty miles from the U.S.-Canada border. Plattsburgh is a state-supported comprehensive institution, accredited by the Middle States Association of Colleges and

Schools. Part of the State University of New York (SUNY) system, Plattsburgh offers nearly sixty major fields of study, with a primarily residential student population of about 5,500.

Plattsburgh first offered distance courses in 1989, and has been expanding its distance learning program since 1994. Classes are offered with a real-time, two-way interactive videoconferencing system, through e-mail distribution/discussion lists, and on the Internet. The university has a typical semester distance learning enrollment of more than 500—about 200 nursing and 300 education and management students. Options for students in this program include using distance learning technologies or meeting at one of the distance site campuses with traveling Plattsburgh faculty or local instructors. Students generally attend videoconferencing classes in groups, but work more independently in the e-mail and Internet courses. The five distance site classrooms are all located within this rural area of upstate New York, at other SUNY two- or four-year colleges, with which Plattsburgh negotiated agreements on classroom use and library access.

Organizationally, distance learning is part of the Center for Lifelong Learning, which offers many courses and degree programs. Students receive library services jointly from Plattsburgh's Feinberg Library, where services are coordinated by the outreach librarian, and their site library. Library faculty teach a required one-credit course, LIB101 Introduction to Library Research, previously described by Carla List (1995). Additionally, the Division of Library and Information Services (LIS) offers many research and computing workshops each semester.

CRITICAL ISSUES AND RESPONSES

The critical issues facing information literacy librarians vary from institution to institution. Certainly the priority given to each issue is dependent on the institutional mission, student profile, academic programs, and institutional readiness for service delivery. A review of the literature, the co-authors' experiences, and librarian survey responses resulted in the identification of several critical issues faced by most distance learning instruction librarians. These issues can be organized into the following three categories:

1. administrative/organizational issues
2. information literacy/pedagogical issues
3. instructional technology/logistical issues.

A description of the issues will help librarians develop an information literacy program for distance learners, as there is considerable overlap with those faced in the development of on-campus instruction. Experienced instructional librarians will quickly recognize these issues but may not be prepared to respond easily with effective strategies, so details of how these issues are defined and addressed by distance librarians may provide time-saving guidance.

Administrative/Organizational Issues

Critical administrative/organizational issues include strategic planning, short- and long-term budgeting, professional and clerical staffing, institutional and library mission statement development for distance learning, professional development activities, technology purchases, and promotion and marketing of courses. Additional issues include copyright compliance, course scheduling, department and individual workloads, and academic review and approval for credit courses. For libraries, issues of research database license agreements, off-campus network access, and contracts and coordination of services with other institutions may be added to the list.

Most institutions have a designated distance learning administrative office that may exist as an academic dean's office, a lifelong learning or continuing education office, a separate distance learning office, or even a sponsored research office in the case of grant funding. It is important that the instruction librarian know which office to approach, as coordination with this unit is essential if the library is to contribute to the academic success of the distance learners. There are many variations on this unit's relationship with the library, but library administrators usually have the most contact with the institutional distance learning office. Library administrators, then, need advice and recommendations from instruction librarians as distance learning planning begins.

Early involvement of librarians in distance learning planning and individual course development has enormous payoffs for the institution in terms of increased quality of services and even in the simple availability of services to off-campus students. After-the-fact involvement usually results in course research assignments that are difficult to support, inaccurate faculty and administrative assumptions about student access to information tools and resources, and no instruction opportunities for librarians charged with supporting distance learning. A recent article on distance learning policy issues neatly lays out the important policy and planning issues for distance learning administrators, and argues that student support services (including library services) are "often overlooked" and are "central to the success of any distance learning program" (Gellman-Danley and Fetzner, 1998). Librarians must be alert to rumors of distance learning program development, involved in recommending library funding in grant proposals, and diligent about asserting the role of the library in the earliest planning stages.

Strategic planning, budgeting, and staffing should be given high priority by library administrators, since decisions made in these areas have far-reaching impact on an instruction librarian's ability to provide the necessary services. Institution distance learning offices and library administrators can address these issues on a broad scale, but only the instruction librarians can address them in the details of their programmatic efforts. While administrators address institutional missions, instructional librarians must address the instructional mission. While administrators may provide an institutional copyright policy and legal guidelines, instruction librarians must detail exactly how these guidelines will be interpreted and followed in their instruction sessions, research guides, and Internet pages. All broad administrative and organizational issues have details and raise questions to which instruction librarians will be called upon to respond.

Administrative/Organizational Responses

Each of our three representative programs (UNET, NSU, and Plattsburgh) operates from a designated office with either full- or part-time librarians responsible for library services for distance learners. Their administrative structures are different, yet in all three cases the librarians emphasize the importance of focused attention on distance learning. The size and geographic reach of a distance learning program significantly shapes its instructional services. The two larger programs highlighted in this chapter (UNET and NSU) have full-time dedicated staff, whereas the smaller program (Plattsburgh) has a more distributed model with an outreach librarian who is also responsible for interlibrary loan operations.

The Off-Campus Library Services Program Office coordinates information literacy instruction at UNET. This office serves a large student population and offers a broad range of degree programs. The Assistant Dean for Off-Campus Library Services for UNET develops the instructional mission and designs the professional development activities. This direct administrative coordination leads to a responsive and effective program.

Nova Southeastern University provides instructional services to its 7,000 distance learners through the Distance Library Services Office at the Einstein Library. When NSU significantly expanded distance learning library services in the 1990s, planning and budgeting were crucial (Tunon and Pival, 1997), since exceptional administrative support was essential in securing additional funds for database purchases.

At Plattsburgh, both the Dean of LIS and the Outreach Librarian maintain regular contact with the Center for Lifelong Learning, which coordinates distance learning for the campus. The Coordinator of Distance Learning staffs an office within the center and oversees course scheduling, recruitment, and distance learning equipment maintenance. The library's instructional services programmatic group works with the Outreach Librarian to address instruction for distance learners, striving for equity and consistency between on- and off-campus learners.

Librarians at all three institutions work collaboratively with faculty and cooperating librarians at distance learning receiving sites to design and deliver information and instruction. Staffing issues have been addressed in different ways. One university recognized the increased overlap between on- and off-campus students and services and folded distance learning instruction into the regular responsibilities of all reference librarians. Another university addressed workload, academic quality, and professional development with a joint labor-management agreement on distance learning. At another institution, the outreach librarian teaches the distance learning sections of a credit-bearing course, and has a reduction in reference desk hours when scheduled for distance learning course-related sessions. All three representative institutions made a significant commitment by hiring outreach or distance learning librarians to coordinate services and to provide direct instruction services to distance learners.

Librarians have developed WWW instructional pages, which are time, and workload, intensive, but cost effective in terms of reduced travel to off-campus sites and their provision of immediate instruction delivery to distance learning students across the globe. This is particularly important for programs serving students taking WWW-based courses. Library instruction is required for some student orientations, which clearly indicates strong coordination and advocacy for information literacy between the library and university academic deans and program chairs.

Faculty in the representative programs are provided with library services information, training, and consultation services regarding intellectual property for their courses. Copyright issues can be addressed by adherence to accepted educational fair use interpretations, password-protected electronic reserves, and closed videoconferencing or interactive television systems. Comprehensive library instruction marketing is often augmented by separate efforts to reach faculty scheduled to teach distance learning courses. Examples include letters and course-related instruction forms distributed to faculty, library Internet pages on instruction services, and guidance to faculty advisors about credit-bearing courses. Instructional programs have been funded as part of a library's overall budget, by separate distance learning grants, or partially by another university office, such as the broader unit responsible for university distance learning.

Information Literacy/Pedagogical Issues

Critical information literacy pedagogical issues include understanding adults and distance learning theories and adapting traditional teaching methods to engage learners at a distance. Instructors must also develop or revise assessment tools, learn techniques for the academic management of multiple distance learning sites and asynchronous learning, and identify appropriate distance learning technologies that will allow the instructor and students to meet the instructional objectives. For course-related or course-integrated instruction, additional issues of collaboration with faculty and the development of content-specific instruction guides are also critical. Priority in addressing these issues will again be determined by each institution's mission and student profile, but the literature suggests that most instructional librarians leap (or are pushed!) into adapting their traditional teaching methods quickly in response to an immediate program need. It is usually when programs reach a critical mass that an institution will budget for professional development in distance learning pedagogy or offer course release for development activities. Librarians have used methods such as reading books and journals and attending conferences and workshops to develop the important pedagogical skills needed to provide high quality distance learning instruction.

It is vital in all this to remember that distance learning requires a change in orientation. While information literacy instructional objectives are usually the same, instructional delivery methods do impact course design and timing, and can even affect the core pedagogical issues of what to teach, how to teach it, and how to assess student learning. It is important to consider delivery format (interactive television, compressed video, print guides and handouts, printed course packs, or Internet applications such as e-mail, chat, or Web-based course management systems) when planning instructional sessions and materials. Although it would be ideal to determine and then select the most appropriate format for the instructional objectives, the instruction librarian may not have such a choice. In the case of course-related instruction, the librarian may choose to use the same format as the content course, since students will be familiar with it and will be better able to concentrate on the concepts being presented and discussed.

Adult learning theories recommend shaping instruction to accommodate the needs of self-directed learners. When planning information literacy sessions for distance learning programs with many adult learners, the instruction librarian is well-advised to consult the literature on adult learning and instructional design. As Malcom Knowles stated in the title of one article, "Adults Are Not Grown-Up Children as Learners" (Knowles, 1983: 4). Communication and interactions take a new shape in distance learning, particularly with adult learners. Knowledge-building and information-exchange opportunities should be developed not only between the instructor, the course materials, and the student but also between students. Assignments that include group projects, discussions, and student presentations are excellent ways to keep students engaged and learning from each other, as adult students bring significant career and life experiences to their coursework.

Pay special attention to interaction when designing instruction for distance learning. As stated in a recent review article, "In a traditional classroom environment, the community is 'built-in' to the instruction and occurs to some degree with little or no additional planning or effort. In asynchronous learning environments, communities have to be specifically designed, developed, and implemented" (Moller, 1998: 117). Moller provides many citations recommending and evaluating interactive activities such as collaborative projects, sustained computer-conferencing dialogues, student-student writing critiques, and social and academic support and encouragement. She identifies online classroom conversation opportunities as highly valuable in creating a community where learners are ready and able to learn.

Academic preparation for a distance learning course includes not only content analysis and lesson design but also additional interactivity or feedback to keep learners engaged, and special attention to graphical design, for interactive-television or compressed-video formats, and to page layout and design, for Internet formats. As more distance learning faculty embrace Web-based courses, librarians are moving into cyberspace with them for information literacy instruction. The pedagogical advantages include consistency with academic course format; anytime, anywhere access; and an ever-growing body of Web-based information resources to tap into. Learning and fluency are enhanced when the teaching techniques closely match the real applications of new knowledge and can be facilitated by teaching information literacy on the Internet, the current research tool of our new information age. Dynamic Web pages allow the display of both teaching materials and immediate practice opportunities (through hypertext links and multiple open windows), which can clarify and reinforce instructional objectives. Librarians at Northwestern University wrote that their "Class and Academic Web pages are, in essence, the transformation of the library instruction handout from a print document to a more dynamic HTML document" (Sedam and Marshall, 1998: 257). Web-based courses for distance learners are best supported with Web-based information literacy instructional efforts, and many librarians are moving in that direction.

Selection of the Web as an instructional format must not mean, however, that librarians focus exclusively on teaching students how to use it. In a 1996 lecture, Cerise Oberman cautioned librarians against linking instruction to research tools instead of to research and information-management concepts. In the 1970s, "the convergence of learning theory and concepts of information led to the recognition of the importance of critical thinking skills" (Oberman, 1996: 319). She pointed out that with the arrival of CD-ROMs, online catalogs, the Internet, and now the World Wide Web, instructors are feeling pressure to focus on the use of electronic research tools. "We risk losing sight of the concept of information access, retrieval, and evaluation that will serve our users long after a particular interface ceases to exist" (320). Instructors working with distance learning students need to be particularly conscious of this issue, as they may encounter technology and electronic tools in many areas—while designing their instruction sessions, teaching their classes, and instructing students to use electronic resources. It is essential that librarians continually remind themselves that learning the technology interfaces may provide students with immediate research results, but will not sustain them through even four years of undergraduate work, given the pace of technological change.

Information Literacy/Pedagogical Responses

Information literacy instruction is provided by the three representative programs in several ways: on-site instruction at the off-campus centers, in-class instruction from the campus providing interactive television or videoconferencing classrooms, and as part of a college experience or summer institute class. Guides for online catalogs and research databases are distributed to students in print and Internet formats. Web-based instruction is under development by librarians as both systemwide and library initiatives. Content for information literacy instruction is most often the same as that for on-campus students, with additional guidance for distance students on resources that meet their specific needs included in handouts and instruction sessions, especially logistical instructions.

Librarians make site visits or use computer-conferencing software to deliver instruction to students in programs that do not require any on-campus components. In a number of programs, efforts are made to work collaboratively with faculty to integrate library instruction where possible. Site visits can be particularly important in establishing good working relationships with local librarians, who often assist students in using the host library's Internet resources. Specific examples of Internet-based instructional services include NSU's Virtual Reference Assistant, Internet pathfinders, Internet-based tutorials, and help pages. Internet or Web-based instruction can be very closely integrated into an academic Web syllabus, with immediate and repeated access to library and information-research concepts and guides directly from the course Web pages. Students can move easily between course materials, readings, assignments, and active Web links to information literacy instruction and information resources.

Some institutions have clearly defined their instructional goals, which provide librarians with an important framework for program design and assessment. Representative instructional goals include: to provide library instruction to all students, to integrate library instruction into the curriculum of all programs, to enable all members of the college community to achieve information and computer literacy, to improve the methods used to deliver training, and to provide students with a variety of alternative methods for library instruction.

The pedagogical issues critical to distance learning require new instructional skills and techniques. Librarians should be given opportunities to learn videoconferencing software, adult learning theory, and graphic design for television, as well as to work with a remote site facilitator. For example, librarians and other faculty at one institution participated in a half-semester training course for interactive videoconferencing in which faculty were reminded to change instructional activities every ten minutes and to engage students by asking direct questions. Short lessons using active learning techniques were recommended, as these methods are more appealing to adult students. Faculty were advised that adult students are more likely to challenge the instructor's lectures, demand detail and clarity in assignments, and bring their own varied experiences to the classroom—yet these students are apprehensive about academic assignments, less confident in their writing and research skills, and very pressed for time.

Adult student characteristics influence course design and instructional pedagogy for information literacy instruction for distance learning. Course lectures have been transformed into short interactive lessons, interspersed with group-learning practice activities to keep student attention and to generate feedback and questions quickly where facial expressions are not immediately clear. Research tool-specific assignments have been replaced with general research assignments to accommodate the variety of resources at distance site libraries, and at one institution, the final traditional bibliography was adapted into a research narrative focusing on process throughout the research project rather than on selection of the bibliographic items.

In the best of circumstances, students would be offered a variety of opportunities to participate in library instruction. Librarians would design instruction to accommodate diverse learning styles and be available at the point of need. Just-in-time help sheets and one-on-one reference would offer assistance at the point of need. Instruction programs would be structured so that librarians had at least one chance to reach all students in a program. Librarians would be available to students for additional training where and whenever possible.

Course-related sessions conducted in distance learning courses have covered topics from general research strategies to specific library services. Librarians may meet with students at distance sites to conduct library tours and demonstrate the use of the electronic resources available. Site librarians may conduct additional tours and research sessions specific to their libraries. All three representative program librarians produced videocassettes to provide distance students with visual tours of the campus libraries and some basic instruction. Videocassette tours have recently been replaced with Internet virtual tours, using more current delivery methods for the same purpose.

Information literacy classes can require students to work through all six levels of Bloom's cognitive learning domain, from knowledge acquisition to evaluation and synthesis (Bloom, 1956). Students should be able to demonstrate learning and achieve competence in basic research concepts and strategies. Classes should offer opportunities for students to apply knowledge to new or different research situations. Class structures should be simple, usually with presentations of new material, demonstrations of its application to research, and class learning activities for guided practice. Students can then be given assignments for independent or group work that will reinforce or expand their new skills. With distance learners, general assignments should provide enough structure for learning the important concepts and skills along with enough flexibility for students working in libraries with different information resources. For example, a lesson might require students to search an online database relevant to their topic, rather than requiring all students to search the same database, so that students can utilize the different information resources they have available. Internet proxy services or remote student authorization for licensed databases may make this consideration less important.

Institutional changes may prompt a library to begin rethinking its instruction program for distance learning. Several situations pose new challenges for instructors:

- additional distance learning courses from several college departments
- new possibilities for instruction delivery
- development of new Web courses that might not incorporate library research, but turn instead to the Web alone for information.

Faculty need regular reminders that distance learning students have access to the library's resources and that they can request instruction services for their distance learning sections. The head of Distance Library Services at NSU explains her approach as dependent on the program. She takes responsibility for making sure that instruction is scheduled for the off-campus students.

She does not wait for the faculty of on-campus students to request training, but actively promotes and even (politely) badgers faculty to schedule training.

Instructional Technology/Logistical Issues

Instructional technology issues are quickly identified as critical in planning and implementing information literacy programs in distance learning. These issues stand out by virtue of their immediacy and usually demand a significant amount of faculty and librarian attention. While selecting distance learning technology is an administrative issue, implementing and incorporating use of the technology is an instructional issue.

Broad issues affecting technology incorporation include transmission quality for videoconferencing systems, technical training and support for all distance learning formats, technology backup systems (mirror Web servers for Internet courses, videotapes of interactive television or videoconferencing sessions, alternate T-1 lines, modem ports, and authentication databases), and computer network management. Technology at the originating campus is only one part of the distance learning equation, however; there must be equal concern and attention given to technology issues for the distance learner. Access, reliability, interactivity, computing support, authentication costs, and training in technology use and database protocols are just some of the important issues that impact learner success.

Logistical issues for distance instruction are often connected to the technology format. These issues include distributing instructional materials, whether in print, on video, or online, coordinating academic schedules in multi-institutional or collaborative programs, timing lessons for videoconferencing, coordinating multiple sites, scheduling Internet resources updates, and linking users with the appropriate service offices for assistance. For credit-bearing coursework, or any instructional session where librarian feedback is desired, mechanisms for quick delivery and return of assignments must be established.

Many of these issues will be directly addressed by institutional support offices, such as computing or academic administration. Nonetheless, instruction librarians need to make recommendations for technical and logistical systems that meet the needs of information researchers and instruction sessions. Instruction librarians need to be fully aware of the schedules and support mechanisms in place in order to directly assist students and to make the most appropriate referrals. Additionally, librarians will likely continue to be the initial or only campus contact person (other than the course instructor) that a distance learning student may be aware of. An active instructional program ensures high visibility to instructional librarians, and a correspondingly high number of requests for technical or logistical assistance may come from both faculty and students.

Instructional Technology/Logistical Responses

Courses are delivered to distance learners via the Internet, interactive television, and videoconferencing. A well-developed interactive television system combines voice, video, computer-graphic displays, and even Internet conferencing systems to deliver high-quality telecourses. Off-campus librarians regularly avail themselves of high-tech and traditional technologies in their efforts to reach distance learners so as to have alternate formats for diverse learning styles and technical ability, as well as ready back-up in the event of technology failures.

Many students never come to the host campus, so librarians need to make site visits or use Internet conferencing technologies to deliver instruction. Instructors use a wide variety of distance technologies, making professional development and support a critical technology issue. Technologies vary according to the program and model and include compressed video, desktop videoconferencing, NetMeeting, PlaceWare, audiobridge, Embonet, online chats, e-mail, and Webboards. Librarians must gain proficiency in whatever technologies are used by an academic program. "Librarians have had to be prepared to deliver everything from hands-on training and live demonstrations to slide shows and transparency presentations" (Tunon, 1998: 118).

Compressed videoconferencing is not always transmitted at broadcast quality, and the resulting delay in video can create a disconcerting blur and confusion until participants adjust. Instruction may have to be paced to account for the delay, graphics may need longer display times, and special equipment is needed to transmit computer images properly. A teleconferencing system for distance learning may impose some restraints on an instructor's ability to lecture, but offers superior interactivity between instructor and student. It also provides the essential student-to-student, real-time interaction that is designed into some curricula. Librarians may prefer the Internet over videoconferencing for information literacy instruction, so that students will have more of an opportunity to learn library research skills while using an important library research tool as their course medium.

Librarians, faculty, and students need access to computing support services for using computers, networking, or educational technology. For interactive television course development, studio production staff and graphic and multimedia designers are essential assistants for faculty as they prepare and deliver their courses. At one university, the Academic Logistics/ Teleservice Office handles exam and course materials distribution, while the User Support Web pages list services for students and faculty including user support for online conferencing, frequently asked questions (FAQs) for Web pages and using e-mail, and interactive television documentation for setting up and troubleshooting equipment.

If the library instruction-program model uses distance-site librarians, students have a ready resource for assistance with their technological-access and logistical questions. The off-campus librarian can offer training to site staff and librarians to ensure clarity and proficiency in technical skills and library policies and procedures. Librarians may encounter the logistical issue of scheduling staff site visits as well as scheduling sessions when students attend orientations or summer institutes. One university community is provided with technological resources and support by their Office of Information Technology and Media Services, which coordinates technology training, runs a help desk, and provides computing and network services. Internet research databases are protected by password authorization systems that require up-to-date student/faculty databases for accuracy. Each technological investment requires ongoing attention to update, upgrade, and fully utilize its capabilities.

A separate office for distance learning was established at another institution to provide distance site coordination, equipment maintenance and troubleshooting, academic scheduling and registration for distance learners, and print and video material distribution. Back-up materials—either printed display handouts or videotapes of instructional sessions—are regularly mailed to site facilitators. Other offices at that university provide computing and network support, maintaining contact with the outreach librarian for coordination. Technical and logistical issues have continued to appear with each new instructional format and each new academic program, requiring continued creativity on the part of distance learning instructors.

TRENDS AND DIRECTIONS

As noted throughout this chapter, libraries are delivering services and instruction to increasingly broad audiences with disparate needs and resources as a result of distance learning initiatives at their institutions. These changes and their attendant issues can be catalysts for serious and thoughtful consideration about what we do as librarians and how we do it. They can also, however, lead to frustration, discouragement, and heavy workloads if the planning, resources, or expertise are not in place to effect positive and progressive implementation of new services and programs.

In the fall of 1998, a survey was posted on the Bibliographic Instruction List (BI-L) and Off-Campus Library Services List in order to identify issues and possible trends faced by libraries that are having to adapt or create equitable, though not necessarily equal services, resources, and instruction for distance learners engaging in the educational process via distributed learning models (see Appendix A at the end of this chapter). Despite myriad methods of delivering instruction—including off-site classrooms with live instruction, interactive video, Web-based instruction, e-mail, Web-based conferencing, video-conferencing, online chats, and satellite television broadcasts— and the differences among the responding libraries, a common thread of critical concerns and issues emerged that mirror the issues raised throughout this chapter.

Almost without exception, every responding library noted administrative or organizational issues at the forefront of the implementation of distance education and services. The key phrases were "more staff, more funding, more training, and more resources!" Libraries have taken a variety of approaches in dealing with this. The University of Wyoming, which is the only four-year public university in the state, offers 217 distance courses. In response to such a large offering, the library has designated the Library Outreach Services Office to handle "delivery of books, journals, and audio-visual materials, course related reference and research services, electronic access to library catalogs and indexes, [and] library instruction" (Lange and Kearley, 1998). Although other libraries have integrated these services into already existing departments or programs, having an established office to handle distance education issues for the library has the effect of legitimizing the issues and work it takes to implement new programs and services. The University of Wyoming respondents noted that, as a result of the mission of this office, services are well-publicized, there is effective coordination with instructional designers and faculty, there is effective cooperation with academic and public libraries throughout the state, and the library is actively involved in the planning process for outreach services. It also seems that the respondents were able to articulate a more comprehensive list of needs and planning initiatives, perhaps as a result of clearly identifying the context of issues surrounding distance learning at their institution. Additionally, they note that "as increasing numbers of institutions of higher education offer distance education the competition for students will increase. The ability to offer a full array of library services including instruction may become a selling point for distance education programs" (Lange and Kearley, 1998).

All the respondents had adapted their distance learning instruction to whatever delivery methods their institutions endorsed. This means instruction is happening over the Web, via interactive video, in person at far-flung locations, over the telephone, via e-mail or postal service, and on television. No matter what the method, the most common pedagogical issue in distance learning library instruction is how to teach the students effectively. Most libraries noted that the core goals and objectives of library instruction are the same for on-site and distance learners; the problem is how to both teach content and assess outcomes when your students may have very little, or at least very disparate, library contact and access to databases or other technology in the course of their studies. Mark McManus of the

State University of West Georgia says that "librarians must be able to relate to student's instructional needs at any point" and that there need to be "measurable indices" so that we know if the instructional needs of distance learners have been met. He goes on to say that "librarians will need time to develop and test software and pedagogical methodologies and the freedom to discover techniques and strategies to impart the knowledge about the academic communication process" (McManus, 1998).

Unfortunately, time was one commodity most respondents regarded as lacking in the planning of instructional content and delivery. As one librarian noted, while Web delivery was well-liked by students, it was time intensive for the librarian to write and mount content as well as to manage the flow of information created in this format. Dan Ream at Virginia Commonwealth University noted that beyond the difficulties faced by adapting or creating instruction in a new delivery mode, the demographics of the distance students are different: "These are mostly returning/adult students who are not comfortable with computers and they are very motivated and appreciative of instruction" (Ream, 1998). He went on to say that the librarians do more instruction on computer basics than with traditional students, and that the timing of instruction is especially important. The implication is that they need not only library instruction but computer instruction as well. Finally, Dee Mooneyham of Taft College cautioned that "distance learning is not for everyone . . . many students just don't have the self-motivation to stick with the course" (Mooneyham, 1998).

Instructional technology and logistical issues were also identified as significant areas of concern and change. While all respondents stated that they were having to learn to use and manipulate new technologies, a point reiterated several times was the need to develop better licensing agreements for the provision of online resources for distance learners, which is also an administrative and pedagogical concern. This is reinforced by the number of students with access to computers. At California State University, Chico, a recent study showed "that some 80% have access to computer technology" (Power, 1998). Access to more resources also reinforces the legitimacy of the education distance learners engage in and receive, and may be an essential part of that "full array of services" noted by the University of Wyoming. A second point that appeared frequently is that librarians felt they needed more training in and better access to technology used in delivering distance education. One respondent stated that none of the videoconferencing technology used on campus was available in the library.

Distance learning and its attendant issues and problems are a challenging development for most academic institutions. It signals a marked shift in the traditional academic models and sends teachers and students into uncharted territory. Despite changes in technology, delivery method, pedagogy, and student demographics, our role as librarians in the intellectual and academic pursuits of students remains essentially the same: to fulfill the needs of students through service and instruction. Mark McManus states that "while there may be differences between traditional and off-campus students these are not as important as the similarities" (McManus, 1998). And as noted above, the most common responses to distance education initiatives are the need for "more staff, more funding, more training, and more resources." When asked what resources he thought librarians need to successfully provide instruction to distance learners, Dan Ream summed it up best: "Same as always."

REFERENCES

American Library Association. 1989. *Presidential Committee on Information Literacy: Final Report.* Available online at *www.ala.org/acrl/nili/ilit1st.html* [cited 1999, June 14].

Association of College and Research Libraries. 1997. *Guidelines for Instruction Programs in Academic Libraries.* Available online at *www.ala.org/acrl/guides/guiis.html* [cited 1998, December 10].

———. 1998. *ACRL Guidelines for Distance Learning Library Services.* Available online at *www.ala.org/acrl/guides/distlrng.html* [cited 1998, December 10].

Bloom, Benjamin Samuel. 1956. *Taxonomy of Educational Objectives: The Classification of Educational Goals.* New York: D. McKay.

Dasher-Alston, Robin, and Gerald Patton. 1998. "Evaluation Criteria for Distance Learning." *Planning for Higher Education* 27 (Fall): 11–17.

Gellman-Danley, Barbara, and Marie Fetzner. 1998. "Asking the Really Tough Questions: Policy Issues for Distance Learning." *Online Journal of Distance Learning Administration* 1 (Spring). Available online at *www.westga.edu/~distance/danley11.html* [cited 1998, June 12].

Jayne, Elaine A., Judith M. Arnold, and Patricia Fravel Vander Meer. 1998. "Casting a Broad Net: The Use of Web-Based Tutorials for Library Instruction." In *The Eighth Off-Campus Library Services Conference Proceedings,* compiled by P. S. Thomas and M. Jones, 197–205. Mount Pleasant: Central Michigan University.

Knowles, Malcolm S. 1983. "Adults Are Not Grown-Up Children as Learners." *Community Services Catalyst* 13 (Fall): 4–8.

Koha, Kay. 1996. "Foreword." *Peterson's Distance Learning 1997*. Princeton, N.J.: Peterson's.

Lange, Karen, and Jamie Kearley. 1998. E-mail survey sent to author, November 15.

Lebowitz, Gloria. 1997. "Library Services to Distant Students: An Equity Issue." *The Journal of Academic Librarianship* 23 (July): 303–308.

List, Carla. 1995. "Branching Out: A Required Library Research Course Targets Disciplines and Programs." *The Reference Librarian* 51/52 (1995): 385–98.

Lowe, Susan. 1995. "Collaboration with Faculty: Integrating Information Literacy into the Curriculum." In *The Seventh Off-Campus Library Services Conference Proceedings*, compiled by C. J. Jacob, 257–60. Mount Pleasant: Central Michigan University Libraries.

———. 1998. E-mail survey sent to author, November 15.

———. 1999. E-mail survey sent to author, April 6.

McManus, Mark. 1998. E-mail survey sent to author, November 19.

Moller, Leslie. 1998. "Designing Communities of Learners for Asynchronous Distance Education." *Educational Technology, Research and Development* 46: 115–22.

Mooneyham, Dee. 1998. E-mail survey sent to author, November 23.

Oberman, Cerise. 1996. "Library Instruction: Concepts and Pedagogy in the Electronic Environment." *RQ* 35 (Spring): 315–23.

Power, Colleen. 1998. E-mail survey sent to author, November 11.

Ream, Dan. 1998. E-mail survey sent to author, November 11.

Sedam, Rebecca E., and Jerilyn Marshall. 1998. "Course-Specific World Wide Web Pages: Evolution of an Extended Campus Library Instruction Service." In *The Eighth Off-Campus Library Services Conference Proceedings*, compiled by P. S. Thomas and M. Jones, 251–58. Mount Pleasant: Central Michigan University.

Slade, Alexander L. 1998. *"Draft Guidelines for Library Support of Distance and Distributed Learning in Canada."* Available online at *http://gateway1.uvic.ca/dls/guidelines.html* [cited 1998, December 10].

Snyder, Carolyn A., Susan Logue, and Barbara G. Preece. 1996. *Role of Libraries in Distance Education. SPEC Kit*. Washington, D.C.: Association of Research Libraries, Office of Management Services.

Steffen, Susan S., and J. Marshall. 1993. "The Schaffner Model of Library Services." In *The Sixth Off-Campus Library Services Conference Proceedings*, compiled by C. J. Jacob, 273–79. Mount Pleasant: Central Michigan University Libraries.

Tunon, Johanna. 1998. E-mail survey sent to author, November 11.

Tunon, Johanna, and Paul Pival. 1997. "Library Services to Distance Students: Nova Southeastern University's Experience." *Florida Libraries* 40: 109,118.

APPENDIX A: SURVEY

1. Briefly describe your institution and library.
2. Briefly describe the distance learning program at your institution.
3. Briefly describe your information literacy or bibliographic instruction program for both on and off-campus students (e.g., course-related, Web tutorials, guides, etc.).
4. Does your program have specific goals and objectives? If so, what are they?
5. Are these the same for distance learners as for on-campus students? If they are different, please explain.
6. What are your instructional methods and pedagogies? Are they the same for on- and off-campus students? How?
7. How satisfied are you with your distance learning instruction? What has worked well? What could use improvement?
8. How do you see your instruction program for distance learning students changing in the next 2–3 years? (Please be as specific as possible.)
9. What resources do you think librarians will need in the next 2–3 years to successfully provide instruction to distance learners as you envision it?
10. Other comments not covered by the questions above are most welcome.

Meeting Adult Learners, Wherever They May Be: If It's Thursday, It Must Be Thermopolis!

Katherine Holmes and Cynthia Farr Brown
Lesley College

Since 1981, Lesley College has offered off-campus master's degree programs to thousands of adult learners in locations far from the main campus in Cambridge, Massachusetts. More than half of Lesley's 6,000–plus students earn their degrees in these programs, which are now running in thirteen states as well as throughout Massachusetts. The majority of these students seldom, if ever, set foot on the Lesley campus or in the library. Yet the nature of their educational programs requires the use of library resources and materials, which poses a challenge: how to deliver quality library services to a graduate student population whose knowledge of library research, comfort with technology, and access to library resources vary widely. This chapter describes a four-year collaboration between a librarian, Katherine Holmes, and a faculty member, Cynthia Brown, working together to teach library-research skills—first within a single course, and then evolving to encompass the core courses of a large academic program.

WHY THERMOPOLIS?

Lesley College was one of the pioneers of a particular kind of distance education, whose main features may be summarized as:

- intensive delivery, in which two weekends of course meetings replicate the traditional forty-five hours of seat time spread over thirteen- or fourteen-week semesters on-campus
- learner-centered pedagogy
- geared to adult learners—working professionals whose experience is validated and incorporated into instruction
- cohort-based—the same group of students takes each course at the same time, going through the entire program together and building a collaborative, supportive group dynamic
- sites dispersed at 125 locations across the United States
- core faculty fly to sites from the Lesley College home campus, and adjuncts travel from all over the country.

In attempting to meet students where they are, Lesley College identifies communities and sites, such as Thermopolis, Wyoming, where professional-development programs are needed for teachers and other human-service professionals. These communities differ widely in terms of access to academic libraries, museums, and other research facilities: Some off-campus students can access excellent local academic libraries that have signed service agreements with Lesley College; other students can access good libraries only if they are willing to travel an hour or more; and there are some sites so remote that there is no academic library for miles around, as in Thermopolis. The challenge is to establish an infrastructure based on collaboration within and outside the institution in order to provide library services and support to students at a distance (Paul and Brindley, 1996).

In addition, students bring a wide variety of skills and expectations; many of them are returning to graduate work after ten to twenty years' absence from academia, with little or no experience of the Internet or other electronic resources (Cooper et al., 1998). Mandell and Herman assert that "opening the academy to non-traditional students in non-traditional delivery, requires greater support of students once they're inside" (1996: 3). This is particularly true for library use, as libraries are nearly unrecognizable from the institutions most students used even five years ago.

THE INTENSIVE WEEKEND FORMAT

The intensive weekend format presents particular challenges for library instruction. Courses meet for two intensive weekends, about a month apart. Prior to the first course meeting, students receive a syllabus, purchase textbooks, and begin working on assignments, before even meeting the instructor. The intensity of 22.5 hours of class in a single weekend makes library visits and presentations hard to schedule. Between the two course weekends, and after the second weekend, students complete their coursework in a time frame that may span almost three months. The month's interval between classes can be a long time for students lacking confidence in the research process, when face-to-face contact with instructors and librarians is not possible. While telephone, e-mail, and the Web enable contact with faculty and librarians between weekends, the authors find it particularly important to build students' research and library skills during the first weekend so students have maximum independence.

HOW DOES LESLEY COLLEGE SUPPORT THESE STUDENTS?

Ludcke Library, the home library of Lesley College, has developed a number of services to deliver library materials, resources, and assistance to students in a commitment to provide needed services that are equivalent to on-campus resources. The ACRL *Guidelines for Distance Learning Library Services* stipulate that "the instilling of lifelong learning skills through information literacy instruction in academic libraries is a primary outcome of higher education, . . . of equal necessity for the distance learning community as it is for those on the traditional campus. . . . Effective and appropriate services for distance learning communities may differ from, but must be equivalent to, those services offered on a traditional campus" (Gover, 1998).

Toward that goal, Ludcke Library's services include World Wide Web access to online catalogs and databases, with a growing array of full-text options; e-mail and toll-free telephone reference service; and interlibrary loan and document delivery for journal articles and ERIC documents. The hardest service to offer from a distance is instruction. Students need to learn information literacy skills to design search strategies, evaluate resources, and integrate information effectively in assignments. Ludcke librarians do some sessions off-campus and invite groups on-campus whenever possible. But Thermopolis is a long way from Cambridge, and just one of dozens of remote sites.

The Authors' Collaboration

The authors have collaborated for four years to deliver library instruction in a specific program, Curriculum and Instruction, in Lesley's School of Education. That collaboration began with support of a single required course in educational research, and expanded in the 1998–1999 academic year to include the five required core courses of the whole program; it was then redesigned to meet a number of instructional and program outcomes. Faculty recognized the need to integrate technology objectives seamlessly into the learning outcomes of the program in order to enable their teacher/learners to utilize technology effectively in their own classrooms. The authors endeavored to apply some of what they learned from the earlier, one-course collaboration to the larger task of weaving library instruction and access into the whole program of study.

INFORMATION LITERACY STEPS

In the Educational Research & Evaluation course, the authors co-teach an information literacy skills process loosely adapted from the Big Six Skills Approach (Eisenberg and Berkowitz, 1988). Students are led through the following action steps:

1. BRAINSTORM your topic.
2. Read BACKGROUND materials.
   - *Encyclopedia of Educational Research*
   - *Encyclopedia of African American Culture & History*
   - *Encyclopaedia Britannica*
   - *Facts on File Education Dictionary*
3. Consider and evaluate all MEDIA.
   - Print
   - Audio-Visual

- Electronic
- Interviews
4. EVALUATE potential sources.
   - Scholarly versus general content
   - Journals versus books
   - Internet versus print
5. Identify and locate TITLES.
   - Library catalog
   - Subject databases
   - ERIC
6. EVALUATE findings and adjust strategy.
   - Which resources respond to your research question?
   - Is more information needed?
   - What strategies would help find that information?
7. SYNTHESIZE the information.
   - What are common themes?
   - Where are contradictions?
   - How to resolve the two?
8. EVALUATE the process.
   - How efficient was the process?
   - How successfully did it answer your research question?
   - How would you do it differently next time?

The authors have co-taught most of these steps. The librarian tends to focus more on search strategies and evaluating information, whereas the faculty member leads the analysis and synthesis processes. Brainstorming, problem solving, small-group work, and hands-on practice are featured in every session. PowerPoint presentations, handouts, and homemade videos reinforce the concepts. World Wide Web pages support student research during and after the course (Brown, Gannon, and Holmes, 1998; Holmes, 1998).

Information literacy concepts now span the five core courses of the Curriculum and Instruction Program. Faculty and librarians have collaborated to build a matrix of learning strands, including a Research Strand that integrates technology and library literacy into the core curriculum. Faculty travel to off-campus sites with library videos and handouts, promote student research through library Web pages, and support each other in this new curriculum.

Professional literature offers limited evidence of faculty/librarian collaboration for library instruction with off-campus or distance learners. Susan Barnes at Linfield College collaborates with faculty to teach information literacy in the Re-Entry Program (Barnes, 1998), which brings off-campus students to campus once a year for training and support. The uniqueness of the Holmes and Brown collaboration is in library instruction amid the challenges and opportunities posed by delivery at off-campus sites.

STRATEGIES FOR LIBRARY INSTRUCTION

A variety of strategies have been devised to bring library instruction to students and to extend the learning necessary for students to become more independent researchers. The following points document the current state of the collaboration.

Collaborative Curriculum Development

Under Brown's leadership, the core courses in the Curriculum and Instruction sequence were recently redesigned around a matrix of learning strands that make explicit the technology skills and information literacy concepts required in each course. Holmes joined the faculty in this redesign, as the following sequence of competencies was developed for the five courses:

1. Dimensions of Teaching and Learning
   - Access to Ludcke Library and online resources
   - Writing abstracts
2. Curriculum, Assessment, and Instruction
   - Simple World Wide Web search
3. Dimensions of Equity
   - Advanced Web search
   - Evaluate online resources
   - Read/critique original research
   - Annotated bibliography
4. Classroom and School Inquiry
   - Extensive use of library and online resources for research proposals
5. Action Research and Seminar

- Use of library and online resources for group projects focused on substantive change and implementation
- Generic software applications, such as word processing and spreadsheets, that have been identified as tools for students to master as they learn to manipulate and present the information.

Shared Teaching

Whenever possible, the faculty member and librarian share the teaching role in class. Students see the give and take of shared teaching and learning; they see the power of collaboration modeled in practice. Brown and Holmes benefit from their enjoyment of each other, and from the heightened energy and creativity engendered by the collaboration.

Instructor/Librarian in a Box

Newly available technology led to the creation of the first of a series of "Look Over My Shoulder" videos in which the librarian models searching in Web-based resources. These homemade videos utilize PowerPoint slides, direct video-to-computer transcriptions, video clips, and voice-over narration. The class can literally watch over her shoulder as the librarian goes into the Web, opens a database, tries search strategies, and evaluates resources. Now each instructor who teaches the first course in the program takes a copy of the video and the accompanying handouts to class for viewing and discussion. Students have computer lab access during this course and time to try out the skills modeled in the video as they begin the first course assignments. Student and faculty response has been overwhelmingly positive. More videos are planned to address other online information searching and evaluation. Where online access is lacking, PowerPoint presentations have been provided to faculty on disk or overhead transparencies.

Migration to the Internet

Increasingly, the library is accessing Web-based resources that are available to all students, whether on- or off-campus. As this chapter goes to press, the library will nearly triple the number of full-text databases available to students, including a full-text database of scholarly education journals. A Web site of Library Research Guides oriented around particular topics, information-literacy processes, and geographic areas provides strong support to off-campus students, including a guide to full-text resources on the World Wide Web (Holmes, 1998). These pages are linked to the Lesley Website and the library Web pages and are among the most heavily used on the Lesley College Website.

Evolving Document Delivery

The library is piloting electronic document-delivery services to enhance traditional interlibrary loans. Articles are obtained from full-text databases or purchased through Web-based vendors and mailed or e-mailed to students. With a microfiche duplicator currently on order, large ERIC documents will be delivered to students via fiche.

Linking Instructors to Libraries

The authors have teamed to link teaching faculty with local libraries for instruction. Program faculty are encouraged to make time for instruction; individual and group training sessions are provided for faculty; funding has been located to pay for fee-based instruction sessions; and the library negotiates with academic libraries local to off-campus sites to deliver instruction sessions that meet specific course objectives.

Student Response

Students have for the most part responded enthusiastically to the steps described above and are quicker to see the connections between library skills and processes and the work they are being asked to do. After the first course, for example, one student wrote in her reflection paper, "Learning how to do research through the Internet [to access library databases and other Web sites] was one of the best things I could ever have learned." She went on to talk about not only the deep content available but also how her mastery of the tools to use that content has evolved after only one course using the integrated approach. Another student in the same section of the same course reinforced the idea of the skill-based learning that takes place through this approach, referring to it as "a whole new knowledge of search skills" using the computer.

WHAT ASSUMPTIONS NEED TO BE ADDRESSED?

The fluidity of the instructional situation, coupled with identified characteristics of Lesley students as they learn library research, led the authors to look at long-term, facilities-independent solutions to the issue of library instruction. In order to assure that library instruction is available when and where students need it, a number of assumptions had to be addressed. The first assumption was that library instruction and the skills associated with it, including evaluation and application of information gleaned from library searches, was "someone else's responsibility"—the sole realm of either library or teaching faculty. The authors' collaboration models the interdependence of library research and classroom instruction. The communication engendered allows for program decisions to be informed by academic resource decisions, and vice versa. In the off-campus environment, instructors must act "in loco librarian" to meet students' needs, just as they must offer support in other basic academic skills such as writing, reading, and oral presentation. The weekend model, in short, does not lend itself to hard boundaries between roles. The person available on-site must respond to a wide range of needs, regardless of the particular hat she wears at the moment. Faculty and librarians need to share responsibility for library instruction, rather than leaving it to librarians alone (McNeer, 1991)—or worse, leaving it out entirely.

The second assumption was that there is not enough time in the intensive weekend format for library instruction, or that an hour's quick orientation "in someone else's class" will suffice to prepare students to function in the complex world of electronic information. On the contrary, library instruction must be integrated throughout the program and be delivered at the time of need. Timely library instruction may, in fact, be the most time-efficient way to avoid hours of "first aid" tutoring from a distance after the weekend is over.

In order to integrate library instruction with program outcomes and course objectives, it is necessary to engage all program faculty in a dialogue on information literacy and training on library resources. Faculty can no longer fall back on the library strategies from their own graduate work, when indexes were in print, library catalogs were in drawers, and computers had punch cards. Faculty must understand information literacy processes and be familiar with current research tools. They must encourage students to utilize appropriate resources through carefully crafted assignments and learning activities. Faculty and librarians need to be engaged in conversations throughout the academy on information literacy and on the integration of technology and information literacy in the curriculum. Many faculty need hands-on training in information tools and search strategies. Supportive instructional resources must be available for faculty to meet library instruction needs as they arise, both planned and unanticipated (Herrington, 1998). Where available, library professionals located near off-campus sites must be contracted (paid!) to deliver library instruction in local facilities. The library is piloting several such instruction contracts with academic libraries.

A number of new initiatives at Lesley College are beginning to address these concerns. Faculty are being encouraged to consult with librarians early in the curriculum development process. Librarians and faculty are working together to imagine how library instruction and services will evolve in the future. New initiatives for integration of technology and information literacy across the college curriculum offer exciting opportunities for future collaboration.

Administrative support for the authors' collaboration has been substantial from Ludcke Library, the School of Education, and the college leadership. In the early stages of the collaboration, support was limited to encouragement and congratulations. As the work expanded to include other faculty, the School of Education funded a faculty retreat to enable faculty and the librarians to work together on the redesign of the core curriculum. The school paid honoraria and travel expenses so that senior adjunct faculty from around the country could participate with core faculty based in Cambridge. The authors received an Academic Technology Grant from the college to develop software and video support; the grant money purchased software, paid the authors for time above workload, and paid for video editing. Both the School of Education and the library have provided honoraria for contracting with off-campus librarians, and recently the director of Ludcke Library has joined Holmes to negotiate with other library directors for off-campus library instruction.

WHAT IS AHEAD FOR LESLEY COLLEGE?

Several factors are important to the success of the instruction methods proposed, and will continue to be critical as collaborations grow and develop.

Faculty/Library Collaboration

Not only must faculty continue to undertake some of the tasks of library instruction, they must also articulate information needs to the library in order to meet the outcomes of each course and of the program of study as a whole. For example, one faculty member has collaborated with librarians to develop her own library instruction presentation to demonstrate some of the library reference tools she uses in her course on early childhood observation and assessment. While she prefers that students see these tools in a library setting, that is not always possible or practical. The overhead transparencies and interactive lesson she is developing will be an effective substitute. This type of activity is expected to increase.

Changing Student Profile

Program goals must continue to evolve to meet the changing needs of students. For example, with each year, more and more students are at least minimally computer literate when they enter the program. In the early days of this collaboration, few students had computer skills and even fewer used the Internet. Library instruction often had to begin with "This is the mouse." In contrast, many current students have ready access to computers and use the Internet for e-mail and information. With these students, instruction can begin at a higher level.

Patterns of Student Behavior

During instruction sessions, however, the authors have observed patterns of student learning behavior that mitigate against successful library research and pose particular challenges for library instruction:

- Limited vocabulary: Brainstorming synonyms for keywords is often seen as a superfluous step, even though modeled during instruction.
- Can't be bothered with Boolean: Students have difficulty applying newly learned search strategies such as Boolean logic. Even with structured hands-on practice, they tend to fall back on natural-language strategies, with predictable results.
- Seeing the trees and not the forest: It's difficult for students to grasp how articles relate to one another or to their topic. If the population or setting is slightly different from theirs, they fail to see the connections.
- All or nothing: Students swing between finding too much information with no way to distinguish among sources, or thinking there is nothing available on their topic. Both responses are common in electronic searching.
- Needles in haystacks: Many students insist on ordering articles or hunting down books without carefully analyzing abstracts. They order everything hoping something will apply.
- Superficial analysis: Students often judge a piece based only on the title, failing to read and reflect on the abstract and subject headings.

Guaranteeing Student Access to Computers

Effective delivery of library services and instruction via the Internet depends upon ensuring that each student has computer access at home or at work, and preferably both. One day soon, this may mean that students will be required to lease or buy computers as part of the program. An equal challenge is to assure access to computers at the Lesley sites for library instruction and hands-on practice, and to maintain that access consistently throughout the program.

Using Emerging Technologies to Present Information

The video series described earlier makes sense as an easily accessible, easily updated, and relatively inexpensive way to provide instruction. However, emerging digital technologies will open other powerful and inexpensive ways to communicate information to and with students. Media such as audio compact disc, digital versatile disc (DVD), interactive CD-ROM, and DVD-ROM will enable easy delivery of tutorials, self-paced instruction, and video clips (ACRL Media Resources Committee, 1999). It should even be possible to prepare a common script and set of activities, and leave "frames" or spaces for custom lessons, activities, and virtual tours of physical libraries that are focused on program specialization and local resources. The advantage of these formats over Web pages includes more reliable access and the ability to include more elaboration of content. Streaming video over the Web is possible, but neither fast nor reliable; a video clip on DVD or even CD-ROM is currently a better solution.

Staying Open to Possibilities

A powerful result of the last four years is the understanding that the pace of change is rapid and the directions it will take are unpredictable, particularly when technology is concerned. Four years ago no one was predicting component prices would fall so fast that one could buy a very functional computer for less than $1,000. There was no apparent appetite for high-speed Internet connections into private homes. DVD was still on the drawing board, and the World Wide Web itself was just emerging from its infancy. There was no such thing as "e-commerce." Television had just begun the diversification process promised by satellite-based delivery of channels and services. And databases offered little more than citations and abstracts.

Current trends in technology have potential implications for Lesley College and any institution seeking to provide distance-mediated library instruction:

- 500 channels of cable: Will this mean new and more focused opportunities for private, and/or for-profit, educational providers?

- E-commerce: Figuring how to sell micro units of copyright and reprint rights over the Web may mean students will have full access to more and more published text.
- Computing as appliance: Internet service may cease to be freestanding and instead be attached to cable service, free in exchange for advertising, or subsidized by state governments as an essential communications utility.
- ILL from home: Commercial vendors will provide document delivery services directly to students. A book will be ordered over the Internet, charged to the library, shipped to the student, who either keeps the book or sends it back to the library. (The cost of the book may be cheaper than the cost of a single traditional interlibrary loan transaction.) Electronic books are already available on the Internet, "purchased" by libraries and accessed from users' home computers a page at a time.

WHAT IS THE FUTURE OF LIBRARY INSTRUCTION FOR DISTANCE LEARNERS?

Library instruction of the future can no longer waste scarce time and resources on the tool-based approach. Gone are the days when library instruction meant a superficial "covering" of a laundry list of reference books and databases, truncation symbols and descriptors. The list is simply too long, especially when Internet search engines are included. Instruction must focus on the concepts that students can apply to any research tool, since it is impossible to anticipate what research tools current students may use in ten years. "A new model of library instruction calls for instructional librarians to focus on the system," rather than the tool, to empower students to draw from that system the information needed, at the precise moment of need, in the most useful format for that individual (Herrington, 1998: 384). Fast becoming a buzzword on campuses, our goal now is to make information literacy a living reality in the academy. Collaboration between faculty, librarians, and students will go a long way to further this goal.

As Lesley College continues to offer its programs at sites like Thermopolis, collaborations between librarians, faculty, and students hold the promise for enabling a new generation of teachers and learners who are not only computer literate but also understand and benefit from the power of information in their lives.

REFERENCES

ACRL Media Resources Committee. 1999. *Guidelines for Media Resources in Academic Libraries*. Association of College and Research Libraries. Available online at *www.ala.org/acrl/guides/medresg.html* [cited 1999, September 16].

Barnes, Susan, Katherine Holmes, and Mem Stahley. 1998. "Library Instruction at a Distance: The High Tech/High Touch Mix." In *Proceedings of the Eighth Off-Campus Library Services Conference*, 183–96. Mt. Pleasant: Central Michigan University.

Brown, Cindy, Marie Gannon, and Kathy Holmes. 1998. *EEDUC 6009: Educational Research and Evaluation Home Page*. Available online at *www.tiac.net/users/ludcke/C&Ihome.html* [cited 1999, May 5].

Cooper, Rosemarie, Paula R. Dempsey, Vanaja Menon, and Christopher Millson-Martula. 1998. "Remote Library Users: Needs and Expectations." *Library Trends* 47 (Summer): 42–64.

Eisenberg, Mike, and Bob Berkowitz. 1988. "Library and Information Skills Curriculum Scope and Sequence: The Big Six Skills." *School Library Media Activities Monthly* 5 (September): 26–28.

Gover, Harvey. 1998. *ACRL Guidelines for Distance Learning Library Services* . Association of College and Research Libraries. Available online at *www.ala.org/acrl/guides/distlrng.html* [cited 1999, September 16].

Herrington, Verlene J. 1998. "Way beyond BI: A Look to the Future." *Journal of Academic Librarianship* 24 (September): 381–87.

Holmes, Katherine. 1998. *Library Research Guides*. Available online at *www.lesley.edu/faculty/kholmes/libguides* [cited 1999, May 5].

McNeer, Elizabeth J. 1991. "Learning Theories and Library Instruction." *Journal of Academic Librarianship* 17 (November): 294–98.

Mandell, Alan, and Lee Herman. 1996. "From Teachers to Mentors: Acknowledging Openings in the Faculty." In *Supporting the Learner in Open and Distance Learning*, edited by Roger Mills and Alan Tait. Washington, D.C.: Pitman.

Paul, Ross, and Jane Brindley. 1996. "Lessons from Distance Education for the University of the Future." In *Supporting the Learner in Open and Distance Learning*, edited by Roger Mills and Alan Tait. Washington, D.C.: Pitman.

Conclusion: Summary and a Look Ahead

As noted in the introductory chapter, the one sure aspect of user education is change. The formal label of librarian as teacher may be fairly new, but the concept has been with the profession since its inception. As librarians, we have the skills (or the where-withal to gain them) necessary to meet the demands of a constantly changing environment. Knowing that change is inherent in what we do, we can be much better prepared to put that change to positive use in our instruction programs.

The preceding chapters have, we hope, given the reader some new insights into, and ideas and directions for, teaching in libraries. The groups of students discussed here will proliferate; never again will we see classes of homogenous, college-ready eighteen-year olds—if, in fact, we ever really did. What has changed is our ability to identify and address these students more effectively. The diversity of students in higher education will continue to provide us with an ever-changing audience, with different capabilities, needs, and learning styles.

Technology will also continue to change, and perhaps diversify. Our students' skills with these technologies will also continue to grow; five years ago many of us were teaching the "what is a mouse" section at the beginning of each class, whereas that is now much more the exception. In some cases, our students are more technologically savvy than we are. This means we can increasingly spend our teaching time connecting students with content, and with the process of finding, evaluating, and using that content, rather than with specific keystroke instruction.

Keeping students as the focus of our teaching is a theme repeated in every chapter of this book. It does not matter what technology, if any, is used in the classroom—from online access to video presentations to handouts or overhead transparencies— if we don't have the students and their needs and capabilities in mind when preparing for the session. Some advance thinking about the audience goes a long way toward a successful instruction interaction, and the techniques discussed here should assist in that. From working with student support units across campus to using diverse vocabulary during sessions, there are many appropriate methods for effectively reaching and teaching heterogeneous student groups.

To know if instruction is effective, it must be evaluated. For a program to change in response to user needs, it is necessary to know if those needs are being met. The thought of programmatic evaluation may be intimidating, but it can be broken down into manageable parts. Sometimes the best feedback is anecdotal—when students start asking higher-level questions at the reference desk, or when you as the instructor see that "aha!" of recognition flash across a student's face during a session. While many of the chapters emphasize ideas for instruction and program development more than in-depth evaluation methods, readers who would like to learn more will find a number of valuable sources on evaluation available in the library and education literatures.

It is also important to update our teaching skills and to be aware of changes occurring in education, and not only in academic settings. Public libraries are increasingly experiencing a demand for instruction by a wide variety of users, and public librarians can also strengthen their teaching programs by incorporating new methods and concepts. A regular check of the library literature can yield useful resources; keep in mind that the literature of education also provides vital information on the characteristics of students and their changing needs, as well as new teaching techniques.

User education is one of the most prominent ways to put a human face on what a library is and does. It provides us as librarians with the opportunity to showcase the access, collections, and services that might otherwise be ignored by users. We can successfully connect our diverse users with the information that they require by identifying those users and their needs. Once these elements are known, we can construct or adapt existing programs to meet these needs. It bears repeating that this is a continuous process, not a one-time task; however, by incorporating these activities into our professional lives, we will ensure better-informed and satisfied users as well as our own sense of a job well done.

Index

About the Authors and Editors

Cynthia Farr Brown is Assistant Professor and Interim Division Director of the Curriculum and Instruction Program, Lesley College School of Education, Cambridge, Massachusetts. She teaches and researches in the areas of teacher research, adult learners, technology in education, the history of education, and U.S. social history. Her teaching takes her all over the country and lets her experience the frontier of integrating electronic library resources into graduate education.

Diane DiMartino is an Associate Professor in the Library Department at Baruch College, City University of New York, where she has worked since 1986. She has headed computerized information services in addition to reference services before assuming a newly created position as coordinator of graduate services in 1998. She participates in workshops and bibliographic instruction programs. Her MLS is from Pratt Institute and her MPA from Baruch. Since the early 1990s, her primary research and publication have been in the area of ESL issues and library technology. In 1995, her co-authored article (which appeared in *College & Research Libraries*), "CD-ROM Search Techniques of Novice End-Users: Is the English-as-a-Second Language Student at a Disadvantage?" was selected by ALA's Library Instruction Round Table as one of the twenty best papers of the year. She is currently the chair elect of ACRL/NY's metropolitan area section.

Karen E. Downing has been Assistant to the Director for Cultural Diversity and Staff Development Officer at the University of Michigan, University Library since 1995. Previously, she was the Coordinator of Academic Outreach Services and Research Library Resident, Coordinator of the Peer Information Counseling Program at the Shapiro Undergraduate Library, University of Michigan. Her expertise lies in the area of multicultural library services, such as peer-information counseling, instruction for diverse populations, interracial research issues, minority recruitment, and diversity-related programming. Her publications include "Multicultural Services at the Undergraduate Library," which appeared in *Cultural Diversity in Libraries* (Neal-Schuman, 1995); *Reaching a Multicultural Student Community: A Handbook for Academic Librarians*, co-authored with Barbara MacAdam and Darlene Nichols (Greenwood, 1993); and "Instruction in a Multicultural Environment," co-authored with Joseph Diaz in *Learning to Teach* (ACRL, 1993). She has served on a number of national committees related to cultural diversity. In 1988, she won the University of Michigan Women of Color Leader of the Year award.

Holly Heller-Ross has been the Outreach Information Services Librarian at Plattsburgh State University of New York since 1994. She previously worked as the Circuit Rider Librarian at the CVPH Medical Center Library in Plattsburgh. Her areas of specialty include information literacy, library services for distance learners, and interlibrary loan. She has published in the *MC Journal: the Journal of Academic Media Librarianship*, and has an article accepted for publication in the *Journal of Library Services for Distance Education*. She holds an MLS from SUNY Albany and a BA in Environmental Science from Plattsburgh State University.

John W. Holmes is a reference librarian and the User Education Coordinator for the Odegaard Undergraduate Library at the University of Washington in Seattle. Since arriving in Seattle in 1996, he has taught several hundred course-related library skills workshops and trained colleagues and students to teach several hundred more. In addition, he has taught information and communication technology courses in the UWired program, a collaborative information literacy initiative that incorporates campus computing, undergraduate education, and the university libraries. Beyond his contributions to campus information-skills curricula, Mr. Holmes is also the instructor of Librarianship 560: User Education, Issues and Practice in the University of Washington School of Library and Information Science. Before arriving in Seattle, he spent seven years training undergraduate students to perform library public service, including peer tutoring and beginning instruction, at Michigan State University.

Katherine Holmes is Assistant Library Director at Lesley College in Cambridge, Massachusetts. Prior to that she held the position of Off-Campus Services Librarian. Her primary responsibility remains coordinating library services for off-campus students and distance learners in fifteen states and several countries. She has presented at ACRL national conferences in Detroit and Nashville, as well as the Off-Campus Library Services conferences in Kansas City, San Diego, and Providence. Her presentation at the ACRL 1999 conference was a workshop entitled "Using All Your Smarts: Multiple Intelligences for Diverse Library Learners." She is active with the Distance Learning Section of ALA/ACRL. Ms. Holmes holds a Master's degree in Library and Information Science from Simmons College in Boston, and a BA in French, English, and Education from Kalamazoo College in Michigan. Her presentations can be viewed on her home page at *www.lesley.edu/faculty/kholmes*.

Trudi E. Jacobson has been the Coordinator of User Education Programs at the University at Albany since 1990. Previously she was the Reference Services Coordinator at Siena College, Loudonville, NY. She has written numerous articles about user education that have appeared in both library and education journals such as *College & Research Libraries, The Journal of Academic Librarianship, Reference Librarian, Research Strategies* (the key journal for user education librarians), *Education, College Teaching,* and *The Teaching Professor.* She was a member of the *Research Strategies* Editorial Board from 1994 to 1997, and currently serves on the Advisory Board of *Urban Academic Librarian.* She is active in the Association of College and Research Libraries' Instruction Section, and has been chair of a number of committees, as well as Secretary of the section from 1993 to 1994. Since 1995, she has taught the User Education graduate course at the

School of Information Science and Policy at the University at Albany. In 1998, she received the School of Information Science and Policy Distinguished Alumni Award from the State University of New York at Albany's Nelson A. Rockefeller College of Public Affairs and Policy. She frequently gives presentations and workshops on topics relating to user education.

Julia Kiple has been the Reference and Instruction Librarian at Carleton College in Northfield, Minnesota, since January 1999. She previously worked as Reference and Instruction Librarian at the State University of New York at Plattsburgh. Her areas of expertise are information literacy and reference services. She holds an MLS and a BA in English, both from the University of Iowa.

Cheryl LaGuardia has been a practicing librarian for over 20 years. She is presently Head of Instructional Services for the Harvard College Library, Harvard University. Previously she worked in reference, library instruction, online services, collections, interlibrary loans, and circulation at the University of California, Santa Barbara and at Union College in Schenectady, NY. She has written and edited the column, "Database & Disc Reviews" for *Library Journal* since 1992, and in 1996 she was awarded the Louis Shores/Oryx Press Award by RASD for her reviewing. That same year she received the school of Information Science and Policy Distinguished Alumni Award from the State University of New York at Albany's Nelson A. Rockefeller College of Public Affairs and Policy. In 1998 she was the co-recipient of the first Janice Graham Newkirk Research Award of the Eastern New York Chapter of the Association of College and Research Libraries. Cheryl is a contributing author to *Library Journal* and other library magazines, and is on the editorial boards of the *Journal of Academic Librarianship* and *RSR: Reference Services Review*. She is the Editor-in-Chief of *The New Library* book series for Neal-Schuman Publishers, Inc., and has published several books, the most recent of which include: *Becoming a Library Teacher; Recreating the Academic Library: Breaking Virtual Ground; Finding Common Ground: Creating the Library of the Future Without Diminishing the Library of the Past*, and *Teaching the New Library* (Neal-Schuman, 1996–2000).

Katy Lenn is Reference Librarian, Education and Linguistics Subject Specialist at the University of Oregon Library. Her expertise lies in the areas of disabilities, distance education, and the instruction of senior citizens. Her articles have appeared in *Wilson Library Bulletin* and *Reference Librarian*. She has presented at the 1992 and 1997 national ACRL conferences, Online Northwest (1990–1999), Loex of the West (1998), and the Oregon Library Association (1996).

Sara McDowell recently assumed the position of Staff Training and Development Librarian at Ryerson Polytechnic University in Toronto. Previously she held the position of Access and Information Services Librarian at Trent University, Peterborough, Ontario. At Trent as well as at Ryerson, she has been actively involved in all aspects of the bibliographic instruction program. Ms. McDowell has additional teaching experience as a Japanese language teacher and an ESL instructor. She holds a Master of Information Studies, Library Science Specialization, from the University of Toronto, as well as an MA in Japanese Studies, and a community college certificate in Teaching English as a Second Language to Adults. She has a strong interest in diversity, both in bibliographic instruction and in other aspects of her work. At Trent University she developed a program of instruction for lesbian, gay, and bisexual students. Ms. McDowell also worked with the local lesbian gay bisexual transgendered (LGBT) community group to establish a LGBT lending library. She presented her work at Trent in a poster session at the Workshop in Instruction in Library Use (WILU), Kingston, 1998. At the same conference, she also presented, with colleagues, the Trent University Library Orientation Program for first-year students, of which she was one of the developers.

Ilene F. Rockman is Deputy Director and Head of Instructional and Interpretive Services at California State University, Hayward. She was previously the Associate Dean and Interim Dean of Library Services at Cal Poly, San Luis Obispo. She has also worked in the libraries of Washington State University, the University of Southern California, and the Los Angeles Public Library. Her recent instructional activities have focused on providing campus leadership to incorporate information competence initiatives across the curriculum; actively working with discipline-based faculty members to reconceptualize and redesign individual courses and degree programs offered at the undergraduate and graduate levels to include information competence principles; reaching out to community colleges to assist in the articulation of information literacy courses for transfer students; encouraging the development of Web-assisted information-competence courseware; and assessing the impact of credit-bearing, information competence classes linked to freshmen learning communities. She is the editor-in-chief of *RSR: Reference Services Review*, and is on the editorial board of *Library Hi Tech*. Her articles have appeared in *Library Administration and Management, The Journal of Library Administration, The Reference Librarian, RSR: Reference Services Review, RQ* (now *RUSA Quarterly*), *Library Journal, Library Trends, College & Research Libraries, College & Research Libraries News*, and *Education Libraries*.

Kwasi Sarkodie-Mensah is the author of some two dozen articles, several book chapters, and close to 100 book and video reviews, as well as numerous presentations to a variety of audiences. His writings have appeared in sources such as *Research Strategies, Reference Librarian,* the *Horn Book Guide, Video Rating Guide for Libraries, College Teaching,* and *Library Journal*. The forthcoming issue of the *Reference Librarian*, edited by Dr. Sarkodie-Mensah, addresses challenges faced by librarians when it comes to dealing with adults in the era of technology. He is Manager of Instructional Services at the O'Neill Library, Boston College, and an Adjunct Professor in the College of Advancing Studies, Boston College's Evening College. Before coming to Boston College in 1992, he was the Coordinator of Bibliographic Instruction at Northeastern University from 1989, and Public Services Manager at Xavier University, New Orleans, from 1986 to 1989. His dissertation on international students and U.S. academic libraries encouraged other academic librarians to develop services for this population. He is active in the Instruction Section of ACRL, the Library Instruction Round Table, and the New England Bibliographic Instruction Committee. Dr. Sarkodie-Mensah holds a Bachelor's degree from the University of Ghana (1979), with additional course work in French and Spanish from institutions of higher education in the Ivory Coast, France, and Spain. His MSLS is from Clarion University (1983), and he holds a Ph.D. from the University of Illinois (1988) in library and information science. He has traveled to Belize, Jamaica, and the Dominican Republic with Boston College's Ignacio Volunteers.

David A. Tyckoson has been a Reference Librarian for over twenty years, during which time he has helped thousands of students learn the academic research process. He is a leader in the field, having published numerous articles on reference services and information technology. His most recent work, "What's Right with Reference," which appeared in the May 1999 *American Libraries*, reviews the basics of reference service in light of recent reform efforts. Prior to his appointment at Fresno State, he was at the University at Albany as Business Bibliographer and Head of Reference.

Helene C. Williams has been the English Studies Librarian at the University of Washington Libraries since 1995. She came to UW after serving as Bibliographic Instruction Coordinator at Northeastern University in Boston and also at Michigan State University. She has been involved with the nationally recognized teaching and technology program known as UWired since 1996, working to improve collaboration between students, faculty, and librarians by effectively incorporating technology into the curriculum. She also teaches the graduate research methods course for the UW English department and provides user education sessions for both upper-division and graduate English courses. As a member of the Management of Instruction Services Committee of the Association of College and Research Libraries, she coordinated the proposal and program development phases of a joint Instruction Section/Library Administration and Management Association institute, Managing Educational Services: Teaching and Learning in Libraries. Since 1998, Ms. Williams has headed the UW Libraries usability team, conducting task-based user testing of the UW Libraries Information Gateway. She has presented widely on her teaching and usability activities, and co-edited the proceedings for the 1996 LOEX of the West conference, *Collaboration and Instructional Design in a*

Virtual Environment. In her spare time, she develops collection-development policies for Web-based resources and manages the humanities collections fund.

Lucinda R. Zoe has been an Assistant Professor in the Library Department at Baruch College, City University of New York, since 1994. She is the Electronic Information Specialist/Instructional Services Librarian at Newman Library, teaching in Baruch's credit course and bibliographic instruction programs. She holds a doctorate in Library and Information Service from Columbia University and an MLS from the University of Kentucky. Research interests include international information systems and services, the provision of information technology and services to diverse communities, and the impact of native language on end-user searching in multicultural environments. She previously served for two years as the Information Officer for the International Women's Tribune Center and the United Nations Development Fund for Women (UNIFEM).